THE SCOPE
OF FACULTY
COLLECTIVE
BARGAINING

Contributions to the Study of Education

Black Students in Higher Education: Conditions and Experiences in the 1970s
Gail E. Thomas

THE SCOPE
OF FACULTY
COLLECTIVE
BARGAINING

An Analysis of Faculty Union Agreements at Four-Year Institutions of Higher Education

Ronald L. Johnstone

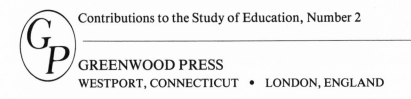

Contributions to the Study of Education, Number 2

GREENWOOD PRESS
WESTPORT, CONNECTICUT • LONDON, ENGLAND

Library of Congress Cataloging in Publication Data

Johnstone, Ronald L
    The scope of faculty collective bargaining.

    (Contributions to the study of education ;
no. 2 ISSN 0196-707X)
    Bibliography: p.
    Includes index.
    1. Collective bargaining—College teachers—
United States. 2. Collective labor agreements—
Education, Higher—United States. I. Title.
II. Series.
LB2335.875.U6J63   331.89 '04137812 '0973   80-27440
ISBN 0-313-22918-X (lib. bdg.)

Library of Congress Catalog Card Number: 80-27440
ISBN: 0-313-22918-X
ISSN: 0196-707X

First published in 1981

Greenwood Press
A division of Congressional Information Service, Inc.
88 Post Road West, Westport, Connecticut 06881

Printed in the United States of America

10 9 8 7 6 5 4 3 2 1

To
Kirsten, Donna, and Kenneth

CONTENTS

TABLES

ACKNOWLEDGMENTS

I am pleased to single out three individuals and four organizations, each inextricably tied with the others, for special acknowledgment: Norb Musto in the spring of 1976 provided the initial encouragement to begin the study; Kenneth Melley had a vision of ways in which such a study could aid faculty collective-bargaining agents nationwide; and William Owen opened doors and provided encouragement as the study progressed. Each of the following organizations, with which Musto, Melley, and Owen were associated, made contributions toward a summer research grant that enabled this study. These are the Central Michigan University Faculty Association, the Ferris State College Faculty Association through the Michigan Association for Higher Education, and the National Education Association. My appreciation to all is both deep and sincere. None should be blamed for any inaccuracies, overstatements, understatements, or any other flaws in the study, but all should be credited with providing significant encouragement and help at crucial stages along the way.

INTRODUCTION

As both the faculty and the representatives of the administration and the board of trustees of any given college or university with collective bargaining approach contract negotiations, they always come with a list of ideas and items they would like to see included in any final agreement. Without question the faculty perceive some problems they want redressed. In fact, faculty initially view the adoption of collective bargaining very explicitly as a problem-solving mechanism. They have specific goals they want to reach —increases in salary, an improved grievance system, more faculty responsibility for academic planning, or a larger contribution toward their retirement annuity. On the other hand, the administration and board will certainly want the agreement that ultimately will be negotiated and approved not to weaken their authority and control over the institution. Further they want to avoid giving up too much on economic and other matters despite the fact that collective bargaining has arrived on their campus.

But as each party begins to develop its proposals and later as active negotiations begin and they confront the other's proposals, each must reconsider how reasonable the items appear to be. Are we asking too much or too little? Is this item or that one normal and common in a collective-bargaining agreement of this kind, or is it unusual, unique, even bordering on the absurd? In short, what have others done? And how do we compare? It is precisely such questions that this book attempts to answer.

I have conducted a content analysis of the universe of the most recent (those available in printed form as of December 31, 1979) collective-bargaining agreements at four-year institutions of higher education in the United States. I have not sampled these institutions but investigated all of them, with a 95 percent rate of return. The number of agreements actually in force as of December 31, 1979, to the best of my knowledge was ninety-four. However, I was unsuccessful in obtaining five of these either because of oversight or because repeated requests both to the institution's administration and the collective-bargaining agent went unanswered. Thus eighty-nine agreements constitute the data base here.

Other four-year institutions have approved collective bargaining, of course, some as long as five or six years ago. In some cases, however, questions about the legitimacy of the selection of an agent or what the nature of the bargaining unit should be (for example, whether it should include chairpersons) were and still are being raised in specific court cases. Such litigation has delayed the process of bargaining a first agreement or keeping a first agreement in force (the Nebraska State College system and Boston University are examples). These institutions where faculty have voted in favor of collective bargaining but where the negotiation of a first agreement has been delayed numbered twenty-two as of December 31, 1979. Included are institutions that only recently adopted collective bargaining and although they were into negotiations had not yet completed and approved a first agreement by my cutoff date (the University of Maine is one of these).

There are many more individual institutions with a collective-bargaining agreement with its faculty than the 94 I mentioned. Many agreements cover multi-institution college and university systems. For example, one agreement for the State University of New York system serves and represents 32 separate colleges and universities; there are 8 colleges included in the New Jersey State Colleges agreement; 14 in the Pennsylvania State Colleges agreement; and so on with Minnesota, Connecticut, South Dakota, Illinois, Florida, City University of New York, and a few others. In fact, the ninety-four agreements represent 258 separate institutions. Thus, eighty-nine agreements in this study represent 95 percent of all the agreements in force at four-year institutions of higher education in the United States. But these eighty-nine agreements in turn actually cover 253 campuses or 98 percent of all unionized four-year campuses as of December 31, 1979.

Although it may have been legitimate to use the larger number of 253 individual institutions as the divisor when calculating percentages, I wanted to avoid the built-in redundancy of that approach and the undue influence that the large systems would have on the direction of the data. Therefore I chose to consider only the agreements themselves, not the separate institutions; hence the eighty-nine (95 percent of the ninety-four) agreements that constitute the universe of our content analysis.

In attempting to answer the question of what has been bargained, I have had in mind both faculty and administrators in three primary settings. First are those who come out of the same experience as I do: being part of an institution that already has experiences with faculty collective bargaining.

These are the faculty at the 258 institutions covered by ninety-four separate agreements that make up the universe of the study. Although they have some experience—in some cases with five or six agreements already having been negotiated—even these bargaining teams are mapping new territory each time an agreement is negotiated because they are unlikely to have complete answers to the questions of how unusual or unreasonable, on the one hand, or how commonplace or eminently reasonable, on the other, any given proposal or demand might be. Neither party to negotiations gets very far into either proposal writing or the subsequent negotiations themselves before asking such questions. Even parties with experience in collective bargaining will look to see how others have handled issues they view as salient. Then they can create their own proposal or demand.

Second are those faculty and administrators who are approaching negotiations for the first time. Where do they start? What is reasonable, perhaps even without question, to include in their package of demands? What is it reasonable to stand adamantly against? Faculty in this situation of first-time negotiations may have naively optimistic visions of what to expect. And administrators may have exaggerated fears. Solid data on what has gone before and what has been done elsewhere should help both parties.

Third are those faculty and administrators and boards of trustees only now considering the collective-bargaining mode for their campus. Perhaps an election has been formally requested or perhaps the subject recently has been introduced to the faculty, and their informal discussions are only beginning to include references to collective bargaining. In these cases (the most numerous of the three sets of audiences we have in mind) the faculty are interested in reliable answers to what they might reasonably expect of collective bargaining. How substantial might the salary raises be? Is it possible to provide for significant faculty participation concerning primary personnel decisions and academic planning of the institution? Can grievance procedures be established that include binding arbitration as the final stage? How many of the horror stories with their specters of time clocks, lowest-common-denominator models of scholarship, productivity measures, and elimination of merit pay should be believed? How much can they realistically dismiss as the rhetoric of fear or perhaps as simply representing an administrative perspective? On the other hand, how much of the scenery painted by faculty union organizers is virtually unattainable? Who can be believed? What can be believed?

I hope that this analysis will provide both firm data and substantial generalizations for faculty and administrators to assess realistically both their present situation and what might be possible in the future. I shall describe the actual outcomes to date of collective bargaining in the four-year college and university segment of higher education in the United States and answer a variety of questions. What has been bargained? In what manner or form? How frequently? At what type of institution? And in many cases—where?

Both the faculty, on the one hand, and the administrators and boards of trustees of four-year colleges and universities, on the other, will be in mind throughout this study. I expect the data to be equally useful to both. But it is only fair to mention that my original interest in and direct involvement with collective bargaining has been as a faculty member; I have participated as a faculty member in negotiations and have been president of a local faculty association. On the other hand, my present position is an administrative one—one that some will note hints of a bit of irony—and involves carrying out and implementing tasks that are demanded by a collective-bargaining agreement. As such, my aim has been to be nonpejorative and to present an objective approach. Some of the findings will bolster faculty positions, and some will reinforce administrative positions. I trust that reliable, representative information and data will serve the needs of both parties to negotiations.

THE SCOPE
OF FACULTY
COLLECTIVE
BARGAINING

1. INTRODUCTION TO COLLECTIVE BARGAINING IN HIGHER EDUCATION

Collective bargaining in higher education began at a time that logically would seem to have been the unlikeliest. In the mid-1960s higher education was in a boom period. There was some student unrest and protest, to be sure, but despite the disenchantment of a few, students were flocking to college and university classrooms in unprecedented numbers; faculty were in demand and could move fairly readily from one school to another; new construction was commonplace; and growth, expansion, and optimism were implicit assumptions. In such a seller's market so far as faculty were concerned, collective bargaining seemed unnecessary.

Many faculty were deeply concerned with other issues that had come to supplement their traditional preoccupation with the tasks of teaching and research. The Vietnam war was in process. As it became more and more unpopular, its merits were debated with increasing heat. A great deal of that debate occurred on college and university campuses and absorbed the attention and energy of many faculty—some as active participants, many others as interested observers, all as commentators and evaluators.

Therefore one might have predicted reasonably that the topic of collective bargaining would come in only a distant fourth or fifth in the hierarchy of faculty attention—behind the war issue, the student revolts, and a faculty member's own teaching and research efforts. Not only was higher education riding a crest of expansion and growth, but faculty had more than usual to absorb their attention and action. Nonetheless collective bargaining in higher education was both born and nurtured during this expansionary period and apparently ranked quite high in the minds of a significant number of faculty.

In part, this development occurred because of factors that were quite distinct from the other developments within higher education. It also appears to be true that unionizing efforts in higher education began at least in part as a type of spin-off from the most newsworthy movements in higher education in the 1960s.

History of Collective Bargaining in Four-Year Institutions

Even if I expand the universe to all institutions of higher education and include the two-year junior and community colleges, the beginning of collective bargaining goes back only to 1963. In that year the faculty at Milwaukee Technical Institute, a two-year college, organized for purposes of collective bargaining,[1] and the United Federation of College Teachers, Local 1460, an American Federation of Teachers (AFT) affiliate, was formed in New York City.[2] The first four-year institution at which the faculty organized was the U.S. Merchant Marine Academy, organized in 1966 by the AFT,[3] but with an initial agreement not negotiated and signed by all parties until February, 1968.[4] Actually the Merchant Marine Academy is an atypical case so far as institutions of higher education are concerned in that governmental control and regulations allow less autonomy and less faculty control, even under collective bargaining, than is true at most public and private four-year colleges and universities.

Thus if we regard the U.S. Merchant Marine Academy as a special case, or if we consider the date of the signed agreement as more significant than the date of organization or approval of a bargaining agent, then the signing of an agreement in the summer of 1967 at Bryant College of Business Administration, a private college in Rhode Island, would make that school the first more-or-less traditional four-year college or university with collective bargaining.[5] Following shortly in 1969 were the large City University of New York system, Central Michigan University, and Southeastern Massachusetts University. By the end of 1970, the faculty at these institutions, plus St. John's University, had successfully negotiated their first agreement with their employing institution. Collective bargaining in the four-year segment of higher education, both public and private, was definitely under way. By mid-1972 the number of four-year colleges and universities with collective bargaining had increased tenfold; at least forty four-year institutions had chosen a bargaining agent and had begun negotiating an agreement.

By January 1, 1979, faculty at a minimum of 116 four-year institutions[6] representing at least 258 campuses[7] had approved collective bargaining, and currently organizing efforts are underway at dozens of other schools; the legislatures of several states have proposals before them that would provide the enabling legislation for collective bargaining by public employee faculty members; boards of trustees are deciding what stands to take with respect to collective bargaining and, in some cases such as various state universities in Ohio, whether to agree to a representative election and possibly whether to bargain with the faculty collective-bargaining representative even in the absence of enabling or mandatory collective-bargaining legislation. In calendar year 1978 twelve four-year schools voted in favor of collective bargaining for the first time, three switched agents or reaffirmed one, and five rejected collective bargaining. The twelve first-time favorable elections represent twenty-two separate campuses, an increase of 10 percent over the number of unionized campuses in 1977.

Although such growth may not seem phenomenal (certainly not all campuses, or even a majority, have yet approved of collective bargaining), it is definite and steady; growth has hovered around an average rate of 10 percent per year for the past ten years. Further, the growth has also been fairly substantial when one considers that legislation enabling faculties to bargain collectively at state-supported schools has been withheld in over one-third of the states. Even when such legislation has been passed, the boards and administrations of many institutions have opposed the movement and have filed suits requiring clarification from the courts with regard to definition of the bargaining unit or the scope of bargaining or have challenged the election of the collective-bargaining representative, in addition to asserting as much contrary moral suasion as possible. No doubt the collective-bargaining phenomenon will continue to grow, though not likely by any longer leaps and bounds than it has already demonstrated.

Factors Leading to Collective Bargaining

The Growth Factor

Of prime importance in understanding why faculties increasingly have been attracted to collective bargaining is the rapid rate of growth of higher education in the 1960s and most of the 1970s. Not that growth is a direct cause of collective bargaining. Rather, it is indirect, much in the fashion of an early variable in a causal chain that has collective bargaining as its end. This growth has two forms—in the size of a host of individual colleges and universities and in the sense of the emergence of the large multiversities. At such multiversities great numbers of both students and faculty gather in one place, but the location of the seats of administration and policy-making power is not just across campus but often across the state, scores of miles away.

During the last ten to fifteen years the number of faculty teaching and doing research in higher education has nearly doubled (from 354,000 full-time faculty in 1965 to an estimated 623,000 in 1978); the current fund expenditures of colleges and universities have increased even faster (from $12.5 billion in 1965-66 to $42.6 billion in 1976-77, or more than an eight-fold increase if we go back to 1959-60 when the total expenditure was $5.6 billion); the number of students increased from 5,921,000 in 1965 to 11,415,000 in 1977, and 12,087,200 in the fall of 1980.[8] In a comparable time period, grants and gifts grew phenomenally also, increasing fivefold from $382,569,000 in 1959-60 to $2,105,070,000 in 1976-79. Property values grew from $18,893,385,000 to $85,486,550,000 in the same time span.[9] Such figures are evidence of phenomenal growth. But as Joseph W. Garbarino observes, "It was a brief golden age."[10]

Such growth resulted in a pair of distinctive though related developments. First was a breakdown on many campuses of collegial relationships between faculty and administrators. Second was the shift to professional management techniques on the part of college and university administrators.

Decline of Collegiality

By *collegiality* I mean a relationship of mutual respect and reliance between faculty members and administrators, where each feels the other is a trusted partner in the educational process. The administrator in a collegial situation is likely to be a person who rose through the ranks and now heads a unit or function within the college or university as a dean, vice-president, provost, president, or other high-level administrator. This person has been given the faculty's mantle of acceptance and respect through what was likely a protracted process of searching for an outstanding scholar who also had a reputation for strong teaching skills, as well as some previous administrative experience. When that president, provost, or dean comes to call you by your name and perhaps knows those of your spouse and children as well, when you have eaten dinner in his home, and when he personally saw to it that you got an extra $100 in merit pay last year, it is hard to present him with a collective-bargaining petition and demand to submit to written contractual language what has been tacit during these many years of collegiality.

But as numbers grow large, as personal anonymity sets in, as bonus seems to accrue only to a small cadre in an inner circle that does not include you, or as what Garbarino calls "changes in function" occur, the collective-bargaining option begins to look more attractive. Changes in function include such developments as a two-year college converting to a four-year institution, a four-year college adding one or more doctoral programs, or a teachers' college expanding its function to focus on liberal or applied arts programs, perhaps adding a professional school or two as well.[11]

Any such changes result not only in intrafaculty conflict over curriculum, admission requirements, criteria for tenure and promotion, and the like, but because of increasing size and increasing complexity, the gap between faculty and administration widens. As goals broaden, as more committees are formed, as additional levels in the administrative hierarchy are inserted, the rank-and-file faculty are separated from the administration and vice-versa. The idea of collegiality in such situations, although not an absurdity, does lose in the translation and cannot endure in its old form or at its old level.

At one extreme so far as structural changes that negatively affect collegiality are concerned has been the creation in many states of multicampus college and university systems. In the seven-unit state college system in Minnesota, for example, all schools for one hundred years had operated under a single board of trustees.[12] But the day-to-day operations, including personnel decisions and setting salaries, were conducted fairly independently at each of the colleges. Collegiality had meaning in such settings. But in 1968, in an effort to increase efficiency and create greater unity, the state established a central office with a single chancellor and an additional administrative hierarchy to which comparable hierarchies at each of the seven campuses had to report. As would be expected, collegiality was reported to break down under these circumstances.[13] More than five years of lawsuits and legal haggling over the definition of the bargaining unit and whether each campus should negotiate separate agreements or whether a single unit-wide agreement would do—a five-year period when academic senates were deemed superfluous—and one hardly is surprised that collegiality was an early casualty in Minnesota.[14]

Collective bargaining might intrude at the point where collegiality either begins to break down or is declared absent. It may come because some of the faculty feel threatened by the changes or because the idea of it, though perhaps suggested long before, can now be considered more seriously because the collegiality that collective bargaining might be viewed as threatening or even destroying already has been significantly eroded by other changes. William McHugh reminds us that we are observing almost a classic case of the shift from *gemeinschaft* to *gesellschaft* relationships and that a fragmentation is taking place.[15]

Academic Specialization and Professionalization

Another factor that is conducive to collective bargaining among faculty but clearly is not the fault of administrators or boards of trustees or anyone in particular, for that matter, is the knowledge explosion in every field of academic research and endeavor. The rapid increase of specialization has tended to separate colleagues on the same campus, even within the same department, and gives specialized academics a greater degree of colleagueship with fellow specialists on other campuses than members of their own department or institution. Often this process is called professionalization, that is, faculty identify more closely with others in the profession than with members of their department or other colleagues on campus.

It might seem that such a phenomenon would inhibit the formation of a collective-bargaining unit because such fragmentation and atomization would be inimical to joint action with local colleagues. In all likelihood it did at first. Certainly it did not lead to collective bargaining when academic specialists could move about fairly freely from one academic position to another. But as the job market tightened, as supply-and-demand ratios tipped away from the supplier (the faculty) to the employer, faculty began to realize that they had some commonalities of interest with those people around them whom they hardly knew: their faculty colleagues on the local campus. And because for many, their former allegiances had been to faculty within their specialized academic area and not to the institution at which they taught and conducted research (an institution that included the administration), they did not even need to break a relationship. They simply broadened slightly their perception of collegiality to include the faculty at their own institution and followed routes that would benefit this collective. The possibility of faculty collective bargaining could be very attractive in this context, particularly when administrative or board of trustee provocation was present and could be identified and used as catalyst.

Increasing Bureaucratization of Academic Administration

As faculty were beginning to experience changes in self-perception and function, a parallel situation was occurring with administrators. As the organization grows larger and as governmental regulations and paperwork seem to increase at almost a geometric rate, the need of the academic organization for business-like management becomes more and more like that of almost any other large organization. When this happens, a greater chasm erodes between faculty and administration. Administrators begin to lose the traditional sense of being among peers and become managers. Colleges and universities become bureaucratic; the levels of authority increase and, implicitly, greater distances grow between the faculty and the top administration. Committees expand, a parallel need for coordination arises, and as Garbarino observes, there is a need for consultation that "results in delay, compromise, and referrals before an action can be taken."[16] Potential administrators often are scrutinized more carefully by boards of trustees for the number of short courses they have taken at a business school than for the number of scholarly monographs and articles they have produced in their field of academic specialization.

This development corresponds fairly closely to the bureaucratic model presented by Max Weber and applied specifically to academic governance by Frank R. Kemerer and J. Victor Baldridge. Kemerer and Baldridge have identified these prominent characteristics of the bureaucratic model: (1) there is a formal hierarchy with detailed bylaws and organization charts that specify levels of authority and role relationships among members; (2) there are formal channels of communication to be followed; (3) authority relationships, although not always clearly defined, are present nonetheless; (4) carefully specified policies and rules govern much of the work of the organization (there are deadlines to meet, records to keep, periodic reports to submit, and so on); and (5) decision making tends to occur in a relatively routine, formalized fashion using councils and procedures established by institutional procedures and bylaws.[17]

Although this bureaucratic or management model does not adequately describe or explain all that goes on in an institution of higher learning—not even all the decision making, let alone the multitudes of other actions that are carried out in classrooms, department meetings, cafeterias, lounges, and so on—nonetheless it has become more and more descriptive of what goes on and how decisions are made in colleges and universities in this country. The people at the upper levels in this hierarchical structure are becoming increasingly conversant with the techniques of management that are common to large corporations.

This shift to bureaucratic management patterns never goes unnoticed by faculty; some among them will be quick to point out that the collegial process has been betrayed, that academic freedoms and professional integrity are threatened severely, and that the distinctiveness of an academic community of scholars is fading as the university becomes just another big business. Such a view is reinforced by the pressures of governmental rules and regulations that require more and more paperwork, the financial problems that demand superior accounting and budget-management procedures, and the growth in size and complexity that seems to require delegation of specialized authority to various offices within the administrative hierarchy.

In the face of such developments, a great many faculty begin to think that collective bargaining may be a way to bring them more directly back into the decision-making process. They may wonder if these professional managers can be trusted with academic decisions. Do they have sufficient experience with the academic subculture of higher education? Will they be sensitive enough to the many nuances of academic training and performance? Will they see the college as an organization of a different order from commercial and productive enterprises? Dare we think of them as one of us, or are they interlopers?

Rise of Other White-Collar Unions

Although so-called white-collar unions go back as far as the beginning of the union movement in the United States (certainly as far back as the 1880s and 1890s, possibly as early as 1865), growth was slow and gradual.[18] By 1964, estimates put union membership by white-collar employees in the United States at 11 percent.[19] A significant precipitating stimulus for adding to the ranks of white-collar unions came with President John F. Kennedy's executive order of January 17, 1962, concerning "Employee-Management Cooperation in the Public Service." Everett M. Kassalow points out that this act shifted the position of government from one of mere tolerance to actual encouragement of collective bargaining as the appropriate, normal way of handling employer-employee relations.[20] As a consequence, white-collar union membership increased substantially. By 1978 it was reported to be 18 percent.[21] And among certain categories of white-collar workers, the proportions were dramatically higher. For example, although including some blue-collar workers, the proportion of local, state, and federal employees stood at 39.2 percent in 1976.[22] Among public school teachers the proportion with membership in a professional association stood at 83.1 percent in 1976 (71.1 percent belonged to the National Educational Association (NEA) and 12.8 percent to the AFT). Such growth in white-collar unions suggests that unionization by non-blue-collar workers was gaining favor fairly dramatically during the 1960s and early 1970s. So for college faculty to think of unionization for themselves by the late 1960s and the 1970s was not as absurd a thought as it would have seemed to be earlier.

Substantial unionization of teachers at the primary and secondary levels is itself relatively recent.[24] For example, the NEA, the largest teachers' professional association and the national affiliation for 1,679,689 teachers, did not begin to embrace collective bargaining for teachers until 1961.[25] This rapid and substantial unionization of teachers is significant with respect to college faculty for two reasons. First, it was an example of a somewhat comparable profession. And its successes, particularly in bargaining economic benefits, were common knowledge. Second, many faculty, particularly those at teachers' colleges and those universities emerging out of this status, had themselves been members of an AFT of NEA union local before moving on to college teaching.

In short, the social stigma of union membership was gradually eroding. Some professors began to think of union affiliation, particularly when it seemed to promise improvement in salary and benefits and might provide a fuller participation in one's own destiny through involvement in institutional decision making.

Enabling Legislation

Nearly everyone who has asked why collective bargaining began in the mid- to late 1960s and not earlier (or later) lists at least two factors that relate to developments within the legal arena or context. First is what we might call the *cultural litigious orientation*, a term describing the apparent willingness of many people to file a suit against almost anyone and in favor of almost anything. Second, specific legislation was passed that allowed collective bargaining for public employees and faculties of higher education in particular.

Only slightly more than twenty years ago (in 1959) Wisconsin became the first state to approve a public employee collective-bargaining statute. Even more recently (1965) the first state statute (Michigan) was formulated to apply specifically to postsecondary faculties. By 1978, thirty-two states had enacted laws that have been interpreted to include the faculties of colleges and universities among the category of public employees who have the right to bargain collectively. Most of these statutes are of a permissive nature; they do not explicitly list faculties of institutions of higher education. Only five call out the faculty of postsecondary institutions explicitly. In 1970, a National Labor Relations Board ruling established the principle of non-profit private educational institutions being required to bargain with their employees under federal, not state, laws. Robert K. Carr and Daniel K. VanEyck make the interesting observation that apparently no one realized at the time when Cornell University (joined by Syracuse University) had requested federal jurisdiction rather than state oversight that a wide door was being opened to the entire private college and university sector to bargain with faculty should those faculty through proper procedures and with appropriate numbers request it.[26]

Although fundamental questions about the legal requirement of private colleges to bargain with faculty are being raised as a consequence of the U.S. Supreme Court's 1980 *Yeshiva* decision,[27] much of the interpretation of that decision has centered around its narrow applicability. The decision concluded that the Yeshiva faculty had sufficient managerial functions as to be part of management and not employees as traditionally defined. The decision is quite specific and appears to be far from automatically applicable to faculty collective bargaining at other private colleges and universities.

The point to be made with respect to enabling legislation is simple: permissive legislation was a necessary condition before collective bargaining in higher education could get underway. Only rarely has the collective-bargaining process and relationship been undertaken by faculties and administrations or boards of public institutions in states without such legislation. Ohio is the notable exception. Two of its universities, Youngstown State and Kent State, and their faculties have reached collective-bargaining agreements, and other state colleges and universities in Ohio are considering it, but without the enabling or permissive legislation yet in effect.

The existence or presence of collective-bargaining organizations such as the AFT, the American Association of University Professors (AAUP), and the NEA and their active recruitment efforts on college and university campuses across the country have been important too.[28] Their competition for members and for exclusive rights to represent faculties has involved not only the expenditure of considerable sums of money and the investment of many persons' time, but promises undoubtedly were made and expectations sometimes raised beyond abilities to produce beneficial changes. Nevertheless the outcome of such competitive efforts was to heighten the awareness of collective bargaining on the part of many faculty and move them from ignorance and indecision to affirmation of the collective-bargaining mode for higher education, at least for the local embodiment of higher education where they had found their niche.

Faculty Salary Erosion

Probably the most important background factor in encouraging some faculty to flirt with and/or embrace collective bargaining is the economic fact that inflation has been eroding the salary increases that faculty have been given.

In 1963 faculty salaries, adjusted for increases in the consumer price index, began a declining rate of gain. And in 1973 their increases were not enough to counterbalance the rate of inflation; faculty salary gains resulted in a net loss of buying power. The data in table 1 show that once the break-even point had been passed, faculty salaries have remained at a net loss level ever since.

TABLE 1
Percentage Changes in Purchasing
Power of Faculty Salaries

1972-73 TO 1973-74	1973-74 TO 1974-75	1974-75 TO 1975-76	1975-76 TO 1976-77	1976-77 TO 1977-78	1977-78 TO 1978-79
−3.6%	−4.8%	−1.0%	−1.0%	−1.3%	−3.3%

SOURCE: W. Lee Hansen, "An Era of Continuing Decline," *Academe* 65 (September 1979): 324.

As faculty began to search for solutions to such economic frustrations, some turned to collective bargaining. Many of them had an image of other white-collar workers, teachers in particular, gaining appreciably so far as salaries are concerned under collective bargaining. Although such gains appear to have been not nearly so great as popular perceptions would suggest, the perceptions themselves were encouraging.[29]

Thus the economic fact of a significant erosion of faculty salary buying power teams up with one or more (almost always more) of the factors presented earlier, and a collective-bargaining experiment is begun at yet another campus. What we have is not only multiple causation in the sense that several of these factors are present when a faculty votes to approve collective bargaining, but they are always in a particular combination and intensity. Thus on one campus, faculty salaries may have been keeping up with inflation modestly well, but the administration may have frightened most faculty by firing several of them without consultation with any faculty representatives and on the basis of a declared financial exigency that most faculty do not believe exists. At another institution, faculty may be on good terms with the administration and hope to remain so, but salary erosion in the face of inflation has been greater than at many other institutions and the faculty believe that collective bargaining might enable the administration of their institution to extract a larger appropriation from the state board of education or legislature. These same faculty perhaps perceive that other teachers in the community have made substantial economic gains since they adopted collective bargaining. Further, the institution is but one of several state institutions under a state board that faculty find impossible to reach through any mechanism available to them up to now.

Two points are important here. First, we always need to think of multiple causation when asking what prompted a group of faculty to organize for purposes of collective bargaining. Second, it would be the rarest of situations when faculty economic needs and concerns did not figure prominently in that decision.

Sons and Daughters of the Age

Faculty, no less than anyone else in society, are sons and daughters of the age in which they live. What has occurred in the social environment of American citizens has affected faculty as much as any other category of persons. Thus the student and youth activists of the late 1960s and early 1970s and their success in gaining rights for students and helping to undermine support for American involvement in Southeast Asia did not go unnoticed by faculty. Similarly, within the last twenty-five years minority groups have achieved dramatic gains because of activist, aggressive tactics by the civil rights and black power movements, the women's movement, the gay liberation movement, and others. Some faculty have realized that action can bring results, and collective action can bring even more results.

At the same time, confidence in government at all levels has declined, and this distrust has spilled over to the relationship of faculty to their administration and board. Faculty have not proceeded particularly swiftly in this regard. They tend to be loyal, and perhaps in some senses naive, in terms of administrative actions. On balance they have given administrations and boards of trustees every opportunity to prove worthy of the implicit trust faculty are so willing to give. But the combination of emphases within society such as "look out for number one," "be assertive if you ever hope to succeed," and what I shall shortly describe as academic "atrocities" have stimulated more than a few faculty to try to assume a more direct involvement in their futures than ever before. One needs only to add other facts of contemporary life such as a litigious citizenry, rights for everyone, and rising expectations, and it is hardly surprising that faculty have joined in the race.

Yet faculty by and large are relatively passive. Majorities of them are not easily provoked to aggressive action. What is usually necessary is that they perceive themselves as victims of an administrative "atrocity"—something they perceive as heinous.

Administrative "Atrocities"

By "atrocities" I mean something less than a literal definition of the word and a knowledge of its referents in history would suggest. Also my description of certain actions as "atrocities" is not an objective assessment by me or anyone else; it is simply a way of describing how many faculty on the scene perceived and described events that immediately preceded the approval on their campuses of the collective-bargaining approach to problem solving. A more objective term might be "provocation."

An almost-classic example is what James P. Begin, Theodore Settle, and Paula Alexander report about Rider College. They state that in efforts by the administration and board to upgrade the tenure and degree qualifications of the faculty but without providing what the faculty regarded as an appropriate grandfather clause, the faculty felt it was being treated unfairly and high-handedly by the administration and board. The "atrocities" in this case occurred when some faculty were denied tenure or promotion on the basis of new rules adopted by the board. These individual acts were enhanced by a general conviction on the part of the faculty that its counsel and advice largely were ignored with respect to determining the means and nature of faculty evaluations, with respect to the appointment of administrators, and with respect to resource allocation.[30]

In the New Jersey State College system the "atrocity" appears to have been the faculty perception that gross discrimination had been perpetrated against them by the legislature in 1966 when the faculty at Rutgers University and the Newark College of Engineering (now the New Jersey Institute of Technology) were granted substantial salary increases through special legislation, but a similar bill for the state colleges was allowed to die in committee. At the earliest possible date following this action, the Association of New Jersey State College Faculties won the right to represent all six state college campuses for purposes of collective bargaining. Begin, Settle, and Alexander repeatedly assert that it was the arbitrariness of this salary action and the subsequent failure in attempts to resolve the issue that precipitated the turn to collective bargaining in the New Jersey State colleges.[31] There were abetting factors, of course: reorganization of the Board for Higher Education, repeated derogatory comments about the state colleges' faculty by the new chancellor, and retirement or resignation of five of the six college presidents.[32] But the principal "atrocity" appears to have been the legislative action on salaries in 1966.

At Central Michigan University the "atrocity" was the action by the board of trustees in the spring of 1968 that abolished the existing salary schedule. Many faculty viewed this action as insensitive, in part because an ad hoc university senate committee that had been working since early in the fall semester to make recommendations for a revision of the salary schedule was ready to report to the senate in April. But the faculty had hardly begun to discuss the recommendations of the salary schedule committee when the board on April 17 abolished the schedule yet had no alternative salary plan to substitute for it. An administrative officer reportedly told the board after its action that it had just asked for collective bargaining. And indeed the faculty began immediately to move toward collective bargaining (enabling legislation had been passed in July, 1965). On September 24, 1969, the faculty approved collective bargaining, and their local agent, affiliated with the Michigan Education Association/NEA was authenticated.

At the University of Massachusetts freezes of faculty salaries, the establishment of de facto tenure quotas, and cutbacks in budgets for secretarial services, telephone, and other faculty services together constituted the administrative-board-governmental "atrocity" that precipitated the approval of collective bargaining by the faculty there in 1976.[33]

My point is that for faculty to approve collective bargaining and to expend the time, energy, and money required to get a collective-bargaining organization underway, they need provocation. A catalyst is needed to get the action going.

We now turn to the results of that action—not simply the formation of faculty unions and their gaining recognition as bona-fide representatives of faculty for purposes of collective bargaining—but to go one step beyond that to the outcomes of that bargaining. What has been bargained? What has been accomplished? We proceed now to an analysis of what is essentially the universe of collective-bargaining agreements in the four-year college and university sector of American higher education.[34]

Notes

1. Joseph W. Garbarino, *Faculty Bargaining* (New York: McGraw-Hill Book Company, 1975), p. 51.

2. Everett C. Ladd and Seymour M. Lipset, *The Divided Academy* (New York: McGraw-Hill Book Company, 1975), p. 249.

3. Garbarino, *Faculty Bargaining*, p. 51.

4. Robert K. Carr and Daniel K. VanEyck, *Collective Bargaining Comes to Campus* (Washington, D.C.: American Council on Education, 1973), p. 17.

5. Ibid.

6. Reported to be 139 as of June 20, 1980, by *Chronicle of Higher Education* 20, no. 19 (July 7, 1980): 7-8.

7. Abstracted from *Directory of Faculty Contracts and Bargaining Agents in Institutions of Higher Education* (New York: National Center for the Study of Collective Bargaining in Higher Education, 1979), pp. 1-29.

8. Jack Maganell, "Fall Enrollment Sets Record Despite Fewer 18-Year Olds," *Chronicle of Higher Education* 21, no. 12 (November 2, 1980): 3-4.

9. Statistics abstracted from *Yearbook of Higher Education 1977-78*, 9th ed. (Chicago: Marquis Who's Who, 1977), pp. 585-623; and *Yearbook of Higher Education*, 11th ed. (Chicago: Marquis Who's Who, 1979), pp. 653-74.

10. Garbarino, *Faculty Bargaining*, p. 3.

11. Ibid., pp. 12-14.

12. Bimidji State University, Mankato State University, Metropolitan State University, Moorhead State University, St. Cloud State University, Southwest State University, Winona State University.

13. *NEA Advocate* (June–July 1978): 4.

14. Edward B. Ehrle and Jane F. Farley, "The Effects of Collective Bargaining on Department Chairpersons and Deans," *Educational Record* 57, no. 3 (1977).

15. William F. McHugh, "Faculty Unionism and Tenure," *Journal of College and University Law* 1, no. 1 (1973): 46-73; and Frank C. Serry, "Reflections on Faculty Unionization: Academic Implications," *Liberal Education* 64, no. 2 (1978): 171-81.

16. Garbarino, *Faculty Bargaining*, p. 10.

17. Frank R. Kemerer and J. Victor Baldridge, *Unions on Campus* (San Francisco: Jossey-Bass, 1975), p. 16.

18. Everett M. Kassalow, "White-Collar Unionism in the United States," in *White Collar Trade Unions*, ed. Adolf F. Sturmthal (Urbana: University of Illinois Press, 1966), p. 319.

19. Kassalow, "White-Collar Unionism," p. 338.

20. Ibid., pp. 336-37.

21. John T. Dunlop, "Past and Future Tendencies in American Labor Organizations," *Daedalus* 107, no. 1 (Winter 1978): 79.

22. John F. Burton, Jr., "The Extent of Collective Bargaining in the Public Sector," in *Public Sector Bargaining*, ed. Benjamin Aaron, Joseph R. Grodin, and James L. Stern (Washington, D.C.: Bureau of National Affairs, 1979), p. 17.

23. Marsha A. Ream, *Status of the American Public School Teacher, 1975–76* (Washington, D.C.: National Education Association, 1977), p. 156.

24. Roots of the AFT go back to 1897 with the formation of the Independent Chicago Teachers Federation, although the AFT itself did not formally organize until 1916. Although its national membership reached 9,300 in 1921, membership did not move ahead substantially again until after World War II. Cf. Kassalow, "White-Collar Unionism," p. 325.

25. *NEA Handbook, 1977–78* (Washington, D.C.: National Education Association, 1977), p. 143.

26. Carr and VanEyck, *Collective Bargaining Comes to Campus*, pp. 46-73.

27. National Labor Relations Board v. Yeshiva University, 100 Supreme Court 856, February 20, 1980.

28. McHugh, "Faculty Unionism and Tenure," pp. 46-73.

29. The following studies show a positive effect of unionization upon salaries of teachers, though the magnitude has not been so great as some might have predicted. W. Clayton Hall and Norman E. Carroll. "The Effect of Teachers' Organizations on Salaries and Class Size," *Industrial and Labor Relations Review* 26, no. 2 (January 1973): 834-41; Hirschel Kasper, "The Effects of Collective Bargaining on Public School Teachers' Salaries," *Industry and Labor Relations Review* 24, no. 1 (October 1970): 57-72; David B. Lipshy and John E. Dratning, "The Influence of Collective Bargaining on Teachers' Salaries in New York State," *Industry and Labor Relations Review* 27, no. 1 (October 1973): 18-35; Robert J. Thornton, "The Effects of Collective Negotiations on Teachers' Salaries," *Quarterly Review of Economics and Business* 11, no. 4 (Winter 1971): 27-46; Robert N. Baird and John H. Landen, "The Effects of Collective Bargaining on Public School Teachers' Salaries: Comment," *Industry and Labor Relations Review* 25, no. 3 (April 1972): 410-17.

30. James P. Begin, Theodore Settle, and Paula Alexander, *Academics on Strike* (New Brunswick, N.J.: Institute of Management and Labor Relations, Rutgers University, 1975), pp. 17-34.

31. Ibid., pp. 84-89.

32. Ibid.

33. *NEA Advocate*, October 1978, pp. 1 and 4.

34. See the Introduction to this book for a description of the universe of faculty collective-bargaining agreements.

2. RIGHTS OF FACULTY

To speak of the "rights" of faculty is to open a door on most everything a faculty person does. The term can include rights to compensation for one's work, rights to a variety of fringe benefits, rights to be considered for promotion, rights to participate in the governance of the institution, and so on. Each of these rights is important, and most will be considered later in this book. The subject of this chapter, however, is more general and contextual. It looks at both the consensus and the diversity that have resulted from collective bargaining in higher education so far as the general climate or environment (what I might simply call the academic environment) that faculty members can expect and within which they work and what rights of due process faculty members can expect when they feel grieved (that is, when they believe their rights have been violated or when their normal expectations appear to have been denied).

Academic Environment

One right of faculty members begins before a particular person arrives on campus or is ever even considered for a position on the faculty. Actually I am speaking of a pair of rights that a person can expect both when first approaching the institution and later as a part of it: that affirmative action will be pursued by the institution in a search for potential faculty members, its hiring of new faculty, and its promotion and tenuring of faculty who meet the criteria, and that it will not engage in discrimination in pursuing these activities.

Affirmative Action

Although affirmative action is a highly current issue on campuses and has been absorbing a great deal of attention, the subject has been included in relatively few collective-bargaining agreements. In fact, only 10.1 percent (nine agreements) have explicit language concerning affirmative action. The phrasing ranges from the terse statement that "this agreement accepts and adopts the principles and guidelines of affirmative action"[1] through reference to a specific affirmative-action plan already in existence that is incorporated into the agreement, as in the University of Scranton Agreement, which states that the advertising of vacancies shall be in accordance with the university's affirmative-action plan,[2] to a fairly strong contractual position as negotiated at Hofstra University. The Hofstra Agreement requires the president of the university to appoint an affirmative-action officer as recommended by a five-member affirmative-action committee. This committee reviews and suggests revisions to the current affirmative-action plan for the university, conducts an ongoing review of affirmative action on campus, supplies faculty with an annual written report, and develops recommendations for affirmative-action programs and projects.[3]

Other agreements generally state that both the board and the faculty collective-bargaining representatives are committed to the principle of affirmative action. And one agreement goes beyond such general statements and details the state and federal laws and regulations that provide protection and remedies in the area of affirmative action.[4]

That few collective-bargaining agreements have specific clauses on affirmative action does not suggest that affirmative-action plans are in operation on only a few campuses. It would be a rare campus that does not have one of some kind at least on paper or in the minutes of some campus body.

Nondiscrimination

It is quite another story with respect to the issue of nondiscrimination. Most contracts (87.6 percent) speak to this. In most cases the statement is fairly standard and straightforward, noting that both the institution and the collective-bargaining representative commit themselves to the principle of not discriminating against either a current member of the bargaining unit (faculty) or an applicant for a faculty position on the basis of sex, religion, age, national origin, or race. Some agreements also add such criteria as political belief, political affiliation, sexual orientation or preference, veteran status, and physical handicap. The Park College Agreement adds marital status, membership in a lawful organization, and familial relationship to another employee.[5] Somewhat over half (53 percent) of those schools that have any contractual language at all on the subject of nondiscrimination go even further and specify that the board-university shall not discriminate against any bargaining-unit member on the basis of membership in a labor organization (such as the one that is party to the contract).

A few agreements insert the phrase "or nonmembership" in a labor organization. This is relevant at institutions where a substantial number of faculty members have held back from union membership for ideological reasons, for pragmatic considerations such as saving the cost of union dues, or other reasons. For example, the agreement at Cooper Union states, "Neither Cooper Union nor the Federation shall interfere with, restrain, or coerce the employees in the bargaining unit because of membership or nonmembership in the Federaion."[6]

Besides the principle of justice and fairness that is involved in making a contractual commitment not to discriminate, at issue here is the establishment of a grievance base. When the principle of nondiscrimination is contractualized, the bargaining-unit member has, unless specified to the contrary in the agreement, recourse in the college or university grievance system to redress if discrimination is alleged. This is supplemental to recourse provided by the state and federal government. Some contracts, however, specify that grievances pertaining to personnel decisions (promotion and tenure) shall not be allowed; decisions are final. Thus a primary area within which discrimination might be alleged is placed outside the grievance system.

Although a few agreements make some general statements about faculty rights (such as being provided a suitable environment within which to do academic work or being promised to be consulted when annual budgets are prepared or when changes in academic policies are proposed), most deal with fairly specific topics or areas.

Academic Freedom

A prime consideration is the principle of academic freedom, included in the collective-bargaining agreements of a high proportion of colleges and universities (78.7 percent). Some are brief; they mention the concept of academic freedom and either assume that it has a commonly understood meaning (sixteen contracts) or make reference (seven cases) to another document or statement in which academic freedom is defined, with commitment to that definition now made explicit in the collective-bargaining agreement. In the Adelphi University Agreement, both parties state that they support the principle of academic freedom as set forth in the 1940 Statement on Academic Freedom and Tenure formulated jointly by the Association of American Colleges (AAC) and the AAUP and incorporated in appendix A of the Adelphi University Personnel Plan.[7] Thirty-three collective-bargaining agreements define the concept of academic freedom but rely heavily nevertheless on common understandings of the principle. Another twenty-one (30 percent of the agreements that include reference to academic freedom) make a somewhat lengthy presentation of the concept. Two schools quote in its entirety the 1940 AAUP Statement on Academic Freedom that several others make reference to.

Many collective-bargaining agreements couple statements on academic freedom and the right of faculty to pursue knowledge untrammeled, with parallel statements of the responsibility of faculty members to be knowledgeable about their subjects, to be fair, to avoid introducing controversial subjects that are outside their training and expertise into their classes, and to clarify that when they speak outside the confines of the institution as a citizen, they are not to be identified as a representative of that institution. A full 75.7 percent (fifty-three of seventy agreements that consider this issue at all) parallel such freedom with responsibility. A typical example is provided in the academic-responsibility paragraph in the agreement for the New Jersey Institute of Technology:

The concept of freedom should be accompanied by an equally demanding concept of responsibility. The college or university teacher is a citizen, a member of a learned profession, and an officer of an educational institution. When he speaks or writes as a citizen, he should be free from institutional censorship or discipline, but his special position in the community imposes special obligations. As a man of learning and an educational officer, he should remember that the public may judge his profession and his Institution by his utterances and should make every effort to indicate that he is not an institutional spokesman.[8]

That 78.7 percent of all agreements have language on academic freedom means that 21.3 percent (nineteen institutions) do not. But lest we jump to conclusions about the potential for violation of academic freedom at these institutions, we need to think about at least three important unknowns with respect to this issue. First, we do not know whether this absence of an academic-freedom section is by deliberate design or by simple oversight. Second, if by design, we do not know if it is because one of the parties to the agreement wished not to be tied down to an academic-freedom clause, or if it is because one of the parties felt that the academic-freedom principle is so basic in higher education and so widely subscribed to that it is not necessary to contractualize it. Third, we do not know whether the faculty at these nineteenth institutions have the protection of other documents, such as a set of board of trustees' policies or an academic senate constitution that includes the principle of academic freedom. Statements in such documents do not have the legally binding force of a collective-bargaining agreement, but any such references would be evidence of commitment to academic-freedom principles in these institutions. In short, although faculties would be well advised to include an affirmation of academic freedom in their collective-bargaining agreement, one cannot automatically infer a lack of commitment to such principles at those institutions where the principles have not been explicitly contractualized.

Personnel Files

An issue of traditional concern to faculty members is their personnel file. Its contents are important, probably vital, in decisions on retention, tenure, and promotion made at the administrative and board levels that are above the initially recommending body, the department. Faculty often speculate on its contents. Are there nasty little notes from persons both known and unknown? Are there secret evaluations? Did that former dean with whom I did not get along slip in some derogatory comments? Are there misstatements of fact? Are there significant omissions as far as records of publications and other accomplishments are concerned? If frequency of appearance in collective-bargaining agreements is any measure of importance to faculty, then this issue is indeed important; 75.3 percent of collective-bargaining agreements have contractual language with respect to personnel files. Typically there is great variation in precisely what has been bargained except for the one universal: access on the part of the faculty member to the file. It may be specified that access can occur only during normal business hours, must be requested in writing, cannot be requested more than once a semester, or must provide three or five or some other number of days' notice, but access is guaranteed.

Sixty-two percent of the agreements specify that as a follow-up to access, the faculty member has the right to respond to the contents of the file by appending rebuttals to particular statements in it, explaining and clarifying, or supplementing with additional sets of facts. Several agreements provide a procedure for removal and destruction of material that is erroneous or defamatory. Some specify that any material in the file that has an anonymous source shall be automatically removed. Most of these agreements require that any anonymous material submitted from the point of ratification of the agreement shall not enter the file in the first place.

Several agreements specify that certain file contents can or shall be destroyed following certain activities. At the University of Guam all material shall be destroyed thirty days after the action to which the material was relevant has been completed.[9] At the University of Long Island (Southampton Branch) material will be removed and destroyed when a faculty member's contention that it is inaccurate is sustained through the grievance procedures specified in the agreement.[10] The agreement at the University of Hawaii specifies that derogatory materal shall be destroyed five years after its placement in the file.[11] In the agreement at the College of Medicine and Dentistry of New Jersey, information that is "mutually agreed to be in error shall be corrected or expunged from the file."[12] The Iowa Agreement specifies that any complaints against a faculty member are to be called to the attention of the faculty member in writing immediately upon inclusion in the file.[13] And the Western Montana Agreement says the same thing in another way when it specifies that "complaints or criticisms which have not been made known to the individual concerned cannot be placed in the individual's personnel file or considered in any personnel administration."[14]

Although more than half (53.7 percent) of the agreements that have addressed the personnel-file issue contractually specify a single personnel file, some delineate two files: one to contain confidential preemployment material, the other to include the faculty member's records since employment on campus. The latter is designated as the one to which the faculty member has access. Still other agreements that do not require two separate files make specific mention of confidential preemployment material that is to be kept elsewhere or removed temporarily when the faculty member requests access to the file. One of the clearest descriptions of the distinction between the two files is found in the Lincoln University Agreement:

There shall be a pre-employment file which shall contain all and only materials requested or received by the University in connection with the original employment of the member. Initial letters of recommendation shall be kept confidential and kept exclusively in the pre-employment file. Other materials submitted prior to the member's employment, with the understanding that it be kept confidential, shall be so kept in the pre-employment file. Copies of nonconfidential materials, such as transcripts, curricular vitae, employment records or published materials received prior to the employment of the member shall be kept in the member's official personnel file described below. The pre-employment file shall be kept by the vice president for academic affairs or his designee.[15]

Ten agreements specify in fairly elaborate detail what shall be allowed to constitute the faculty member's personnel file. The agreement at the University of Dubuque is a representative example:

A. Academic transcripts
B. Documents supporting professional training and experience
C. All correspondence relating to employment
D. Copies of all annual contracts
E. All documents relating to personnel matters such as renewal, promotion, tenure, resignation or discharge
F. All records and transcripts supporting a faculty member's continued professional growth after initial appointment
G. Letters of recommendation or nonrecommendation submitted by department and division chairman
H. Other information including, but not limited to, matters dealing with specific competencies, achievement, scholarly research, and academic professional or other contributions; and any statement the faculty member wishes to have entered.[16]

Some agreements designate who shall have access to the file. Others do so implicitly by specifying who shall not have access. An example of the first case is the Fitchburg State College Agreement, which specifies that the official personnel file shall be open to the department chairperson, the departmental evaluation committee, the Special Committee on Tenure, the academic dean, the dean of teacher education, the president or that person's designee, and the board or its designees.

Nearly two-thirds (62.7 percent) of the agreements also provide faculty members with the right to make copies of any or all material in their own personnel file. It will likely be specified that the request shall be written, that access shall be during normal working hours, that some advance notice be provided, and that the cost of the copying shall be the faculty member's responsibility.

The diversity of the combinations of the various personnel file specifications is interesting. Any number of the following specifications may be combined: faculty access, right to respond, right to make photographic copy, distinction between confidential and nonconfidential files or sections of files, who in addition to the faculty member has access, and lists of what shall be included in the file (for example, faculty access and right to respond but nothing else; specification of a single file together with faculty access but nothing else; faculty access and right to copy, but nothing else; and so on).

Only six agreements include all of these features explicitly: Eastern Michigan University, Emerson College, Fairleigh Dickinson University, Long Island University (C. W. Post Center), the University of Massachusetts, and Northern Montana College. Several others have all but one. Central Michigan University and Saginaw Valley State College have all items save a reference to the faculty right to make copies of material in the file. The five Illinois universities under joint contract (Chicago State, Governor's State, Eastern Illinois, Western Illinois, and Northeastern Illinois) and Roger Williams College have all items except detailed specification of the contents of the file. The University of Delaware has all but any reference to whom besides the faculty member shall access to the file be given.

Such distinctions are unimportant in themselves and do not necessarily lead to a judgment that one or the other of these is inadequate so far as the issue of personnel files is concerned. We simply highlight great diversity.

At this point it should be noted that two variables we shall look at with respect to their influence on the types and quality of contractualized items, namely, the relative prestige of the institution and the nature of its support (whether public or private) produce no differences with respect to the personnel file issue.

The Bloomfield College Agreement provides a good example of a highly succinct yet fairly complete statement on personnel files:

Each faculty shall have the right, as often as he desires, to review and copy documents in his personnel file and to place in that file such written additions and responses to material therein as he shall deem necessary. No other personnel file shall be maintained by the administration.[17]

To this one might wish merely to add some specification of what should be included in the file, as well as some restraints on access.

Grievance Procedures

Probably the next most frequently occurring provision in collective-bargaining agreements in higher education institutions is for some type of grievance procedure. Only Ashland College and Bard College could be viewed as exceptions. And they have hearing procedures to handle claims of dissatisfied faculty. Although Ashland's procedure is almost unique and not a pure grievance procedure in that the hearing process appears to be coterminous with the dismissal or termination of a member faculty, Bard's hearing process begins with the request of the faculty member after an action has occurred and seems to function as a grievance procedure.

The presence of grievance procedures in collective-bargaining agreements in higher education is essentially universal, but each grievance procedure is unique. Some are more complex than others. Some are of greater benefit to faculty than others. Some specify binding arbitration as a final solution, while others specify presidents or boards of trustees as the final authority. Some provide for binding arbitration; others forbid it.

Definition

First, what is a grievance and what kind of situations or actions are defined by the agreements as grievable? All collective-bargaining contracts define a grievance in similar terms. For example, the Monmouth College Agreement says, "A grievance is a claim by a faculty member or the Association that there has been a breach, misinterpretation, or misapplication of a specific provision of this agreement."[18] That is, there is a contention by a faculty member or members or their collective-bargaining representative that the board or the administration of the college or university has violated terms or specifications of the collective-bargaining agreement.

That is the starting point. The integrity of the mutually arrived at agreement must be maintained. But following that specification there is considerable diversity. A few agreements distinguish complaints from grievances. The agreement at the New York Institute of Technology defines a complaint as "an informal claim by a member or members of the bargaining unit of improper, arbitrary, or discriminatory treatment by the institution."[19] Parallel to the informal nature of the claim is the specification that the complaint can be carried forward only through the informal stages of the grievance process. A grievance has additional steps.

A far more important distinction is between a grievance based on violation of aspects of the agreement and one based on other policies or established procedures of the institution such as a faculty handbook or printed policies of the board of trustees. Most agreements state that grievances are claims of violation of the agreement and neither affirm nor deny what else might be grievable. But eighteen agreements explicitly state that the established grievance procedures can be used also for faculty allegations of violations of the faculty handbook or board of trustees' policies. A clear example is found in the agreement at the College of Medicine and Dentistry of New Jersey, which carefully lists and distinguishes the two kinds of grievances:

> A grievance is an allegation by a faculty member or the Association that there has been:
> 1. A breach, misinterpretation or improper application of terms of this Agreement or a violation of applicable written College promotion or reappointment procedures.
> 2. An arbitrary or discriminatory or improper application of, or failure to act pursuant to other written policies, rules or regulations of the College, or statutes, which prescribe terms and conditions of employment.[20]

Even more brief but with the same intent is the phrasing in the agreement at Dyke College:

> A "grievance" shall mean a complaint that there has been a violation, misinterpretation, or inequitable application of any of the provisions of this Agreement *or any of the established policies of the Board of Trustees* (emphasis added).[21]

The agreement at Robert Morris College adds a third dimension to what is grievable; it includes grievances that respond to "arbitrary and capricious decisions." Along the same line the University of Lowell and the University of Cincinnati include "academic judgment" grievances in the faculty personnel areas of promotion, reappointment, and so on. But in the agreement at the Connecticut State Colleges, discretionary grievances shall be processed solely with respect to whether the prescribed procedures were followed and whether prescribed criteria were utilized.[22] By way of almost total contrast, however, Southern Oregon State College specifically calls out and prohibits grievances that are of an academic judgment nature. So do several others; Hofstra University, Rider College, Long Island University (Brooklyn Center), Adelphi College, Adrian College, D'Youville College, and Lincoln University all exclude grievances dealing with academic freedom. Wayne State University is unique in one of its exclusions: salary adjustments.

While limiting what can be grieved through the procedures specified in the agreement, seven explicitly refer to supplemental grievance procedures that exist in the academic senate or through other mechanisms at the institution. (I suspect that more than seven not only have a collective-bargaining grievance procedure but a supplemental one as well; however, such alternatives are not referred to in any other collective-bargaining agreements.)

Time Limits

One feature that is universally in evidence in higher education collective-bargaining grievance procedures is careful specification of time limits. Both grievant and respondent at each stage of the grievance process are granted a maximum number of days to present evidence and/or respond to allegations. To exceed these time limits on the part of the grievant is to abrogate the right to grieve further; on the part of the respondent it automatically promotes the grievance to the next level of the process. There is great variation in the precise number of days allowed at each level, though the time periods all tend to be short, by design. Many agreements specify that a basic intention is to handle grievances with dispatch. Table 2 shows time limits on filing grievances after the alleged act occurs. The range is considerable, varying from as few as five days in four agreements to as many as ninety days in two. A one-month interval is the mode. Most agreements specify that these time periods begin when the action alleged to have caused the grievance occurred or when the grievant reasonably could be expected to have learned of the action as a consequence of normal vigilance. Thus the time limits are not necessarily as restricting as they might appear.

TABLE 2
**Number of Agreements Specifying
Time Limits on Filing Grievances**

5 DAYS	10 DAYS	14-15 DAYS	20-21 DAYS	25 DAYS	30 DAYS	40-45 DAYS	60 DAYS	90 DAYS
4	14	11	14	1	26	6	7	2

The state colleges and universities are more likely than the private institutions to provide longer time limits, with the more prestigious universities most likely of all to grant longer time limits: 61.5 percent of the more prestigious state schools allow one month or more; 46.9 percent of the less prestigious state institutions grant one month or more; and only 40 percent of the private colleges allow that much time.

Faculty Involvement

Most grievance procedures specify only the route through various levels of the college or university administration that the grievance must proceed

—chairperson, dean, academic vice-president (provost), president, board—likely ending in binding arbitration if the association (collective-bargaining representative) or the institution so requests. However, thirteen agreements build in a faculty (or at least partially faculty) review process through some kind of faculty grievance committee.

At the University of Cincinnati and Regis College, subcommittees conduct the grievance process from the beginning. At Regis the committee appoints an ad hoc subcommittee to handle a particular grievance when it reaches the formal stage. At Cincinnati there are faculty grievance committees for each college and the librarians, as well as the university-wide Faculty Grievance Committee. Fitchburg State College and Massachusetts College of Art each have a faculty grievance committee composed of five people appointed by the president of the faculty association upon vote of the executive board that comes into the grievance process very early. At the remaining seven schools that have a faculty review process of some kind, the faculty grievance committee enters the process after at least the levels of dean or vice-president for academic affairs have been passed through without satisfactory resolution of the grievance. As such, they tend to be advisory to the president and/or the board. If they are unsuccessful in mediaton and resolution, the grievance can be taken to binding arbitration. Such is the case at Bloomfield College, Bryant College of Business, Eastern Michigan University, Northern Michigan University, and Central Michigan University. At the University of New Haven the decision by four-fifths of a five-person committee is binding. Anything less than such a majority sends the grievance to binding arbitration if so requested by the faculty association. Somewhat similarly at Fairleigh Dickinson University, a majority vote of the six-person faculty Status Judiciary Committee shall be binding upon the grievant, the collective-bargaining agent, and the university. An important though far from debilitating limitation on this committee's deliberations and recommendation is this qualification:

> In making its decision, the Judiciary shall not substitute its judgment concerning the grievant's credentials for that of the committees and the individuals whose recommendations or decisions are under review except insofar as it finds merit to an allegation that a particular action was arbitrary, capricious, or discriminatory, or that it violated department, college or University standards established consistent with terms of this agreement.[23]

The arrangements at Central Michigan University are more complex. Two committees are involved. One, the Contract Grievance Conference, composed of two representatives from the university and two from the association, is invoked in contract grievances if the answer of the contract grievance administrator is not satisfactory to either side. If the recommendation of the conference is not satisfactory to either side, binding arbitration can be invoked. The second grievance committee, the Faculty Review Committee, can be established if there are alleged procedural violations or errors of fact, prejudice, arbitrary or capricious action, or if action is considered violative of academic freedom. Of high significance is the following clause from the Central Michigan University Agreement: "The Faculty Review Committee shall have full power to settle the grievance, including the authority to award tenure, promotion and reappointment. Its decision shall be final and binding on all parties."[24]

Binding Arbitration

Binding arbitration is included in 84 percent of all agreements as the final stage of the grievance process. Most agreements specify that only the collective-bargaining representative or the institution itself can call for arbitration, with costs to be shared equally between the agent and the institution. In addition, these agreements carefully limit the scope of the decision that an arbitration panel can hand down. A phrase like "the arbitrator shall have no authority to add to, subtract from, or otherwise modify this agreement" is universal.

Other Grievance Considerations

A few contracts provide that the institution shall engage in no reprisals against either the grievants themselves or those who aided them in the grievance process. The language in the Rhode Island College Agreement is typical of the sixteen schools that have included this provision:

> No reprisals of any kind shall be taken by the Board or any agent thereof against any party in interest, any witnesses, any member of the Rhode Island College Grievance Committee, or any other participant in the grievance procedure by reason of such participation.[25]

The agreement for the Detroit College of Business defines reprisals as restraining, coercive, discriminatory, or retaliatory action of any type.

Many agreements specify that resort to any other procedure or mechanism (for example, legal action) negates the grievance proceedings and closes them. The agreement of the State Colleges and Universities of the Illinois Board of Governors provides a good example:

> If prior to filing a grievance hereunder, or while a grievance is in progress, an employee seeks resolution of the matter in any other form, whether administrative or judicial, the Board or any University shall have no obligation to entertain or proceed further with the matter pursuant to the grievance procedure.[27]

There is great variation in the amount of space devoted to specifying the grievance procedure in agreements. At one end of the range is Regis College, which devotes 40 percent of its fairly brief agreement to the procedure. At the other end is Quinnipiac College, where the grievance procedure is covered by thirty-six lines, less than 3 percent of the lines in the agreement. The size of the proportion, however, is no necessary indicator of the importance of that item in the eyes of either the faculty or the administration, nor is brevity necessarily an indication of inadequacy. The Quinnipiac Agreement includes all the basic ingredients, save one, that seem to be important. The exception is that of providing a formal definition of a grievance. The agreement includes a commitment to attempting first to use informal procedures for prompt and just resolution of the problem, specification of time limits and a hierarchy of steps, and resort to binding arbitration as the final resolution.

The usual assumption is that a grievant is an employee—in higher education, a faculty member. Therefore agreements specify that the grievance may be filed by individual faculty members, by groups of faculty, or by the collective-bargaining agent that represents the faculty. Most do not feel it necessary to specify that the institution may not file a grievance against the faculty or its representatives. In fact, the University of Dubuque is unique in doing just that when it states very succinctly, "The University may not file a grievance."[28]

At the opposite end and in a nearly unique position is the Central Michigan University Agreement, which not only permits the filing of a grievance by the university, but devotes four paragraphs to the process under the heading "How Central Michigan University May Bring a Grievance." In such a case, grievances go directly to a grievance administrator who coordinates and expedites. This grievance administrator can represent both faculty and administration. The only other agreement to include an explicit provision for the employer to file a grievance against the collective-bargaining agent is in the agreement for the U.S. Coast Guard Academy: "in the case of any grievance involving the interpretation or application of this Agreement which the Union may have against the Employer, or *which the Employer may have against the Union* (emphasis added)."[27]

The best grievance system is the one that never needs to be used. Several agreements speak to this, usually by way of an introduction, when they comment that both parties hope that problems can be resolved through informal procedures and channels. The agreement for the Connecticut State Colleges begins in this way:

> The parties agree that all problems should be resolved whenever possible, before the filing of a grievance, and they encourage open communication between management and members of the bargaining unit so that resort to the formal grievance procedure will not normally be necessary. The parties further encourage the informal resolution of grievances at the lowest possible level.[30]

Conclusions

We have already seen that a clear majority of collective-bargaining teams have addressed issues of fundamental importance to faculty and included them in their agreements. If we wish to speak from the faculty perspective, we can talk about a general level of success in the area of faculty rights. Yet there is no so-called right of faculty that is included in all collective-bargaining contracts. Even such a basic faculty expectation as academic freedom is omitted from 21.3 percent of the agreements. Thus many agreements have a great deal of room to expand the list of faculty rights that are included.

On some issues this expansion may be accomplished quite easily. Perhaps an item was omitted by oversight or because both parties assumed that academic tradition by itself, or what is said in other documents at the institution, would be enough of a guarantee for faculty with respect to particular issues. But on other issues the absence of mention in the agreement is a signal of a stalemate or a lack of consensus between the bargaining teams.

Therefore, we can predict spirited negotiations over any faculty right I have identified here that is not included in a given agreement. The negotiations will be most intense in the area of faculty grievances. Faculty will want to expand the scope of such grievances; administrations will want to set narrower limits. Yet there exists the precedent in one-fifth of the agreements that grievance procedures established by the collective-bargaining agreement can be utilized even when the grievance is with reference to alleged violations of other documents, policies, and principles in effect at the institution. Faced with such data, faculty will probably say, "*as many as* one fifth." Administrators will rejoin, "*Only* one fifth." Compromise and resolution will require long and intricate debate and negotiation.

Along a similar vein, 15 percent of the agreements provide for some kind of faculty review factor to be included in the grievance process. This is a provision that most faculty likely will view as a goal toward which to strive, yet at least some administrations will oppose it.

Thus there is no clear consensus among collective-bargaining agreements in higher education on the nature or scope of faculty rights, nor will there ever be. However, agreements most assuredly will move toward greater consensus once both faculty and administrations know what has been successfully bargained elsewhere. That binding arbitration, for example, is specified as the final grievance stage in 84 percent of the agreements under study will encourage the faculties at most other institutions to push for inclusion of this provision.

Notes

1. Agreement (1976-79), University of New Haven, p. 1.
2. Agreement (1976), University of Scranton, p. 7.

3. Agreement (1976-79), Hofstra University, p. 38.

4. Agreement (1977-80), Central Michigan University, pp. 33-35.

5. Agreement (1979-80), Park College, p. 4.

6. Agreement (1978-80), Cooper Union, p. 3.

7. Agreement (1976-78), Adelphi University, p. 4.

8. Agreement (1977-79), New Jersey Institute of Technology, p. 9.

9. Agreement (1976-79), University of Guam, p. 37.

10. Agreement (1974-77), University of Long Island, Southampton Center, p. 8.

11. Agreement (1977-79), University of Hawaii, p. 26.

12. Agreement (1979-81), College of Medicine and Dentistry of New Jersey, p. 4.

13. Agreement (1977-79), Iowa State Board of Regents' Colleges and Universities, p. 9.

14. Agreement (1977-79), Western Montana College, p. 17.

15. Agreement (1976-78), Lincoln University, p. 6.

16. Agreement (1977-78), University of Dubuque, p. 20.

17. Agreement (1975-77), Bloomfield State College, p. 24.

18. Agreement (1976-79), Monmouth College, p. 18.

19. Agreement (1977-80), New York Institute of Technology, p. 29.

20. Agreement (1979-81). College of Medicine and Dentistry, p. 4.

21. Agreement (1976-79), Dyke College, pp. 29-30.

22. Agreement (1977-79), Connecticut State Colleges, p. 37.

23. Agreement (1977-79), Fairleigh Dickinson University, p. 89.

24. Agreement (1977-80), Central Michigan University, p. 13.

25. Agreement (1975-77), Rhode Island College, p. 43.

26. Agreement (1979-81), Detroit College of Business, p. 6.

27. Agreement (1977-79), State Colleges and Universities of Illinois, sec. 10:2.

28. Agreement (1977-78), University of Dubuque, p. 21.

29. Agreement (1978-79), U.S. Coast Guard Academy, pp. 12-13.

30. Agreement (1977-79), Connecticut State Colleges, p. 37.

3. PRIMARY EMPLOYMENT DECISIONS

Academic personnel decisions encompass not only a series of discrete steps that is greater in number than in many other employment environments but a process that is essentially unique as well. The steps begin with a decision concerning where in the college or university there are or shall be positions available and proceed through the search, the hiring (appointment), the retention (reappointment), the tenure decision, promotion decisions, and finally the granting of emeritus status. There may also be decisions concerning discipline or dismissal because of alleged improprieties performed by the faculty member or layoff, retrenchment, or reallocation because of changes in enrollment patterns at the institution. Faculty are very sensitive to the dynamics of these situations and reflect their concern over these issues in the agreements that have been negotiated.

Initial Appointment

Nearly half (47.2 percent) of the collective-bargaining agreements speak to the issue of the initial appointment of faculty members. The agreements at the private colleges and universities are more likely to do so (60 percent) than are those at the public institutions (39.6 percent).[1] In most cases this section of an agreement specifies that a letter of appointment provide details on such items as the rank at which the faculty member is employed, a statement of tenure status, a description of one's primary assignment, and the date of appointment. In most agreements this section also specifies the criteria so far as training, experience, progress toward various academic degrees, and the like that shall be required for appointment in various ranks. Further, most make some statement to the effect that an appointment letter must state explicitly that whatever in a collective-bargaining agreement relates to a faculty member's rights shall be automatically incorporated into the faculty member's contract, or, if not so stated in the letter, such rights are declared for all faculty within the agreement itself. An example of the former is in the Regis College Agreement, which states that all letters of appointment shall contain the following clause:

> This letter of appointment is offered and accepted subject to the applicable provisions of the Collective Bargaining Agreement 1977-1979 between Regis College and the Regis College Chapter of the American Association of University Professors.[12]

Some agreements specify the approval route that needs to be followed in the hiring of new faculty. Although most require some faculty contribution to the process, the range of democratic involvement by faculty is wide. At the democratic end is the Long Island University (Brooklyn Center) Agreement, which specifies that an applicant must be reviewed and approved by a majority of qualified voters in a department before the name is sent on to the president and the chancellor for final approval and appointment.[3] Similarly the Pennsylvania State Colleges and Universities Agreement says that "a candidate, who may be secured from any source, first must be recommended by the department Faculty."[4] At the other end of the scale is the Florida State University Agreement:

> The Board shall exercise its authority to determine the standards, qualifications, and criteria so as to fill appointment vacancies in the bargaining unit with the best possible candidates. In furtherance of this aim, the Board shall, through the universities, advertise such appointment vacancies, receive applications and screen candidates therefore, and make such appointments as it deems appropriate under such standards, qualifications, and criteria.[5]

In between are agreements such as that at Cooper Union, which states that although the "final decision on hiring of all new full-time Faculty members and professional Librarians shall be made by the President," faculty members shall be consulted prior to making the appointment.[6] At Cooper Union those faculty shall be "appropriate available senior full-time Faculty members."[7]

Reappointment

With respect to the next decision to be made—the annual reappointment decision—only slightly more than half of all agreements (58.2 percent) deal explicitly with this issue. In all, 75 percent of the agreements at private schools do so, but only 39.6 percent of the agreements at public institutions. Of those that deal with this issue, quite understandably most merge their discussion of reappointment with that of tenure, since at some point a decision not to renew a faculty member's appointment is implicitly not to grant tenure.

A universal feature for those contracts containing clauses on the reappointment issue is some specification of dates within the February 1 to April 1 range on annual reappointments. Some specify criteria for evaluating the probationary faculty member, and some also specify a process. One of the most orderly and clear is in the University of Dubuque Agreement. There the procedures for handling first-year probationary appointments are as follows:

The department and division chairpersons and the Academic Dean will meet with each first-year probationary faculty member no later than December 15 to evaluate and discuss the faculty member's professional performance. At this conference, the faculty member's teaching, scholarship, and other professional activities will be assessed.

Such evaluation will result in a written statement of the faculty member's professional effectiveness. If that effectiveness is inadequate in any respect, the faculty member will have the opportunity to set down in writing a plan to remedy those inadequacies and insure continued professional growth.

Recommendations for renewing contracts of first-year-probationary faculty members shall be submitted by department and division chairpersons to the Academic Dean. These evaluations will include a statement on the professional growth of the probationary faculty member since the conference referred to in B, 1 above. Letters of reappointment or non-reappointment shall be issued by the Academic Dean not later than March 1. A copy of each letter of non-reappointment shall be sent to the Association. [8]

Undoubtedly many institutions have a process described in a faculty handbook or similar document but do not contractualize it. In only a few cases are such faculty handbook procedures referenced in the collective-bargaining agreement. Some agreements specify a review or hearing process that a nonreappointed faculty member may request. The grievance procedure is available in many contracts though seldom specifically referenced when the agreement discusses nonreappointment. An exception is Loretto Heights College where the grievance procedure through level one, division head or dean, is open to a faculty member who is not renewed in his or her first year; level two, college president, for those in their second to fourth year; and level three, binding arbitration, for those in their fifth year. Also an exception is the agreement at Cooper Union, which specifies that faculty members who believe that the proper procedure was not followed may process their contention through the grievance procedure. [9] Less clear is the provision in the Pratt Institute Agreement: "Any determination which is arbitrary, capricious, or discriminatory shall be subject to the grievance procedure."[10] It is not clear whether the arbitrary, capricious, or discriminatory nature of decision must be proved before a grievance can be filed or if allegations alone would suffice.

At the other end of the scale are six schools that state specifically in their collective-bargaining agreements that nonreappointment decisions are not grievable through regular grievance procedures. An additional four specify that no personnel decisions shall be grievable.

Tenure

Most academics regard tenure as a decision of the highest order. This view is stated succinctly in the Framingham College Agreement: "The granting of tenure is the single most important type of decision made in an educational institution. Barring unforeseen circumstances, tenure obligates the institution for the employment of the faculty member for the balance of his professional life.''[11] The D'Youville College Agreement adds that tenure is a privilege, not a right, and lists the standard areas in which judgments are made: "Tenure is status granted by the college in recognition of sound scholarship, enthusiasm for teaching, professional attitude, teaching skill, and esteem of students and peers.''[12] Among the agreements is a fairly high degree of consensus that tenure is not only something to be granted faculty members who are qualified but that it should be made part of the collective-bargaining agreement as well. Not all institutions agree, however; 20.2 percent do not include specific language on tenure. Of these eighteen institutions, three make a clear reference to rules, principles, definitions, and procedures with regard to tenure that are included in a faculty constitution, faculty handbook, or the like and provide that alleged violations of those provisions shall be grievable, or in some manner incorporate them into their collective bargaining agreement. At one institution, a letter to faculty notes that a letter of agreement in which there shall be a commitment not to change present practices shall be written once the formal agreement is ratified. For seven others we can infer from the agreement the existence of principles and procedures with respect to tenure (often in state law), but they are not explicitly stated. For all intents and purposes, then, only 7.9 percent (seven) of the agreements do not include reference to tenure. Three of these probably have tenure (Ferris State College, Roger Williams College, and the State University of New York System); four probably do not (Goddard College, the U.S. Merchant Marine Academy, the U.S. Coast Guard Academy, and Wentworth Institute of Technology). In short, most collective-bargaining agreements in higher education include tenure as a negotiated item. As such, William McHugh's prediction in 1971 that "tenure is likely to become a major negotiable issue when faculty bargaining arrives on campus" was prescient.[13] A major reason for the high level of interest in negotiating tenure is, of course, that the conditions conducive to unionization are much the same as those that encourage the contractualization of tenure.[14]

There appears also to be high consensus on the fundamental purpose or intent of tenure. The Bard College Agreement, for example, says, "Tenure has one purpose and justification: to insure the adherence of the college to its stated policy of academic freedom. It is not justified as or intended to be a compensation for low salaries or a reward for long and faithful service."[15] And the Framingham College Agreement states:

> The serious decision of granting tenure demands that the President, before making recommendations to the Board, have substantial evidence determined through professional evaluation, that the candidate will be a constructive and significant contributor to the continuous development of high quality education in the institution.[16]

The Connecticut Agreement is even more explicit in emphasizing both the rights inherent in tenure and the responsibilities:

> Since the purpose of the system of tenure is the protection of academic freedom, it shall not be considered a sinecure. It remains incumbent upon the member to maintain and improve professional competence, professional growth, and the excellence which occasioned the grant of tenure to the member.[17]

There is even high consensus on time limits that apply before a tenure decision must be made. The range of the probationary period is from three to seven years; the clear majority (63.6 percent) specify seven years as the maximum probationary period, with a tenure decision required to be made during the fifth or sixth year. Only four agreements are at the low end of three years. Prestige of institution is irrelevant so far as length of the probationary period, but the private colleges are somewhat more likely than state institutions to specify the seven-year probationary period (56.8 percent of the private and 41.6 percent of the state colleges and universities).

Despite fundamental similarities of both intent and process, one area in which substantial differences of procedure stand out is that of the recommendatory process. That is, through what steps or stages of review and recommendation does an application for tenure proceed? The diversity is considerable and seems in significant part to be a function of the size (number of faculty members) of the institution. For example, in small schools it is common for a college- or university-wide committee on tenure to review the applications and make recommendations directly to the dean or president in essentially a two-level process. The faculty at Massachusetts College of Art selects an ad hoc committee for each applicant.[18]

At larger schools the review process commonly involves four or five steps, occasionally even six. Collective-bargaining agreements are likely to specify in considerable detail (covering several pages) the procedures people must follow at each level. Generally the beginning is a departmental personnel committee or committee of the whole that passes a recommendation on to the department chairperson. In some cases the chairperson will forward the departmental recommendation to the school dean, and in others to a school tenure committee and then to the dean. From the dean it may go to a college- or university-wide tenure committee for review, but most commonly it goes directly from the dean to the provost (the vice-president for academic affairs) or the president.

An explicit statement in many agreements and implicit in the others is that tenure can be granted sooner than the five- or seven-year time frame—immediately upon hiring, in fact. The agreement at Oakland University specifies that a full professor is tenured upon employment as full professor whether hired at that rank or promoted later. Further, associate professors automatically are tenured upon the first reemployment after the promotion.[19] In the same spirit, a few other agreements (9 percent) permit the acceptance of some years of prior experience as credit toward the minimum probationary period. The maximum number is almost always three. At Pratt Institute it is two, with prior experience counting at a rate of two for one (that is, four years prior experience counting as two years toward tenure at Pratt).[20]

Most agreements allow grievances regarding tenure to go through the normal grievance process. In fact, 68 percent provide either implicitly or explicitly for the contractual grievance procedure as a recourse if a faculty member feels grieved concerning application of the tenure procedures and criteria. Most make general statements to the effect that the grievance process shall handle alleged violations of any provision in the agreement. Such a statement includes by definition the tenure-awarding process. At least one agreement, however, leaves no doubt that decisions that exude from the tenure process are grievable. The Wayne State University Agreement says:

If, in the opinion of the candidate and the Association, the failure to recommend the award of tenure was, at any level, based substantially on the candidate's exercise of his/her constitutional rights or was due to a violation of this Agreement, the candidate may file a grievance at Step III of the Grievance Procedure.[21]

Others specify clearly that a tenured faculty member who faces termination shall be granted access to the grievance process, but they leave uncertain the grievance rights of nontenured faculty.

Of the 27 percent (twenty-four agreements) that do not provide contract grievance arrangements as a response to tenure decisions, four agreements at least provide for or refer to alternative procedures for hearings and review of decisions. For example, the Ashland College Agreement provides that faculty members denied tenure for what such faculty feel are inadequate or unjust grounds may request a "hearing by the appropriate instructional faculty committee established by the Faculty Senate."[22]

State institutions are noticeably more likely to permit grievances over tenure decisions. Whereas the contracts of 90 percent of the state colleges and universities permit such grievances, only 65 percent of the agreements at private institutions do so.

The grievance provisions relating to tenure (promotion and reappointment as well) in effect through the collective-bargaining agreement at Central Michigan University are unique. One important feature of it is the provision of two alternative procedures for the grievant. When the allegation is one of procedural error, the grievant may proceed through the normal grievance process, which is subject to final binding arbitration. But when the grievant alleges "that a violation of procedural regulations has occurred, or that errors of fact, prejudice, arbitrary and capricious actions, or considerations violative of academic freedom have occurred, any one or more of which materially contributed to the decision," the bargaining unit member may submit the grievance through step 3 of the grievance procedure and then be referred to a faculty review committee. This seven-member committee, selected from a panel of eleven randomly identified faculty members (both the faculty association and CMU Central Michigan University can exercise two peremptory challenges each), has full power to settle a grievance. This includes the authority to award tenure, promotion, or reappointment. Also a faculty committee has the contractualized right to overturn a personnel decision made elsewhere in the institution.[23]

A final issue associated with the subject is that of tenure quotas. Although only two agreements contractualize a quota, administrative personnel at other universities have certainly talked about it. The agreement at Bryant College of Business specifies that there shall be no tenure in a department beyond 65 percent of the faculty.[24] The Monmouth College contract does not specify a quota, but one is assumed because the contract speaks of the "limitations" on the number of tenured faculty that exist at the college.[25]

While most agreements do not speak in any manner to the issue of quotas, two make very explicit statements at a pole opposite that of Bryant and Monmouth. The agreement at Temple University says, "The policy of Temple is not to have quotas limiting the number of persons we can advance to the distinguished status of tenured faculty."[26] And the agreement at Wayne State University says that there shall be no fixed proportion of tenure to nontenured faculty in the university, in any college, or in any department or division.[27]

Promotion

Second in importance to tenure to most faculty members as they look to the future is the prospect of promotion in rank. The issue for faculty who are negotiating collective-bargaining agreements appears not to be how to wrest the ultimate authority from boards of trustees and presidents who always are the official grantors of tenure, but how to ensure significant faculty contribution to the decision-making process.

Some measure of the importance of the promotion issue is indicated by the frequency of its appearance in collective-bargaining agreements; 73 percent of all agreements devote space to some measure of specificity regarding promotion. There is no significant difference by type of institution. Of the state institutions, 77.1 percent speak to the promotion issue, while 70 percent of the private institution agreements do so. Usually included are two sets of statements: one that identifies the set of criteria that shall be used as a base against which to evaluate the faculty candidate for promotion, and one that describes, often in considerable detail, the process of evaluation and decision making that shall be followed.

Although 73 percent of the agreements have included language on promotion, that does not necessarily mean that a lot of material is included or that faculty have gained much as a consequence. In fact, a few agreements are almost amazing in this regard. For example, the agreement for the Florida State College and University system says that the criteria for promotion are to be determined by the board, and the recommendations for promotion are to begin with the faculty member's supervisor, proceed through "appropriate administrative officials," and end with the president.[28] At no point is there any indication, let alone guarantee, of faculty contributions to the recommendatory process. Similarly the agreement at Adrian College states that a faculty member may be considered for promotion "provided he shall prove himself worthy of same to the Vice President for Academic Affairs or his designee during the appropriate evaluation time."[29]

Most agreements, nevertheless, do specify faculty involvement in the evaluative and recommendatory process, usually at one point in the process but at as many as three points (excluding the department chairperson) in at least three institutions (Northern Michigan University, Oakland University, and Southeastern Massachusetts College). Thirty-five percent of the agreements (that is, 45.6 percent of those with contractual language on promotion) specify that either a departmental personnel committee or the department as a whole shall make the initial evaluation or recommendation with respect to promotion and rank for an individual faculty member. Twenty-nine percent (38.2 percent of those with contractual language on promotion) require that a faculty committee representing the total institutional faculty be involved as a filtering and advisory body in the promotion decision process. The committees that work at the institutional level usually are a combination of administrative appointees and elected faculty members. Most often the faculty are elected by a senate procedure; occasionally they are appointed or elected directly by the faculty association or federation. For example, at Robert Morris College, the faculty federation is required by the agreement to appoint a faculty committee on rank.[30] At Wentworth Institute of Technology, all recommendations for promotion are made by a committee that is chaired by the provost and composed of five faculty members: one appointed by the president, two elected by the department chairpersons, and two appointed by the faculty federation (union).[31]

In only a few institutions are quotas established with regard to the number or proportion of faculty at various ranks. In fact, I am aware of only four at which such quotas are contractualized: Adrian College, the University of Guam, Western Montana College, and Robert Morris College. The last agreement specifies only that the college may impose a limit of 20 percent of the total faculty that can occupy the rank of professor.[32]

By way of direct contrast with the four agreements that specify or allow a quota are two that expressly prohibit the establishment of a fixed proportion. The remaining, a clear majority, leave the issue open and rely on noncontractual understandings.

The issue of where the considerations for promotion originate (whether by the candidates themselves on their own initiative, on someone else's initiating recommendation, primarily as a consequence of automatic consideration by virtue of length of time in rank, or some other criterion) has no consensus. In addition to the three specific options just mentioned is the most common alternative of all: not specifying precisely where or how a consideration for promotion is originated (35.3 percent of the agreements that speak to the promotion issue). The next most common point of initiation for a faculty member's promotion in rank is the candidate (25 percent). The department is the next most likely to bear the responsibility—sometimes specifying that the responsibility lies with the chairperson but usually with a department committee (23.5 percent). In 16.2 percent of the agreements, it is specified that consideration and review is automatic for each faculty member on an annual basis.

The question of the grievability of promotion decisions is left open in most agreements. Only 22 percent specify that a grievance or appeal procedures of some type may be followed even if only on procedural, not substantive, grounds.

Clearly the contractual language on the issue of promotion in rank varies. From the faculty perspective the range is from either nothing at all or language that fails to provide explicitly for faculty participation, through a wide variety of faculty committee structures, and finally to explicit specification not only that the primary responsibility for judging the merit of faculty members for promotion in rank rests with faculty but that careful procedures must be followed throughout the process and by all persons involved in the decision. A prime example of contractual language regarding this last point is the Central Michigan University Agreement. After speaking to the importance of both excellent teaching and continuing research by faculty members, and listing broad university-wide promotion criteria such as teaching competence, involvement in university life, and the like, the agreement makes two statements about the special capability of faculty members' promotion recommendations: "Departmental colleagues are best informed and are in the best position to arrive at specific criteria or objectives to satisfy contributions in teaching, research, and related supplementary activities,[33] and "The primary responsibility of judging the extent to which departmental members have pursued their professional university obligations, and have disseminated knowledge rests with the department."[34] A promotion calendar with a series of deadlines for recommendations is provided. And finally the agreement specifies that any changes with respect to promotion policies (as well as tenure and reappointment) shall require agreement among the collective-bargaining agent, the academic senate, and the university administration.

Discipline and Dismissal

It is next to impossible to discuss the subject of academic discipline without also talking about dismissal of faculty members by the academic institution. Discipline and dismissal are essentially synonomous in most agreements. In fact, only 21.3 percent of all agreements discuss discipline as either a general concept or as involving alternatives other than dismissal (27.1 percent of the public institutions, only 12.5 percent of the agreements at private colleges and universities), and 47.2 percent provide a procedure for academic dismissal. The number includes the 21.3 percent referred to previously. The primary function of the contractualizing of discipline in general, and dismissal for cause in particular, seems to be the granting of appeal or grievance rights to the faculty members affected and usually providing a due-process procedure to be followed before the final act of discipline. Although few agreements spend much time talking separately about discipline distinct from dismissal, I will make the distinction and focus first on the general concept of discipline as it has been contractualized.

A few agreements note that academic discipline can take more than one form. For example, the Ferris State College Agreement defines disciplinary action as oral warning, written reprimand, probation, or suspension.[35] The Florida Agreement speaks to suspension with or without pay and specifies that counseling is not considered a disciplinary act.[36] The agreement for Wagner College is most explicit of all in distinguishing various forms of discipline. Although it first takes up discharge and suspension as forms of discipline, later it identifies several miscellaneous disciplinary acts that can be imposed upon faculty for their failure to abide by specific elements of the collective-bargaining agreement:

a)   A letter of warning, a copy of which shall be placed in the faculty member's Performance File for a period of one year and which shall be destroyed at the expiration of that time.

b)   An appropriate fine not to exceed $200, or a proportionate salary reduction where services are withheld.

c)   A letter of reprimand, a copy of which may be placed in the faculty member's Performance File.[37]

All agreements refer to the need for just cause or adequate cause (also called proper cause and good cause) before disciplinary steps can be commenced. But they seldom define adequate cause as fully as does the Oakland University Agreement where just or adequate cause is limited to failure to fulfill professional responsibilities, professional misconduct, conduct punishable as a felony, or conduct violating article 20 of the agreement on work stoppage.[38] The agreement at the University of San Francisco defines just cause as that which is so defined by arbitration case law under the National Labor Relations Act.[39] The agreement at the University of Massachusetts puts discipline within the context of failure to perform the minimum assigned duties associated with faculty work load. Examples included in the agreement are these:

for instructional faculty, the failure to meet classes, keep office hours, advise students and maintain other traditional methods of student-faculty contact; for research/extension/service faculty or librarians, the failure to meet pertinent schedules of work.[40]

So far as procedures for discipline are concerned, a few agreements specify that informal discussion should take place as the first step. Most of the eighteen agreements that speak of discipline as distinct from dismissal specify that after written notice is sent, some time must be granted for the faculty member to respond to the charges. A faculty committee may be called upon at this point. If the discipline (such as suspension) is carried out, then the matter becomes grievable and likely arbitrable as well.

The primary function of the contractualizing of discipline in general and dismissal for cause in particular seems to be the granting of appeal and grievance rights to the faculty member affected. Usually, also, a due-process procedure to be followed before the final act of dismissal is prescribed in the agreement.

Although the agreements exhibit great variation of language and the details of procedures, those that have a dismissal procedure (the 47.2 percent) almost universally prescribe a slow, deliberate procedure that involves careful scrutiny by a representative faculty committee. Universally, the formal charges and the formal faculty review are to be preceded by an informal conference between the accused and what is defined as an appropriate administrative officer (dean, provost, or president). Frequently it is stated explicitly that all parties involved hope that such an informal conference shall resolve the matter.

If a resolution is not reached at the informal stage, commonly the matter is referred to a hearing committee after formal charges have been filed with the accused. In fact, only three of the agreements that have language on dismissal procedures omit a faculty hearing committee. Each of these specifies that if a resolution has not been accomplished following conferences between the parties involved, the issue shall go directly to arbitration. Slightly fewer than half (43.3 percent) of the other agreements that specify a hearing committee of faculty members require the formation of a special ad hoc committee to handle the individual case. The other 56.7 percent specify that an existing committee shall conduct the hearing.

Many of the agreements not only provide for a special informal and/or formal hearing process but specify that following the hearing, if the accused faculty member requests, the normal grievance procedure also can be followed. This process can be activated even after the president and/or board have reached decisions on the basis of the special dismissal review process. Seventy percent of the agreements that incorporate reference to a dismissal procedure specify or at least clearly permit recourse to the regular grievance procedure at some point. An additional 23 percent do not speak to the question or have no another grievance procedure. Most of the institutions included in the 23 percent probably intended that the hearing and review procedure outlined for dismissal cases would suffice and that the grievance procedure would not need to be invoked, but only three agreements explicitly state that the outcome of a dismissal case is not grievable.

The contractual provisions on dismissal are clear that no party to such actions will approach it lightly. The overriding philosophy that is at least implicit in most of the agreements is well stated in the Agreement at the Polytechnic Institute of New York:

In the effective college, a dismissal proceeding involving a faculty member on tenure, or one occurring during the term of an appointment, will be a rare exception, caused by individual human weakness and not by an unhealthful setting. When it does come, however, the college should be prepared for it, so that both institutional integrity and individual human rights may be preserved during the process of resolving the trouble. The faculty must be willing to recommend the dismissal of a colleague when necessary. By the same token, presidents and governing boards must be willing to give full weight to a faculty judgment favorable to a colleague.[41]

Retrenchment

In addition to the concept of dismissal for cause is the possibility of retrenchment, often called faculty reduction, which arises because of financial exigencies and student enrollment declines. Fully 82 percent of all collective-bargaining agreements at four-year colleges and universities have a section devoted to this topic (87.5 percent of agreements at public institutions and 77.5 percent of those at private schools). Some of these agreements require some amount of faculty participation and consultation before a faculty reduction takes place. Occasionally a special faculty or senate committee is established to review the administrative analysis of the problem and its proposed solution (ten agreements specify such a committee). More often the contractual specification is merely for consultation with the collective-bargaining agent and its executive board or a special committee selected by the agent. There are twenty-seven agreements in this category (37 percent of all agreements with a retrenchment section). At Hofstra University, for example, the agreement specifies that "great weight" shall be attached to the collective-bargaining agent's responses to an administrative announcement of financial exigency and the resultant need for faculty reduction.[42] At Fairleigh Dickinson University the bargaining agent has the right to file suit to determine if financial exigency really exists.[43] If it does, then a long series of alternatives to termination must be worked through before retrenchment can occur.

The highest number of agreements (thirty-four) specify or imply that the decision is an administrative one, and they formally provide for no faculty participation. At the University of Guam the president makes faculty reduction decisions without faculty consultation and can do so even without unanimous consent of the deans.[44] At Southern Oregon, the president determines whether a financial exigency exists; the declaration of such a state automatically waives the timely notice provision of ordinary dismissal or reappointment decisions.[45] In the Florida State system, no faculty consultation is required, and there is no requirement to indicate reasons for the declaration of a need for faculty reduction.[46] An extremely clear statement of such administrative prerogatives is contained in the Park College Agreement:

Except as specifically restricted by the provisions of this Article, the College shall have the sole and exclusive right to determine: the need for retrenchment; its scope, extent and effective date; the faculty members to be affected; the courses and programs to be affected; and, all other matters as may be necessary to implementation of retrenchment.[47]

The University of Massachusetts Agreement takes a unique approach. A special committee of five representatives from the administration and five from the faculty association will meet to discuss and submit recommendations in the area of retrenchment.[48] Apparently the negotiators had reached no agreement by the time all parties wished to submit what they had agreed on to the faculty and board of trustees for ratification.

In forty-three collective-bargaining agreements (58.9 percent) a seniority and rank system is listed and required to be followed when faculty reduction is deemed necessary. At Central Michigan University, final determination is based on departmental criteria and priorities for faculty reduction.[49] At Bard College the executive committee of the bargaining agent (the local AAUP chapter) determines who is to be let go or whether salary decreases will handle the matter satisfactorily.[50] At the remaining 38 percent of institutions that have contractualized the retrenchment issue, the questions of how to select persons to be terminated is either left to administrative directive (most often) or left undecided.

Another issue is that of minimum lead time for the retrenchment notice to be given. The range that has been contractualized is from three to eighteen months, with twelve months by far the most frequent time span. Acutally, however, fewer agreements specify a minimum time period for notification than do not (34 percent versus 66 percent).

On the other hand, a large majority of agreements specify a period of time that retrenched faculty shall be placed on a top-priority recall list should the school begin to hire faculty again (59 percent of the agreements that have contractualized anything on retrenchment). The range of time is great: one year in four agreements through two years at twenty-three schools, three years at ten schools, five years at seven schools, and no time limit at all at five schools (except as at Western Michigan University where age sixty-nine is specified as the final point so far as a faculty member continuing on a preferred hiring list).[51]

A significant feature of a few agreements concerns severance pay. Ten agreements have some provision for severance pay. At Monmouth College a retrenched tenured faculty member shall receive one year's severance pay.[52] Temple University has the option of eighteen months' severance pay in lieu of eighteen months' notice for tenured faculty.[53] At Salem College and Worcester College in Massachusetts, the agreements provide for severance pay of up to six months of salary.[54] Robert Morris College will provide a severance sum of $500.[55] Fairleigh Dickinson provides one-year severance pay which it calls a year of terminal leave.[56] Northern Michigan University, Moore College of Art, and Loretto College provide for an amount of severance pay if the notice of termination is short (after February 15 in the Loretto case).[57]

Two agreements link retrenchment to specific enrollment changes. Quinnipiac College specifies that any employee can be terminated at the conclusion of any contract year following a decline of full-time equivalent day students of at least 6.5 percent in one academic year or 8.5 percent over two years.[58] Additional contingencies related to deficit-fund balances are also described. The Western Michigan University Agreement specifies that whenever the student-to-fculty ratio drops below 15.5-to-1, the institution may initiate layoffs.[59]

For none of these issues related to retrenchment is type of institution—the prestige of the institution or its public versus private status—a significant variable.

Retraining and Rehabilitation

To complete the list of personnel items that have been contractualized we turn to faculty retraining and rehabilitation. Two agreements (Framingham College and Salem College in Massachusetts) address the issue of retraining. Retraining occurs within the context of retrenchment and provides for up to two years of tuition at a state or regional institution for a retrenched faculty member in order to acquire new training and skills.[60]

Only one agreement speaks to the issue of rehabilitation. The Moore College of Art Agreement specifies that "the College and the Union agree to cooperate in encouraging employees afflicted with alcoholism to undergo a coordinated program directed to the objective of their rehabilitation.[61]

Conclusion

The fabricators of collective-bargaining agreements in higher education regard the area of personnel decisions of major importance. Clear majorities have incorporated a variety of provisions, particularly with regard to tenure and promotion, but the record is very uneven with respect to faculty versus administrative control over personnel decisions. Certainly the full range—from close to total faculty control over judgment making with respect to promotion and tenure to almost total administrative control—is present. Both extremes have been contractualized. The lesson, particularly for faculty, is clear: to reduce an issue to contractual language is not necessarily to introduce meaningful, significant faculty participation and responsibility. On the other hand, there is certainly comfort here for administrators who fear that with collective bargaining, their traditional prerogatives and responsibilities will be severely curtailed.

It is equally important to observe that the range of provisions for faculty versus administrative responsibility in the area of personnel decision making is very wide, suggesting that the give-and-take in this area will be substantial for a long time to come. At this point a trend is not even clear. Although many agreements provide faculty with the opportunity to decide who shall be retrenched, the administration is likely to be accorded the right to decide whether retrenchment is necessary in the first place. And although grievance machinery has been constructed in a majority of agreements to deal with allegations by faculty of improper procedure or outcome, the latitude for faculty review committees with respect to recommendations may be quite narrow.

Certainly both sides to collective-bargaining agreements in higher education have been hard at work in the area of personnel decisions, but the task of hammering out the compromises that will protect both parties has only just begun.

Notes

1. Beginning here and repeatedly throughout the book's subsequent chapters, I shall make comparisons between public or state and private colleges and universities, and among more prestigious state universities, less prestigious state institutions, and private colleges and technical schools. The institutions comprising prestigious state universities and systems are: City University of New York, College of Medicine and Dentistry of New Jersey, Florida State University System, Rutgers, South Dakota State College and University System, State University of New York, Temple University, University of Cincinnati, University of Connecticut, University of Delaware, University of Hawaii, University of Massachusetts, University of Rhode Island, Wayne State University, and Western Michigan University. The less prestigious state schools are: Central Michigan University, Connecticut State Colleges, Eastern Michigan University, Eastern Montana College, Ferris State College, Fitchburg State College, Framingham State College, Illinois Board of Governors', Iowa State Colleges and Universities, Kent State University, Massachusetts College of Art, Minnesota State Colleges and Universities, New Jersey Institute of Technology, New Jersey State Colleges, Northern Michigan University, Northern Montana College, Oakland University, Pennsylvania State Colleges and Universities, Rhode Island College, Saginaw Valley State College, Salem State College, Southeastern Massachusetts State College, Southern Oregon State College, U.S. Coast Guard, U.S. Merchant Marine Academy, University of Guam, University of Lowell, Vermont State Colleges, Wentworth Institute of Technology, Western Montana College, Westfield State College, Worcester State College, and Youngstown State University. Private colleges and universities are: Adelphi University, Adrian College, Ashland College, Bard College, Bloomfield College, Bryant College of Business, Cooper Union, Detroit College of Business, Dyke College, D'Youville College, Emerson College, Fairleigh Dickinson University, Goddard College, Hofstra University, Lincoln University, Long Island University (Brooklyn Center), Long Island University (C. W. Post Center), Long Island University (Southampton College), Loretto Heights College, Marymount of Virginia, Monmouth College, Moore College of Art, Park College, Polytechnic Institute of New York, Pratt Institute, Quinnipiac College, Regis College, Rider College, Robert Morris College, Roger Williams College, St. John's University, Stevens Institute of Technology, University of Bridgeport, University of Detroit, University of Dubuque, University of New Haven, University of San Francisco, University of Scranton, Utica College, and Wagner College.

2. Agreement (1977-79), Regis College, p. 1.

3. Agreement (1976-79), Long Island University, Brooklyn Center, p. 15.

4. Agreement (1974-77), Pennsylvania State College and University Faculties, p. 11.

5. Agreement (1976-78), State University System of Florida, p. 5.

6. Agreement (1978-80), Cooper Union, p. 5.

7. Ibid.

8. Agreement (1977-78), University of Dubuque, p. 11.

9. Agreement (1978-80), Cooper Union, p. 8.

10. Agreement (1978-81), Pratt Institute, pp. 20-21.

11. Agreement (1977), Framingham College, p. 86.

12. Agreement (1977-79), D'Youville College, p. 12.

13. William F. McHugh, "Effects of Bargaining on Tenure and Other Academic Policies," in *Faculty Bargaining in the Seventies*, ed. Terrence N. Tice (Ann Arbor: Institute of Continuing Legal Education, 1973), p. 120.

14. Ibid.

15. Agreement (1977-80), Bard College, p. 2.

16. Agreement (1977), Framingham College, p. 86.

17. Agreement (1977-79), Connecticut State Colleges, p. 6.

18. Agreement (1973-75), Massachusetts College of Art, p. 44.

19. Agreement (1976-79), Oakland University, pp. 10-11.

20. Agreement (1978-81), Pratt Institute, p. 53.

21. Agreement (1976-78), Wayne State University, p. 49.

22. Agreement (1972-73), Ashland College, p. 15.

23. Agreement (1977-80), Central Michigan University, p. 13.

24. Agreement (1977-79), Bryant College of Business, p. 45.

25. Agreement (1976-79), Monmouth College, p. 15.

26. Agreement (1976-80), Temple University, p. 15.

27. Agreement (1976-78), Wayne State University, p. 43.

28. Agreement (1976-78), State University System of Florida, p. 13.

29. Agreement (1976-79), Adrian College, p. 7.

30. Agreement (1977-80), Robert Morris College, p. 17.

31. Agreement (1978-80), Wentworth Institute of Technology, p. 37.

32. Agreement (1977-80), Robert Morris College, appendix A, schedule III, p. 2.

33. Agreement (1977-80), Central Michigan University, p. 25.

34. Ibid.

35. Agreement (1975-78), Ferris State College, p. 6.

36. Agreement (1976-78), State University System of Florida, p. 15.

37. Agreement (1977-80), Wagner College, p. 26.

38. Agreement (1976-79), Oakland University, p. 39.

39. Agreement (1976-81), San Francisco State University, p. 15.

40. Agreement (1977-80), University of Massachusetts, p. 19.

41. Agreement (1974-76), Polytechnic Institute of New York, p. C-2.

42. Agreement (1976-79), Hofstra University, p. 29.

43. Agreement (1977-79), Fairleigh Dickinson University, p. 98.

44. Agreement (1975-78), University of Guam, p. 4.

45. Agreement (1977-79), Southern Oregon State College, pp. 11-12.

46. Agreement (1977-78), State University System of Florida, pp. 12-13.

47. Agreement (1979-80), Park College, p. 11.

48. Agreement (1977-80), University of Massachusetts, p. 25.

49. Agreement (1977-80), Central Michigan University, p. 29.

50. Agreement (1977-80), Bard College, p. 4.

51. Agreement (1976-77), Western Michigan University, p. 35.

52. Agreement (1976-79), Monmouth College, p. 22.

53. Agreement (1976-80), Temple University, pp. 17-18.

54. Agreement (1976-77), Salem State College, p. 89; Agreement (1974-77), Worcester State College, pp. 93-4.

55. Agreement (1977-80), Robert Morris College, p. 16.

56. Agreement (1977-79), Fairleigh Dickinson University, p. 102.

57. Agreement (1975-77), Northern Michigan University, p. 35; Agreement (1976-79), Moore College of Art, p. 26; Agreement (1975-80), Loretto Heights College, p. 30.

58. Agreement (1975-78), Quinnipiac College, p. 16.

59. Agreement (1976-77), Western Michigan University, p. 31.

60. Agreement (1977), Framingham College, p. 105; Agreement (1977), Salem State College, p. 90.

61. Agreement (1976-79), Moore College of Art, p. 16.

4. COMPENSATION

Compensation is the most immediately visible result of collective bargaining. As a consequence, it is the criterion by which the success or failure of collective bargaining is judged most often. Although I shall attempt to do some evaluating and assessing of the success of collective bargaining in the area of compensation, the task is difficult because it is inherently impossible to determine what kinds of gains a given body of faculty would have netted in any given year without collective bargaining. Would it have been less? Proponents of faculty unionism would assert so. Would it have been the same? Those who suggest this answer point to the budgetary and appropriation limitations that are implicit, particularly in state institutions. If only so much money is appropriated by a state board of education or legislature or if the board of trustees sets a figure, then some would say that compensation provisions for faculty are predetermined and established at a designated level, collective bargaining notwithstanding. Logically there is another possibility: collective bargaining has produced less by way of compensation increases for faculty. Someone might suggest that out of pique perhaps or by way of recrimination on the part of administrations and boards who are unhappy that collective bargaining has come to their campus, their settlement consequently might be less than it would have been without collective bargaining. Yet although an ultimate assessment of the success of collective bargaining in the area of compensation cannot be made, we do have abundant data on what has been contractualized, what proportional salary gains were made in a given academic year, what kinds of merit pay provisions have been made, and the like.

Salary Increments

The most important item in the compensation area is annual additions to base salaries. Most often these are contractualized as percentage increases added to the previous year's base, though often these percentages vary from one rank to another. Some agreements do not include percentages, instead listing specific dollar amounts that shall be added to salary bases. Some agreements employ a third method and present a combination of percentage increases with set dollar amounts. The fourth possibility is no increase at all. There are two variants here. One is at state institutions to leave the salary issue open to legislative determination. The other is to agree contractually that there shall be no salary increase at all in a given time period. Of the agreements made during the time period under study, there is only one instance of the latter. It appears in the Goddard College Agreement which specifies that for the academic year 1976-77 there shall be no increase in salary for faculty, although for the following year $49,830 was committed for salary increases for faculty.[1]

In the majority of agreements, fairly precise figures (whether proportions or specified dollar amounts) are contractualized. Table 3 presents data on

TABLE 3

Frequency of Percentage Salary Increases Negotiated for Recent Academic Years at Four-Year Colleges and Universities

% INCREASE	1974-75 AND 1975-76	1976-77	1977-78	1978-79	1979-80
10.0	1	1			
9.5				1	
9.0	1		1		
8.5	1	1	1	1	
8.0		6	5	3	1
7.5		2		3	1
7.0	4	2	6	5	3
6.5		2	4	1	
6.0	1	4	5	5	1
5.5			3	4	
5.0	1	4	4	1	
4.5		2	1		
4.0			1		
3.5				1	
3.0					
2.5					
2.0					
1.5					
1.0					
0.5					
0.0		1			

Totals					
8.0 or more	3 (33.3%)	8 (32%)	7 (22.6%)	5 (20%)	1 (16.7%)
7.0 or more	7 (77.8%)	12 (48%)	13 (41.9%)	13 (52%)	5 (83.3%)
6.0 or more	8 (88.9%)	18 (72%)	22 (71.0%)	19 (76%)	6 (100.0%)

salary increases. In the table many of the amounts bargained in contracts are actually in excess of the proportions listed. In some cases the compensation package in an agreement includes the equivalent of 2 to 3 percent more than the straight salary item by itself. Frequently a specific dollar figure or a specified proportion is set aside for equity adjustments, increments for promotion or upon earning a terminal degree, or for merit awards. Further, few agreements mention what are commonly called roll-up costs: increased payments by the employer in social security and/or other retirement benefit premiums as a concomitant to increases in salary. Finally, some agreements include reference to increases in fringe benefits either as a proportion of salary or a specific dollar amount. These are increases in total compensation, an expense to the employer, and are of benefit to the faculty but are not included in the proportions listed in table 3. Thus the proportional salary increases in the table are conservative so far as the reporting of economic gains for faculty is concerned.

Although the compensation increases listed in the table are not overwhelming in magnitude, they are nonetheless substantial. Over threefourths (76 percent) of the agreements in table 3 granted a 6 percent or greater increase to base salary. And most of the proportions are supplemented by additional forms and amounts of compensation, such as increments for promotion or earning a terminal degree, equity adjustments, and merit awards. Half (52 percent) of the agreements have granted a financial package of 7 percent or greater, and 25 percent have negotiated an 8 percent or greater financial package.

There is no indication of a downturn in the negotiated salary increases. The averages for the most recent academic years are reported in table 4. The

TABLE 4
Average Salary Increases, by Year

1975-76		1976-77		1977-78		1978-79		1979-80 AND 1980-81	
%	N	%	N	%	N	%	N	%	N
7.0	9	6.6	25	6.5	31	6.7	25	7.1	6

average in any given year has hovered around 7 percent, reaching a low point in 1977-78 at an average increase of 6.5 percent. Clearly no decline is in evidence. In fact, some recent anecdotal information suggests the possibility of substantial increases in negotiations for 1979-80 and 1980-81 agreements. The faculty at the University of Cincinnati, for example, ended a four-day strike with a tentative agreement that would provide a salary increase of about 18 percent by the end of two years.[2] And at Central Michigan University a supplemental agreement that extends the existing three-year agreement by a year provides compensation increases in excess of 9 percent for 1980-81. Although the number of agreements that have negotiated 1979-80 and 1980-81 compensation packages is small and could not be assumed to be representative, the proportions definitely show an increase since 1977-78. Such evidence should curtail any contention that faculty unions make significant salary gains only in the beginning. In fact, some evidence from a few institutions indicates the opposite: economic gains for faculty at some institution have been smaller in the beginning, probably in part because the institution, particularly if small, needed some time to arrange its budget to include substantial raises for faculty. For example, at Goddard College, the only agreement in which a zero dollar increase has been bargained for faculty, $49,830 were negotiated for faculty salary increases the following year. That increase would be $874 each for a faculty of fifty-seven.[3] Probably also it would represent about a 6 percent increase in salary for that year if we also assume an average academic year salary for those fifty-seven faculty of slightly under $15,000.

A comparison of the proportions in tables 3 and 4 with national data presented in table 5 shows that the unionized campuses have a substantial edge over the total list of college and university campuses summarized annually by the AAUP. Although neither category is comprehensive, there are sufficient numbers in each to suggest that the addition of the remaining institutions that were not included because of lack of data would not change the proportions significantly either in absolute terms or on a comparative basis. Additionally the comparative base of all institutions in table 5 is inflated slightly by the presence in that total of many of the unionized institutions that constitute the comparison category of four-year colleges

TABLE 5
Comparative Faculty Salary Increases for
Unionized Campuses and All Campuses

	UNIONIZED	ALL
1975-76	7.0%	6.0%
1976-77	6.6	4.7
1977-78	6.5	5.3

SOURCE: Data for all campuses summarized from the AAUP's annual faculty salary report in *Academe* 65 (September, 1979): 321.

and universities. This has not skewed the proportions very much, to be sure, but we can note nonetheless that inasmuch as the unionized faculties on the average have made larger salary gains than faculties generally, the inclusion of their gains in the total average artificially narrows the gap slightly between the two categories.

These findings are reinforced by other studies of the salary benefits associated with faculty collective bargaining that are based on sample data or intensive studies of single units. An example of the latter is Trevor Bain's study of the economic gains for the faculty of the City University of New York (CUNY). He observes that although faculty unionization appears to have been secondary to political factors in raising faculty salaries at CUNY, it was significant.[4] Incidentally the principal political factor Bain identifies is the pressure for salary parity between the public school teachers of New York City and the college and university faculty in CUNY—all members of the same teachers' union, the AFT.

Robert Birnbaum also has found that unionized faculties have an edge over nonunionized ones in salary gains. In his 1974 study he found a clearcut association between unionization and salary gains at all types of schools (two-year public, four-year public colleges, four-year public universities, and four-year independent).[5] In his follow-up study published in 1976, however, he suggested that the relationship between unionization and compensation might not be so strong as originally reported.[6] Although the relationship continued at four-year public colleges and at independent institutions, the advantage had stabilized at public universities.

In a subsequent study that was similar to Birnbaum's in procedure but with slightly more recent data and employing only four-year institutions, David Morgan and Richard Kearney analyzed the salary increases for the year 1974-75 for forty-six paired union and nonunion institutions. They found evidence to support the contention that unionization improves faculty compensation. Specifically they found that the collectivized faculty had an average edge of $625 over their unorganized counterparts. Further, when compensation was the dependent variable, the union-nonunion measure was the strongest single predictor.[7]

The three categories of institution—more prestigious institutions, less prestigious public colleges and universities, and less prestigious private institutions—show few differences among them in compensation. The proportions of faculties receiving above-average salary increases (7 percent or greater) are: 38.8 percent of the more prestigious public institutions, 46.2 percent of the less prestigious public institutions, and 42.9 percent of the private institutions. Not only are these differences statistically insignificant, but the absolute percentages themselves are very close.

A few other items closely related to increases in annual salary include cost-of-living adjustments, the presence of a salary schedule, and the establishment of minimums and maximums at each rank. Not many agreements—ten of eighty-nine—have included a cost-of-living factor. And even with these there appears to be no clear intent to match cost-of-living increases with corresponding salary increases but simply to add something to salary as the cost of living goes up. For example, the agreement at Oakland University states that there shall be a supplemental payment of one-half of the percentage change in the consumer price index that is above five.[8] And in the Regis College Agreement, one-half of the consumer price index above five and one-half, but only to and including ten.[9] The St. John's University Agreement states that faculty shall receive $10 for every one-tenth of a percentage point increase in the consumer price index in excess of 6 percent, provided such increases shall not be allowed to exceed $40,000 in the university budget.[10]

The establishment or maintenance of a salary schedule in which there are certain automatic step increases at each rank is made explicit in 23.5 percent (nineteen agreements) of the agreements that include any reference to compensation (eighty-one agreements in all), or 21.3 percent of the entire number of agreements in my research universe.

Minimum and maximum salaries, but without a set salary schedule, are specified in a fair number of additional agreements—more with minimums than with maximums. With minimum salaries for each rank contractualized are twenty-three colleges and universities (27 percent of all agreements); ten of these also list maximum salaries. In most cases the minimum salaries established by a collective-bargaining agreement are not very meaningful or relevant because they are set low. In a few institutions, however, the establishment of minimums was a very calculated mechanism by which to raise the salaries of a considerable proportion of faculty.

Merit Compensation

Although the concept of merit pay is anathema to some egalitarian unionists, the evidence from extant collective-bargaining agreements in higher education shows that merit pay is not incompatible with the concept of collective bargaining in higher education. In all, 36 percent (thirty-two agreements) of the agreements under examination in this study have a merit pay component in the compensation package.

The amount set aside for distribution on the basis of merit varies fairly substantially. The smallest percentage appears to be in the Iowa system where the agreement sets the amount of 0.4 percent of total base salary for merit. Several (four) set aside one-half of 1 percent of base. An equal number establish the amount as 1 percent of the base salary. The highest proportion is 3 percent for the institutions in the University of Massachusetts system, but that percentage includes an unspecified amount for adjustment of salary inequities.[11] The Connecticut Agreement also combines merit with salary inequities but in a total amount of 2 percent of total base salary.[12]

Most of the agreements with a merit pay component contractualize specific dollar amounts, but I shall not attempt to summarize these amounts inasmuch as the figures are not comparable unless I could specify the total amount devoted to salaries. For example, the $150,000 set aside for merit at one institution may not be any more per faculty member as a proportion of total compensation than the $5,000 set aside for merit awards at a small college.

Although most agreements simply list an amount or a proportion for merit pay, some include directions for the distribution of that pay. For example, at Rutgers University the agreement specifies that $1,000 shall be given to 130 faculty.[13] At Youngstown State University there shall be ten $1,000 "distinguished-service awards."[14] At Northern Montana State College there shall be ten $500 distinguished-service awards.[15] At Worcester State College there shall be distributed several awards of up to $1,000 in value but to no more than 5 percent of the faculty.[16]

Most agreements are not so specific, however. In fact, while setting a total amount to be allocated for merit distribution, one agreement specifies that the criteria and procedures are yet to be determined. What most do say is something about the composition of the committee charged with the task of allocating the merit monies. One agreement requires an administrative-student committee; four require either a totally faculty committee or one that is primarily faculty; seven establish a committee of faculty and administrators in essentially equal numbers; another seven grant the institution's president or board sole discretion in the distribution of merit. For example, the Iowa Agreement specifies that merit salary distribution shall be "at the discretion of the Board."[17] And at Saginaw Valley State College, raises that recognize "meritorious professional performance" above the regular negotiated salary increase "shall be given by the Administration to faculty members at the sole discretion of the Administration."[18]

Even when a merit pay component has been included in the collective-bargaining agreement, the determination of merit has certainly not been given totally to the faculty. In fact, in addition to the seven agreements that grant the administration or board sole discretion are thirteen (40.6 percent of those with merit pay somehow contractualized) that fail to specify at all how such merit shall be determined.

A merit component has been included in 91 percent of the more prestigious colleges and universities that have adopted the collective-bargaining mode.[19] I assume here that given strong traditions of individual contracts and academic entrepreneurship at such institutions, the only way the collective-bargaining concept would seem attractive to many of the faculty was by a commitment to retain a merit system of some sort. A merit component has actually been negotiated in thirteen of fifteen cases.

The state institutions, in contrast to the private and small liberal arts and technical schools, are the primary ones that have incorporated merit components. While only 12.5 percent (five of forty) of the private and technical schools have negotiated a merit component, 58.3 percent (twenty-eight of forty-eight) of the state institutions have done so.

One final statistical note of interest concerning merit pay is that only one agreement explicitly rejects and outlaws merit pay. The Long Island University (Brooklyn Center) Agreement states, " 'Merit' can be recognized only by appointment, reappointment, promotion and the granting of tenure."[20]

Our conclusion with respect to merit pay is that the concept, although not impressive in its frequency of appearance in collective-bargaining contracts in higher education, nonetheless is compatible with faculty unionism. Clearly a comment that Everett Ladd and Seymour Lipset published in 1973 would be an overstatement today: "Unionization inevitably fosters policies that seek to eliminate salary differentials among those in a given job category, other than those linked to seniority."[21] Such a statement today would have to overlook the substantial number of agreements that have included some form of merit pay. On the other hand, a significant number of faculty unions (36 percent) seem to have striven to provide a solid core salary increase for all faculty, allowing discretionary merit differentials to accrue to a segment of faculty deemed, through some system of assessment, particularly meritorious. In no case is all the salary increase to be distributed according to specific merit considerations, nor is even a majority of salary funds to be distributed on the basis of special merit.

These data suggest that union organizers should be careful in promising to the faculty something that has actually been negotiated in only a minority of agreements. Of course, should either party to an agreement feel a strong commitment to the merit-pay concept, it is certainly possible to negotiate such pay. What probably will be the primary key factor in whether merit pay is included in a faculty collective-bargaining agreement will be the degree to which clear and significant faculty input into the recommendatory process is included. A great many faculty object to a merit system that is entirely administered by the administration or board of the institution. Clearly this issue is far from resolved.

Equity Adjustments

The equity or parity concept fits most stereotypes of union concerns. The concept holds out for fair treatment with respect to salary for people who are equal so far as certain objective considerations are concerned. That is, using criteria such as faculty members' degree status (usually defined in terms of whether the faculty member has an earned doctorate or something less than that), total number of years teaching or research experience, and number of years in rank, a person's salary will be compared with counterparts. Some who are lower, whether by accident of timing (joining the faculty in a particularly lean year when entry salaries were low), being a low-profile faculty member who would rarely ask the administration for any favors, or perhaps even deliberate discrimination by an administrator somewhere along the line, would be brought up to a minimum level appropriate to their degree status and experience. This would be a classic union concern for the underdog.

It is somewhat surprising, therefore, that only one-fourth of all collective-bargaining agreements at four-year colleges and universities have incorporated the equity concept. At least four of these combine merit pay with equity adjustments. Although we are left with eighteen agreements that do distinguish the two and specifically provide for such adjustments, there is considerable variety so far as what is provided. Some agreements provide funds to bring all faculty up to certain minimums on what is or at least amounts to a salary schedule. Eastern Michigan University illustrates this approach to equity when it provides examples such as an assistant professor in the tenth year of service who should be adjusted to $14,200, or a professor in the fifteenth year in rank with a Ph.D. adjusted to $23,700.[22] Other agreements provide for equity adjustments within ranks to put faculty with similar experience and training into better alignment than history and accident might have provided. One agreement defines equity as a sum of money to provide differential pay for what it calls "critical positions."[23] Two agreements limit the amount any particular faculty member can be awarded by way of an equity adjustment in any given year. The Eastern Montana College Agreement establishes a maximum of $1,500;[24] the Monmouth College Agreement sets no more than $300 per faculty member.[25] A few agreements require a joint faculty-administrative committee to determine the distribution. Some specify that equity decisions should be made by the president. A unique splitting of responsibilities is provided by the University of Massachusetts Agreement. During the 1979 and 1980 academic years one-half of the merit-equity funds was distributed to the departments for their allocation and one-half to the provosts and deans for their distribution.[26] The Agreement for the Florida State College and University system not only has the distinction of specifying more money for equity adjustments than any other ($538,381) but specifies that the money be used to correct salary inequities based on sex[27] (the agreement covers nine institutions with about 5,400 faculty members).

The type of college or university, in the sense of the three categories of prestige and support, is a significant factor in predicting whether a particular institution is likely to have contractualized something about equity adjust-ments. The more prestigious state universities clearly are more likely to have the equity concept in their contracts, though even they are below 50 percent (43.8 percent in contrast with 27.8 percent of the private institutions and only 14.7 percent of the less prestigious state colleges and universities).

A few of the remaining 75 percent of the institutions with collective bargaining allocate some funds for equity adjustments without have con-tractualized either the amount or the process in a collective-bargaining agreement. In other words, equity adjustments are made quite apart from the agreement. Further, equity adjustments sometimes have been included in an earlier agreement at particular institutions but not in the most recent one that I have included in my analysis. Nonetheless, although the pro-vision of equity adjustments is a natural issue for which faculties with collective bargaining could bargain, the proportion of agreements with such provisions seems relatively small.

Special Salary Increments

Another monetary item centers around specifying salary increments to accrue to faculty upon promotion in rank and/or upon earning an advanced degree, usually defined as a terminal degree such as a Ph.D. or Ed.D. The most common of the two is the promotion item, which is contractualized in 37.1 percent (thirty-three) of the agreements.

Four basic models have been used. One specifies a flat rate or amount of increase for promotion at any level: for example, $1,000 or 6.5 percent, whichever is larger, upon promotion at the University of Cincinnati;[28] $500 at Bard College;[29] $60 per month in the Illinois Board of Governors' Uni-versities; [30] 5 percent at Southern Oregon State College, Central Michigan University, and Temple University;[31] $625 at Youngstown State University.[32]

The second model, which is the most common (fifteen agreements), is to allocate differing amounts dependent upon the rank to which a person is being promoted. Universally the pattern is to allocate higher amounts the higher the rank. For example, at Saginaw Valley State College, the promo-tion increment for instructors moving to the assistant professor rank shall be $800, for assistant professor to associate professor $1,000, and for associate professor to professor $1,500.[33] These are the largest amounts contractualized anywhere. Close is the provision at St. John's University where the corresponding increments are $750, $1,000, and $1,250.[34] The mode of $500, $600, and $700, respectively, is found at four institutions. The lowest is at Western Michigan University where the increments are $300, $400, and $500.[35] The average in all the institutions above for the first promotion is $457, the second $648, and the final promotion $861. One agreement (the South Dakota State College and University Agreement) specifies an increasing proportion: 4.5 percent, 5 percent, and 5.5 percent, respectively, for promotion to assistant professor, associate professor, and professor.[36]

The third option is to specify that promotions shall elevate the person to the next rung on the salary schedule or to the minimum of the rank to which one is promoted. Nine agreements have some variant on this theme.

The final option, taken by two agreements, is to mention that promotion shall bring with it some amount of increase in salary but not to specify the amount.

A contractualized increase for completion of a doctorate by a faculty member is found in only 14.6 percent of the agreements. Of these thirteen institutions, five grant a flat $1,000 (with one granting $1,500 to assistant professors and $1,000 to associate professors), one $900, one $700, one $625, two $600, one a step upward on the salary scale, and one moves the person to a different salary schedule (the one for holders of a doctoral degree). Finally, one (a Roman Catholic women's college) provides $200 for completion of thirty hours of doctoral coursework but does not provide for additional compensation upon completion of the doctorate.

Compensation for Additional Work

Another set of tasks for which compensation is contractualized in some agreements can be summarized under three headings: overload teaching, summer school teaching, and off-campus (extension) teaching. Three approaches have been negotiated so far as overload compensation is concerned. The most common (in fourteen agreements) is to follow the principal lead of incremental compensation for promotion and tie overload compensation to rank. For example, at the University of New Haven the dollar amounts per credit hour of overload teaching are $261, $304, $364, and $420 for instructors, assistant professors, associate professors, and professors, respectively.[37] At Temple University the corresponding rates are $300, $350, $425, and $500.[38]

The second most common pattern (ten agreements) is to assign a flat dollar amount per credit hour regardless of the rank of the faculty member doing the overload teaching. The range is from a low amount of $100 per credit hour taught beyond thirty for the year at the University of Dubuque,[39] to $300 per credit hour in the Minnesota State College system.[40] The mode is $275 per credit hour.

The third approach is to differentiate compensation for overload teaching between undergraduate and graduate. Only two agreements make such a distinction: Fairleigh Dickinson's Agreement established for 1978-79 the amounts of $240 per semester hour undergraduate and $295 for graduate[41] and Quinnipiac College's agreement set $240 and $270 per credit hour for undergraduate and graduate teaching, respectively, for the year 1977-78.[42]

Six additional agreements must be classified as indeterminate. Either the value of the compensation is not listed (although it probably exists in another document) or the agreement states explicitly that the rate is to be negotiated on a case-by-case basis. The agreement at Loretto Heights College is a case in point. The rate is to be determined mutually on a case-by-case basis between the president or the division head and the faculty member.[43] Or, even vaguer, at the University of Scranton, the agreement says only that faculty shall receive "extra compensation" for overload teaching.[44]

The contractualization of compensation for summer session teaching takes three major forms. The most common pattern (eighteen institutions or 41.9 percent of all agreements with any language on summer session) is to establish a fixed rate (percentage) that is applied to each faculty member's annual base salary. Thus, the higher one's base rate for a nine-month contract, the higher the remuneration per credit hour of summer session teaching. That principle is modified in only one case (Temple University) where a maximum of $800 per credit hour is established no matter how high one's annual salary might be.[45]

Although these eighteen contracts agree that the appropriate way to remunerate summer session teaching is by a set percentage of one's annual salary, the maximum of that percentage varies widely. Table 6 shows this great range of summer session salaries among institutions. The highest is nearly two and a half times the lowest. The average is 17.9 percent, and half of the agreements have contractualized 18 percent or greater.

TABLE 6
Remuneration Rates for Full-Time Summer Session
Teaching as a Proportion of Base Ten-Month Salary

PROPORTION	FREQUENCY
11.10%	2
14.30	1
15.00	2
16.70	3
17.25	1
18.00	1
18.75	1
20.00	2
22.20	3
27.30	1

The next most common approach to summer session remuneration is the flat-rate method—a set amount per credit hour taught regardless of rank or annual salary base. For undergraduate teaching[46] the range is from $225 per credit hour at the Detroit College of Business[47] to $557 per credit hour as an upper limit at the University of Hawaii.[48] The rates are clustered at the lower end, however. Credit hour rates are $225, $240, $251, $283, $300, $302, $333, $400, and $557. The flat rate approach as contractualized so far almost invariably yields less remuneration to faculty than does the percentage rate method. For example, a faculty member with a $15,000 annual salary will earn more teaching six hours in summer session in sixteen of the eighteen schools with the percentage rate method than in seven of nine with the flat rate method. Only the University of Detroit and the University of Hawaii, where flat rates are as high as $400 and $557 per credit hour, would faculty be better off than those at any of the institutions with the percentage rate method (table 6).[49] At a $25,000 salary all faculty at a percentage rate institution (the eighteen) will earn more teaching six hours of summer session than will faculty at any of the institutions but one (University of Hawaii) that pay a flat rate.

The third approach to calculating summer session salaries is to establish a flat rate but one that takes rank into consideration (table 7). This differential flat rate for each academic rank combines the major features of both other methods. Although this approach exceeds by $24 the remuneration deriving from the flat rate alone approach (overall average of $987 com-

TABLE 7
**Distribution of Flat Summer Session Salaries for a
Three-Hour Course, by Rank**

INSTITUTION	INSTRUCTOR	ASSISTANT PROFESSOR	ASSOCIATE PROFESSOR	PROFESSOR
University of Bridgeport	$750	$795	$870	$930
Rider College	770	865	920	1,000
Regis College	800	800	850	850
University of Connecticut	885	990	1,200	1,395
Lincoln University	900	975	1,050	1,125
Wagner College	975	1,050	1,140	1,275
Minnesota State Colleges and Universities	1,000	1,030	1,150	1,272
Oakland University	Varies according to faculty member's precise location on salary schedule			
Average	869	929	1,026	1,121

pared with $963 per three-hour course), the first approach (summarized in table 6), which utilizes a percentage of base salary, produces the greatest remuneration for faculty overall. Five other agreements that speak to the subject have simply contractualized "current rates." The details of current rates are not included in the agreement.

With respect to off-campus, extension, or field service teaching, relatively few agreements—eleven, or 12.4 percent—have contractualized rates for remuneration in this area. Here are the kinds of differences we have grown to expect in the compensation area, except that no agreement establishes a value based on percentage of a faculty member's salary. The choices have been either a flat rate that may establish differing rates per credit hour and by rank or, in one case, payment on the basis of distance traveled. Flat rates range from $200 to $557 per credit hour; the rates by rank average $275 per credit hour for instructors, $298 for assistant professors, $325 for associates, and $350 for professors. One agreement establishes $340 per credit hour at teaching centers fewer than thirty-five miles from the campus, $360 at centers thirty-five to seventy miles from campus, and $380 at centers seventy or more miles from campus. One agreement (Saginaw Valley State College) contractualizes an "energy increment" at fifteen cents per mile for travel outside the three-county area served most directly by the college.[50] One agreement does not specify a salary increment but establishes an on-campus load reduction at the rate of 133.5 percent of the normal load; that is, teaching a three-hour course off campus will count as a four-hour reduction of a twelve-hour on-campus teaching load.[51]

A topic that is not a form of compensation per se but is closely associated with compensation is a provision for a tax-sheltered annuity option for faculty. Sixteen agreements (18 percent) contractualize language in this area. One agreement defines such activity as "a method of delaying taxes on an eleemosynary institution's employee pension plan until the time when the employee retires."[52] That same agreement does not actually provide one, however. Eleven of the sixteen agreements simply state something to the effect that present practice shall continue or that such annuities currently are available. The agreement for the New Jersey State educational institutions states that legislative help shall be enlisted to inaugurate such a program.[53] The Bloomfield College Agreement, for example, authorizes up to 15 percent of salary,[54] and Stevens College authorizes up to 5 percent as a tax-shelter annuity.[55] Undoubtedly a great many more institutions provide this service and have been doing so for years, but regard it as an issue that is not relevant to collective bargaining.

Other Compensation Items

A few additional topics that have been negotiated but infrequently are compensation for independent study and thesis direction, compensation for part-time faculty, chairperson compensation, and limits on total compensation.

So far as compensation for independent study is concerned, the issue has been addressed in only ten agreements (11.2 percent of the total number of agreements). Seven of these provide monetary rewards, and three provide credit toward teaching loads rather than direct compensation. At two of the three branches of Long Island University (Brooklyn Center and Southampton Center) the rate of compensation for faculty is $30 per semester hour of independent study.[56] At the third center, C. W. Post, the rate is a flat $100 per student.[57] At Robert Morris College the rate is one-third of the tuition charged but no less than $25 for each student.[58] Further, ten independent-study students in a given semester shall count as a one-course overload. At Saginaw Valley State College a faculty member shall be paid at a rate of $10 for each student credit hour (s.c.h.) of independent study if the total s.c.h. (including s.c.h. for independent study) credited to that faculty member that semester ranges from 301 to 599. If the s.c.h. total is 600 or more, the rate per s.c.h. of independent study shall be $15.[59] More generous than any of these is the provision at Regis College for a flat payment of $100 per student.[60] Incidentally the Regis College Agreement has a unique provision regarding the conduct of academic workshops by faculty. If a workshop enrolls fewer than fifty students, the faculty member shall receive one-half of the tuition paid for the workshop, less the direct expenses incurred by the activity. If enrollment is fifty or more, the faculty member shall be entitled to 25 percent of the tuition.[61] The most generous provision for remuneration for supervising independent-study students is found in the agreement at Adelphi College. There, if a faculty member has fewer than six semesters of teaching experience, the rate per student is $113. If semesters of experience total six to ten, the rate is $128. If the faculty member has taught eleven semesters or more, the rate is $150 per student.[62]

So far as course load credit is concerned, in ascending order of benefit to faculty are Youngstown State University with one-half hour of teaching credit for each fifteen s.c.h. of independent study,[63] Quinnipiac College with one semester hour credit for every three independent-study students,[64] and Rhode Island College where each independent-study student counts for one hour of credit for the faculty member, though normally these shall not number more than four.[65]

Although eighteen agreements (20.2 percent) speak in some way to the subject of part-time faculty, only six explicitly establish salaries or contractualize salary increases for such faculty. Five speak to the issue of fringe benefits, usually by committing health insurance coverage to them if they teach half-time or more and providing other fringe benefits on a pro rata basis. Nearly all the other references to part-time faculty present truly unique provisions. For example, at Pratt Institute, a part-time faculty member who has served ten or more semesters and passed evaluaton and review can receive what amounts to tenure and is eligible for promotion.[66] Also at Moore College of Art, part-time faculty become eligible for tenure as their fractional time accumulates on a pro rata basis to the standard number of years as designated by AAUP principles.[67] At Saginaw Valley State College the ratio of part-time to full-time faculty shall not exceed the actual ratio that existed in the 1971-72 academic year.[68]. Similarly the agreement at the University of Scranton states clearly that only in emergencies shall anyone beyond the department select a part-time faculty member, and then only for a maximum of one semester.[69]

Chairpersons' compensation is dealt with in the collective-bargaining agreements in only 39.3 percent of the cases (thirty-five agreements). Those thirty-five represent 63.6 percent of the fifty-five agreements that consider the subject of chairpersons in any way. In other words, chairpersons' compensation is not viewed as a highly important topic, but if chairpersons are considered at all, compensation is dealt with two-thirds of the time.

Compensation for chairpersons can take one of two basic forms: monetary compensation or reduction of teaching load. The latter is more common; 48.6 percent of the agreements cite that as the only form of compensation. In addition, three agreements include a combination of reduced load and extra monetary compensation for department chairpersons. One agreement provides a choice between the two, to be made by each chairperson. Twelve agreements (21.8 percent of those that refer to chairpersons in the agreement) list monetary compensation alone as the choice at their institutions. Finally, two agreements admit incapacity to handle the issue and leave the question to be determined.

Another point of interest under the heading of compensation is the occasional limitation placed upon the amount of money faculty members may earn in any given year. This is done in three agreements; two are in Michigan, and the other is the New Jersey State College Agreement. At Western Michigan University, faculty may earn through various supplemental sources such as off-campus, summer session, correspondence courses, and so on no more than 144 percent of their base nine- or ten-month salary without permission of the vice-president for academic affairs. Even with permission, the total cannot exceed 152 percent.[70] At Central Michigan University faculty are limited to 140 percent of their academic year base, with the additional proviso that summer employment by itself cannot accrue to more than 26 percent.[71] In the New Jersey Agreement faculty are limited to 22 percent additional compensation from sources within the institution.[72]

A few rare compensation items point to the great diversity in collective-bargaining agreements of higher education. Although there is a tradition within academe of filling in on a gratis basis for an incapacitated colleague, in the St. John's Agreement faculty will be compensated at the summer session rate when their substitution for an incapacitated colleague during the regular term exceeds two weeks.[73]

Temple University has the right to match a faculty member's written offer from elsewhere to retain that person and may do so without approval of the collective-bargaining agent so long as the agent is informed within ten days.[74] The agreement at the University of Rhode Island goes further; it grants the right to the institution to pay up to $3,500 more than the contractual maximum in order to retain an exceptional person. A further restriction is that such extraordinary salaries shall go to no more than 1 percent of the faculty during a two-year period.[75] Worcester State College has contractualized a "longevity recognition" of $3,000 during the last year of teaching for those faculty with twenty years or more of service.[76] At Central Michigan University a somewhat similar but more valuable provision predates collective bargaining but has also been contractualized for all faculty employed prior to March 1, 1976. The provision is that those who retire at age sixty and above and have ten or more years of service at the university shall receive a retirement service award of 1.5 percent of the faculty's ten-month base salary at the time of retirement multiplied by the number of equivalent full-time years of service at the university.[77] Thus a faculty member who was earning $30,000 at retirement with thirty-two years of teaching experience at Central Michigan University would receive a sum of $14,400 upon retirement.

Commentary

Several agreements have negotiated fairly outstanding compensation packages that place them at or near the top in all areas of compensation—salary increases, retirement benefits, insurance programs, and the various forms of secondary compensation examined in this chapter. The majority, however, are in the middle range so far as assessing the totality of their monetary gains is concerned. None of the agreements touches all of the bases so far as varieties of compensation are concerned. All collective-bargaining agents will find either a new compensation area to work on or a new level to aspire to after using this chapter and the next as a baseline checklist. From the administrative perspective there should be some sense of satisfaction in the sense that no agreement has been too generous. In fact, a considerable number of agreements have settled at a fairly conservative compensation level if all forms of compensation have been taken into account. That is, although faculty unions appear to have made straight salary gains in excess of national averages for college and university faculty, other forms of compensation provide new horizons to which faculty bargaining agents can still aspire. Thus although collective bargaining deserves substantial credit for improving faculty salaries, bargaining in other areas of compensations such as contributions toward retirement programs, the funding of insurance plans, remuneration for additional teaching, and the like has met with only modest success on many campuses. There remain challenges and opportunities for faculty unions on most campuses to keep them busy for a long time with compensation issues alone.

Notes

1. Agreement (1976-78), Goddard College, p. 56.

2. *Chronicle of Higher Education*, November 5, 1979, p. 2.

3. Faculty size at Goddard College listed as fifty-seven full time, *Yearbook of Higher Education*, 10th ed. (Chicago: Marquis Who's Who, 1978-79), p. 510.

4. Trevor Bain, "Collective Bargaining and Wages in Public Higher Education: The Case of CUNY," *Journal of Collective Negotiations in the Public Sector* 5, no. 3 (1976): 207-14.

5. Robert Birnbaum, "Unionization and Faculty Compensation," *Educational Record* 55, no. 1 (Winter 1974): 29-33.

6. Robert Birnbaum, "Unionization and Faculty Compensation: Part II," *Educational Record* 57, no. 2 (Spring 1976): 116-18.

7. David R. Morgan and Richard C. Kearney. "Collective Bargaining and Faculty Compensation: A Comparative Analysis." *Sociology of Education* 50 (January, 1977): 28-39.

8. Agreement (1976-79), Oakland University, p. 47.

9. Agreement (1977-79), Regis College, p. 3.

10. Agreement (1974-77), St. John's University, p. 27.

11. Agreement (1977-80), University of Massachusetts, pp. 35-36.

12. Agreement (1977-79), University of Connecticut, p. 11.

13. Agreement (1975-77), Rutgers University, pp. 5-6.

14. Agreement (1977-81), Youngstown State University, pp. 3-4.

15. Agreement (1977-79), Northern Montana College, pp. 44-45.

16. Agreement (1974-76), Worcester State College, p. 143.

17. Agreement (1977-79), Iowa State Board of Regents' Colleges and Universities, p. 21.

18. Agreement (1976-78), Saginaw Valley State College, p. 116.

19. See chap. 3, note 1, for listing of institutions in the various prestige categories.

20. Agreement (1976-79), Long Island University, Brooklyn Center, p. 36.

21. Everett C. Ladd, Jr., and Seymour M. Lipset, *Professors, Unions and American Higher Education* (Berkeley: Carnegie Commission on Higher Education, 1973), p. 69.

22. Agreement (1976-78), Eastern Michigan University, pp. 19, 59.

23. Agreement (1979-81), South Dakota College and University System, p. 47.

24. Agreement (1975-77), Eastern Montana College, p. 12.

25. Agreement (1976-79), Monmouth College, p. 45.

26. Agreement (1977-80), University of Massachusetts, p. 35.

27. Agreement (1976-78), State University System of Florida, p. 31.

28. Agreement (1977-79), University of Cincinnati, pp. 12-13.

29. Agreement (1977-78), Bard College, p. 7.

30. Agreement (1977-79), Illinois Board of Governors State Colleges and Universities, sec. 11:2.

31. Agreement (1977-79), Southern Oregon State College, p. 14; Agreement (1977-80), Central Michigan University, p. 51; Agreement (1976-80), Temple University, p. 6.

32. Agreement (1977-81), Youngstown State University, p. 3.

33. Agreement (1976-78), Saginaw Valley State College, pp. 115-16.

34. Agreement (1974-77), St. John's University, p. 28.

35. Agreement (1976-77), Western Michigan University, p. 55.

36. Agreement (1979-81), South Dakota College and University System, p. 47.

37. Agreement (1976-79), University of New Haven, p. 10.

38. Agreement (1976-80), Temple University, p. 10.

39. Agreement (1977-78), University of Dubuque, p. 34.

40. Agreement (1977-79), Minnesota State Colleges and Universities, p. 11.

41. Agreement (1977-79), Fairleigh Dickinson University, p. 3.

42. Agreement (1975-78), Quinnipiac College, p. 5.

43. Agreement (1975-80), Loretto Heights College, p. 11.

44. Agreement (1976-indefinite), University of Scranton, p. 12.

45. Agreement (1976-80), Temple University, p. 10.

46. Two agreements establish different rates for undergraduate and graduate courses: the University of Detroit, p. 21, and Fairleigh Dickinson University, p. 3.

47. Agreement (1978-82), Detroit College of Business, p. 14.

48. Agreement (1977-79), University of Hawaii, p. 36.

49. Agreement (1977-79), University of Detroit, p. 21 and Agreement (1977-79), University of Hawaii, p. 36.

50. Agreement (1976-78), Saginaw Valley State College, p. 39-40.

51. Agreement (1977-79), Southern Oregon State College, p. 15.

52. Agreement (1979-80), Park College, p. C-2.

53. Agreement (1977-79), New Jersey State Colleges, p. 58, and Agreement (1979-81), College of Medicine and Dentistry of New Jersey, p. 14.

54. Agreement (1975-77), Bloomfield College, p. 22.

55. Agreement (1976-78), Stevens Institute of Technology, p. 49.

56. Agreement (1974-77), Long Island University, Brooklyn Center, p. 46, and Agreement (1974-1977), Long Island University, Southampton Center, p. 41.

57. Agreement (1977-80), Long Island University, C. W. Post Center, p. 63.

58. Agreement (1977-80), Robert Morris College, p. 19.

59. Agreement (1976-78), Saginaw Valley State College, p. 34.

60. Agreement (1977-79), Regis College, p. 5.

61. Ibid.

62. Agreement (1976-78), Adelphi College, p. 16.

63. Agreement (1977-81), Youngstown State University, p. 30.

64. Agreement (1975-78), Quinnipiac College, p. 25.

65. Agreement (1975-77), Rhode Island College, p. 31.

66. Agreement (1978-81), Pratt Institute, pp. 30-34.

67. Agreement (1976-79), Moore College of Art, p. 3.

68. Agreement (1976-78), Saginaw Valley State College, p. 22.
69. Agreement (1976), University of Scranton, p. 10.
70. Agreement (1976-77), Western Michigan University, p. 52.
71. Agreement (1977-80), Central Michigan University, p. 52.
72. Agreement (1977-79), New Jersey State Colleges, pp. 29-30.
73. Agreement (1974-77), St. John's University, p. 29.
74. Agreement (1976-80), Temple University, p. 9.
75. Agreement (1977-79), University of Rhode Island, p. 36.
76. Agreement (1977), Worcester State College, p. 145.
77. Agreement (1977-80), Central Michigan University, p. 45.

5. FRINGE BENEFITS

The typical fringe benefits associated with employment (various kinds of insurance, contributions toward retirement funds, access to recreational facilities, and the like that are provided employees by their employers as supplements to salary) are not only items of interest and concern to faculty members but are items that those who are responsible for administering and governing institutions of higher learning deem appropriate to include in collective-bargaining agreements. Although what is proper to consider within the scope of bargaining will be debated as long as there is any kind of a union, almost no one debates whether bargaining over fringe benefits is appropriate. The only question is how much is to be gotten or how much is to be conceded.

Medical Insurance

One of the topics of major immediate interest for faculty members in the area of fringe benefits is that of insurance coverage. Heading that list is medical and hospitalization insurance. A full 89.9 percent of all agreements include a section of contractual language on this topic. Only nine agreements make no mention of it. Among the large majority that have contractualized something with regard to medical and hospitalization insurance, there is wide variation in coverage. The diversity centers around such issues as whether coverage and/or payment is for the faculty member alone or also includes spouse and/or other dependents, whether whatever coverage is contractualized is paid fully by the institution or at least partially paid by the faculty member, and whether in multiyear contracts an increase in contributions by the institution to the insurance plan is included.

A fairly large proportion of agreements do not describe the type of coverage or benefits because they either simply reference the plan "currently in effect" or mention the state plan that is mandated for them as a state college or university. Specifically, 21.5 percent of those schools that have contractual language concerning medical and hospitalization insurance (the 89.9 percent) simply refer to existing plans. An additional 20 percent refer to the mandated state plan. The majority of agreements, then (the remaining 58.5 percent or forty-six), describe their medical-hospitalization plans in some detail.

Although a significant number of institutions contribute toward coverage only for the faculty member (39 percent), the majority include dependents (61 percent). The amount required to cover the costs of full family coverage may be met in only a token way, however. Several plans do not pay the full amount for the faculty member, let alone full family coverage. Further, the insurance programs themselves vary tremendously in the breadth of coverage they provide. Thus although an institution might pay a significant portion or even all of full family coverage, the plan itself often provides only limited coverage.

This leads us into the second issue: the ratio of monetary contribution by faculty member to that by the institution. Here there is a very slight edge in favor of fully paid coverage. Fifty-two percent of the agreements that provide sufficient information to judge specify fully paid coverage; 48 percent require that part of the payment be made by the faculty member. That part may be substantial. For example, at Marymount College the agreement specifies that the college shall pay one-third, the individual faculty member two-thirds.[1] At Park College the full cost is to be borne by the faculty member.[2] Many are in the $200 to $400 range of employer contribution, suggesting an equal or probably greater contribution by the faculty member. By way of a few examples, the University of Delaware has agreed to contribute $240 a year toward the State Hospitalization-Surgical Medical Program.[3] At City University of New York, it is $375 for a faculty welfare program, which approximates a medical-hospitalization insurance program.[4] At Adelphi University it is $400.[5]

By way of fairly dramatic contrast three Michigan universities contribute in excess of $1,000 toward the coverage offered. At the top appears to be Oakland University where, effective July 1, 1978, the amount the institution was to contribute was $1,369 for full family coverage for a Blue Cross-Blue Shield Michigan Variable Fee plan with several attractive riders.[6] Next is Central Michigan University. Effective also July 1, 1978, the annual university contributions for full family coverage under a broad and inclusive program underwritten by the Michigan Education Special Services Association total $1,190.16.[7] During the following and final year of the three-year agreement, the annual amount was $1,284.12.[8] At the University of Detroit, effective August, 1978, the amount contributed by the university toward medical insurance program similar to that of Oakland University was $1,051.32.[9]

Higher than these three Michigan universities is the $1,400 contribution toward full family coverage on the part of the college that was contracted for the academic year 1978-79 at Dyke College.[10] Of course, others may be contributing even more, particularly as new agreements are reached where the institution has agreed to pay the full premium for a broad coverage policy but fail to specify dollar amounts.

Of those institutions paying all or a substantial portion of the premium for a faculty medical plan, the ratio is two-to-one in favor of the public institutions over the private colleges and universities.

At several institutions the full single-member premium but only part of the additional for dependents is paid by the institutions. These institutions are in particular contrast to the majority that contribute nothing toward dependent coverage. For example, in the Iowa State College system the agreement specifies $90 annually to be contributed toward the full-family insurance feature.[11] At Quinnipiac College the college pays $100 toward dependents' coverage.[12] At Wayne State University the specification is one-half the cost of adding dependents to the policy.[13]

With respect to the major medical feature of medical and hospitalization insurance, most agreements specify the common limit of $250,000. A few, however, cite a lower limit. For example, the University of Dubuque states a limit of $100,000,[14] and Ferris State College drops as low as $50,000.[15]

With regard to the provision of an inflationary factor to cover the likelihood of increasing premiums over the life of a multiyear agreement, most agreements simply specify that a certain percentage of costs shall be borne by the institution or that the full cost of a specific plan shall be paid by the institution. In several instances, however, specific dollar amounts per year by which the institution shall increase its contribution are included in the agreement. Oakland University, Central Michigan University, and Southern Oregon State College are examples. Faculty members and administrators as well gamble a bit with such an arrangement. If premiums go up faster than predicted, the administration saves and the faculty loses money. If the opposite occurs, the administration loses and the faculty is ahead. In either event the administration at least knows what its cost will be. The experience at Central Michigan University during the second year (1978-79) of the three-year contract is a case in point. The agreement specifies an increase in the employer's contribution of $7.34 per member for full family coverage under the Michigan Education Special Services Association Super Med II Program.[16] The carrier, however, decided that it did not need to raise its rates that year. The result was that whereas Central Michigan University had been paying 81 percent of the premium for the Super Med II coverage, during the academic year 1978-79 it would pay 87 percent.

In the area of medical-hospitalization insurance a few unique features may be of interest. For example, a provision at the New York Institute of

Technology provides that faculty in their first year shall pay the full cost of the existing Blue Cross-Blue Shield plan, that faculty in their second and third year shall split the cost evenly with the institution, and that faculty retained longer than three years shall benefit from fully paid coverage.[17] Another unique feature in the medical insurance area is the provision of the Youngstown State Agreement for the payment by the university of $150 toward an annual physical examination for all faculty.[18]

Dental Insurance

An extension of medical and hospitalization insurance is dental insurance. Some agreements have made an entry into this area, but they are relatively few—only 21 percent of the agreements under study—and most of these are quite nonspecific. At one end of the range is the Minnesota State College Agreement, which speaks only of "limited dental care beneficial to all eligible employees and their families,"[19] and the New York Institute of Technology Agreement, which says only that there shall be a "group dental plan."[20] Equally as nonspecific is the University of Connecticut Agreement, which specifies that a "state determined dental plan shall be provided."[21]

A few agreements specify particular plans. One of these is Bryant College of Business, which identifies in its agreement a Delta Dental Plan at the first level.[22] A majority (74 percent) of the agreements that include reference to a dental plan at all (the 21 percent) do not specify a particular plan. Most frequently the agreement notes a sum to be spent for dental insurane and then establishes a committee or leaves it to an administrative office to determine what the particular plan should be. For example, the Southeastern Massachusetts University Agreement will pay $5.00 a month for whatever the faculty member needs.[23] Southern Oregon State College says the same but specifies $6.00 from August, 1977 to July 1978 and $7.00 a month from August, 1978 to July, 1979.[24] Central Michigan University's contract lists the sum of $100,000 to be contributed by the university for dental coverage for the faculty.[25] Temple University sets aside $250,000 for the same purpose.[26] In each case the amount is the base for a fairly comprehensive dental program. The New Jersey agreements establish essentially a fifty-fifty arrangement for faculty member and institution so far as premium payment is concerned.[27] Probably the smallest faculty gain is in the University of Cincinnati Agreement: faculty shall have the option of a $100 deductible dental plan for which the faculty members shall pay the complete cost.

Agreements in the public colleges and universities are significantly more likely than those from private schools to include a dental insurance provision by over a three to one margin (31 percent public, 10 percent private).

Disability Insurance

Some form of disability insurance is contractualized in 54 percent of the agreements. Of these, 81.3 percent speak of a total disability plan that almost invariably comes into operation after a six-month waiting period. Usually during this period of time a temporary disability plan is in effect. An additional 14.6 percent of the agreements simply specify "existing plan" or with similar phraseology contractualize whatever has been in effect at that institution. One agreement specifies 160 days temporary disability coverage but does not mention long-term disability insurance.

Considering only those institutions that are included in the 54 percent that have contractualized long-term disability insurance, 10.4 percent specify a maximum coverage of 60 percent of monthly income, whatever the amount of income might be. Other agreements specify the standard 60 percent limit but place a ceiling on the amount of payout. One agreement places the limit at $1,000 a month, six (14.6 percent) at $1,500 a month, and four (8.3 percent) at $2,000 a month. The highest maximum is at the University of Bridgeport, where the agreement specifies 60 percent of salary up to $2,000 plus 40 percent of monthly salary in excess of $2,000 but not to exceed $2,500 monthly.[28] Also at the high end is the provision at the Detroit College of Business where long-term disability payment is set at 66 and two-thirds percent of salary regardless of the amount of salary.[29] The remaining 58 percent simply reference the Teachers' Insurance and Annuity Association total disability plan and do not specify the limits.

In most cases the cost of this insurance is borne by the institution, not the individual faculty member. In fact, only 12.5 percent require that some of the cost be charged to faculty members. In one of these institutions the long-term disability plan is optional in the first place. In another the cost must be borne fully by the faculty member.

At 39.6 percent of the institutions where long-term disability insurance is contractualized, a minimum period of service by a faculty member is required before the coverage becomes effective. The range is great. It varies from only fourteen days at Northern Michigan University[30] to three years at Wayne State University.[31] Other specifications are thirty-one days, ninety days, six months, one year (the majority are here), and two years for faculty appointed at a rank lower than associate professor (no minimum service for eligibility at the associate or full professor ranks) at D'Youville College,[32] and two years for everyone at Pratt Institute.[33]

Contracts consummated at the private colleges and universities clearly are ahead of the state institutions here. Seventy-three percent of the former have contractualized disability insurance; only 40 percent of the latter have done so.

Life Insurance

The inclusion of some form of group life insurance in collective-bargaining agreements is fairly common though far from universal. Sixty-three percent of the agreements provide some form of life insurance coverage (60.4 percent of the public institutions and 67.5 percent of the private schools). The specifics of the coverage are not always provided, however. For example, 37.5 percent of those agreements that refer to life insurance at all note only that the insurance will be continued during the life of the agreement "on its existing basis" or "under present terms." The agreements do not indicate whether the coverage is paid in full or even in part by the college or university. Nearly an equal proportion of the agreements (35.7 percent) provide a life insurance program that is paid entirely by the institution. A few (8.9 percent) provide coverage that is paid for in major part by the institution. In 10.6 percent the cost is divided equally between the individual faculty member and the employer. In the remaining 7.1 percent of the schools, faculty members pay the major portion of the cost.

With respect to the amount or value of the insurance there is great variation as well. A full 14.3 percent of the agreements that provide any life insurance coverage at all (remember that 37 percent of all agreements at four-year institutions make no mention of life insurance at all) specify only a token amount. This is a flat amount for all faculty members that is likely less than the annual salary of any regular faculty member (commonly $5,000 or $10,000). Most agreements, however, that provide life insurance at all specify an amount at least equal to a faculty member's full annual salary. Nine agreements (16.1 percent) provide just that. One specifies an amount equal to 1 and one-fourth times the salary; three (5.4 percent) specify one and one-half times the salary; an equal number have contractualized life insurance at two times the salary; and one agreement (1.8 percent of those with language on life insurance) says two and one-half times the annual salary. Five additional agreements specify a minimum amount for all but provide the opportunity of adding additional coverage at the individual's option. Two allow such an option with the institution subsidizing the additional cost, and three allow the option of additional coverage but require that it shall be entirely at the faculty member's expense.

From the faculty perspective, this is an area in which there is a lot of room for improvement. Only 40.4 percent of all collective-bargaining agreements at four-year higher education institutions provide some form of life insurance that is stated to be at least 50 percent paid by the institution, and only 24.7 percent of the faculty at institutions with collective bargaining have a life insurance program in which the pay-out value is known to be at least equivalent to a given faculty member's annual salary.

Other Insurance

Three additional insurance programs need to be mentioned. One, a form of liability insurance that provides monetary protection for faculty when sustaining injury or when property damage is occasioned by them while acting within the scope of their professional responsibility, is contractualized in 9 percent of the agreements (eight agreements). The maximum coverage ranges from $150,000 to $1 million at Oakland University[34] and Temple University[35] respectively. One agreement simply mentions a comprehensive university liability policy that includes faculty, but with no amounts specified. The second additional insurance program covers faculty members while operating state-owned vehicles. The third is eye care insurance, included in the New Jersey State College and University agreement that provides small amounts ($15-$25) on a biennial basis for prescription glasses for faculty and dependents.[36]

Leaves of Absence

Another area of fringe benefits that is of major concern to faculty members is the types of leaves of absence with full pay that are allowed or provided for faculty members. There are, of course, several types of leaves of absence. Some are provided very commonly throughout the labor force (such as leaves for jury duty, for the military draft or reserve requirements, and for funerals or because of bereavement). Although contractualized with some frequency, even such leaves are far from universally provided in the collective-bargaining agreements under consideration. In fact, only 46.1 percent specify leave with either full pay or supplemental pay for court-related obligations whether as a member of a jury or as a witness. These are much more likely to be state colleges and universities than private institutions. Fifty-eight percent of the public institutions provide in the contract reimbursement for court-related leaves; only 30 percent of the private schools do so. In 33.7 percent of the agreements there is provision for bereavement leaves and for attendance at funerals. While time off for a day or two at a time in the face of such an event is almost taken for granted in the academic setting, and we suspect also essentially universally without loss of pay, the fact remains that the conditions are contractualized only a little more than a third of the time. Here there is essentially no difference whether the contract is from a public or a private college or university (35 percent and 30 percent, respectively).

Somewhat more common is the specification of maternity and/or child-care leaves. Essentially half (48.3 percent) of the agreements provide language on one or both of these related issues, with no differences related to type or prestige of institution. But beyond that is little consensus. For example, whereas some agreements specify that sick leave or short-term disability leave with pay can be used in maternity cases, a few state that sick leave cannot be used. Even with those agreements that specify the applicability of sick leave provisions, however, the variation is great. In some it is "sick leave as accumulated or accrued during one's employment to date." In others the paid sick leave begins when a physician so prescribes but ends ten or fourteen days following the termination of the pregnancy, whether through birth, miscarriage, or abortion. The Agreement at the University of Dubuque specifies a maternity leave of ninety days. Any continuation of salary beyond that period shall be at the university's discretion.[37]

Although not nearly all agreements speak to the issue of the applicability of sick leave to pregnancy, almost all prescribe terms and limits on how much other leave (such as leave without pay) can be utilized for this purpose and what the procedure for application shall be. The length of leave without pay ranges from eight weeks (in four agreements), through one semester or its equivalent (in eight agreements), nine months (in two agreements), one year (in eleven agreements), fifteen months (in two agreements), eighteen months (in one agreement), to two years (in five agreements). Almost all of these allow for extensions of the specified time periods. The remainder either omit the time limit or handle the issue along the lines of the agreement at Rhode Island College: "Pregnancy and childbearing shall be considered as a justification of a leave of absence for a female employee for a *reasonable length of time*."[38] If we go with the range summarized above, what is understood to be reasonable ranges from two months to two years.

One other time dimension so far as maternity leaves are concerned is that the required prior notification by a faculty member of need for the leave ranges from two weeks to four months. Most agreements, however, do not specify the minimum terms of prior notification.

Most agreements are nonsexist in their language with respect to the maternity and child-care leave issue. The terminology is usually "faculty member." Agreements occasionally speak of "either parent," particularly if both are faculty members. The nonsexist terminology is of distinct advantage when reference is made (as it frequently is) to the adoption of a child. Only one agreement limits the taking of a maternity and child-care leave in the adoption case to the adoption of an infant (Northern Michigan University).[39] In all the other agreements that address the adoption issue specifically, the reference is to "an adopted minor."

Of considerable interest to many faculty is the issue of whether maternity and child-care leave time will be included as part of the probationary time period before a tenure decision is made or as part of a minimum amount of time in rank before consideration for promotion. Most agreements explicitly exclude the period of such leaves. That is, although the faculty member retains all rights as of the date of the beginning of the leave, plus often the progress along a salary scale that the intervening time period normally would have provided them, the time of the leave will not count in computing probationary periods or minimums so far as time in rank or interims between sabbaticals are concerned.

There are interesting exceptions, however. The agreement at Northern Michigan University specifies that child-care leave beyond one semester shall not count toward tenure.[40] Implicit in that statement is the crediting of one semester of child-care leave toward tenure requirements. At the University of San Francisco, whether the leave (up to one year) will be credited toward tenure must be determined with the dean in writing in advance of the leave.[41] At Temple University the agreement seems to say that the period of leave (probably short-term disability only) shall be credited, but only at the request of the faculty member.[42] Similarly at Emerson College the time shall be credited toward tenure requirements if requested by the chairperson of the affected faculty member's department.[43]

Despite considerable variation, the record is good so far as faculty protection is concerned. Although time limits are firmly in place in many of the agreements, in most cases they can be extended or violated if emergency or special circumstances so dictate. Further, in those agreements that have any language at all on the maternity and child-care issue, the language assures the faculty member that she or he will not lose rights and benefits already earned, nor will the faculty member prejudice her or his case against future earnings of rights and benefits by requiring or requesting such a leave. In addition, essentially all agreements (the nearly half that speak to the maternity issue—48.3 percent) provide for using accrued sick leave before needing, and then at the faculty member's option, to take an upaid leave of absence. Most also state that the woman can work as long as she wishes or her medical adviser considers safe and can return as early as she gives notice of intent.

Sabbatical Leaves

The leave that is probably on the minds of faculty members more often than any other, and the one that has been contractualized more frequently than any other, is the sabbatical leave; we find that 77.5 percent of all the collective-bargaining agreements under study have contractual language on sabbatical leaves (in slightly more agreements from private schools than public institutions—82.5 percent and 72.9 percent respectively). There is considerable variation in the details, with a notable lack of uniformity insofar as the minimum period of time that must accrue before a faculty member becomes eligible for a sabbatical leave. The norm is six years, but this is the case for only 43.5 percent of the schools that have contractual language on sabbatical leaves. In fact, 30.4 percent require a seven-year interim; one agreement even specifies eight years. Another school split the difference between six and seven years and sets the minimum time interval at thirteen semesters.

What is likely to become a faculty goal at a number of institutions is contractualized in six agreements (8.8 percent): a five-year interval between sabbaticals. Actually the number is really four (Bryant College of Business, the Iowa System, Monmouth College, and Bard College) with the Illinois Governor's Universities' agreement specifying that a faculty member becomes eligible for the first sabbatical after five years but succeeding ones follow only every seven years (presumably after six years),[44] and the Robert Morris College agreement, which specifies the same five-year period following initial employment but then requires a seven-year wait before becoming eligible for succeeding sabbaticals.[45]

The remaining 14.4 percent of the agreements that speak to the sabbatical issue fail to mention time intervals. Probably these institutions have strong precedents of past practices that were simply assumed when the agreement was written. Yet without precise contractual language on the issue, faculty are exposed to the possibility of administrative action that they might term arbitrary and capricious.

Another variable is the rate of salary remuneration for faculty during a sabbatical leave. Although the vast majority specify a standard arrangement of one semester at full pay or two semesters at one-half pay (88.4 percent of the sixty-nine agreements that include any language at all on sabbatical leaves), a few institutions provide modifications. In almost all cases modifications are at institutions on a quarter or trimester system. For example, while most institutions on the quarter system provide for a one-quarter sabbatical at full pay, one agreement specifies that the first quarter of sabbatical leave shall be at 80 percent of salary (a two-quarter sabbatical at 70 percent of salary, a three-quarter sabbatical at 60 percent of salary).[46] One institution on the trimester system has contractualized one trimester at 90 percent of salary, two trimesters at 75 percent of salary, and three trimesters at 60 percent.[47] Two agreements stipulate that sabbatical leaves shall be remunerated at two-thirds salary and that the faculty member must take at least a two-quarter leave.[48] There is no difference between public and private colleges and universities on this variable. Equal proportions specify something less than full pay for even a minimum term sabbatical—14.6 percent and 12.5 percent, respectively.

Another variable is the amount of time required of the faculty member to serve the sabbatical-granting institution upon return from such a leave. Although relatively few agreements vary from the standard of either one full year or a period of time equal to twice the length of the leave, three agreements have specified the period of two years of service following the leave regardless of the length of the sabbatical leave itself. One agreement specifies a four-year commitment following return from a sabbatical leave.

A few agreements have established quotas for sabbaticals. These can be in terms of minimum numbers (representing faculty interests and concerns) and/or maximum numbers (representing administrative interests primarily). For example, six agreements limit sabbaticals in the institution to 5 percent of full-time faculty per year. One agreement says that the maximum shall be 10 percent of full-time faculty. At Saginaw Valley College the maximum is set at 12 percent, with the additional proviso that at least 75 percent of those eligible and recommended by the sabbatical leave committee shall be granted a sabbatical leave unless a financial exigency has been declared (financial exigency is defined as a cut in state appropriations of 10 percent or more in a given year).[49] Fairleigh Dickinson University goes all the way to a maximum of one-seventh of the tenured full-time faculty and never less than one in each college.[50] In the opposite direction is the Florida State system Agreement, which sets its maximum at 4 percent of the professional employees.[51] And at the very bottom of those that stipulate a proportion is the South Dakota State College and University system where 3 percent is the proportion that is contractualized.[52]

Some smaller colleges specify actual numbers rather than percentages of faculty who shall be granted sabbatical leaves. For example, at Stevens Institute of Technology[53] and at the Vermont State Colleges[54] the agreements specify that at least one faculty sabbatical shall be granted each academic year. That may be one full-year sabbatical for one faculty member or two faculty members on half-year sabbatical leaves. At Pratt Institute the number per year is set at seven,[55] and at Wagner College three in 1977-78, four in 1978-79, and five in 1979-80.[56]

A feature unique to the Saginaw Valley State College Agreement that most faculty would find attractive is that if a sabbatical is not taken on time, the years shall continue to accrue so that one conceivably could take two sabbaticals close together. The only restriction on the accrual principle is that the two sabbatical leaves cannot be taken consecutively. Another unique feature in the same agreement is that within any given fourteen-year period every faculty must take at least one sabbatical leave.

This, of course, touches on the subject of the purpose of the sabbatical leave. The State Universities of New York Agreement states explicitly, "The objective of such leave is to increase an employee's value to the university and thereby improve and enrich its program. Such leave shall not be regarded as a reward for service nor as a vacation or rest period occurring automatically at stated intervals."[57] Others such as Bloomfield College state that a sabbatical leave must meet the objectives of "professional development of faculty and enhance their effectiveness as teachers and scholars."[58] All agree that included in such professional development could be research, writing, and travel.

The only point of clear disagreement among institutions is whether a faculty member can use the leave to work toward an advanced degree. While most do not address the issue specifically in the agreement (perhaps deferring to policy elsewhere in a faculty handbook), some feature working for an advanced degree as a legitimate sabbatical activity while others explicitly prohibit such an activity on a sabbatical leave. For example, in the Rhode Island College Agreement, "work on doctoral dissertations or comparable activities to complete a doctorate" is listed as one of four legitimate categories of activity on sabbatical leave.[59] In direct contrast the agreement at the University of San Francisco says, "Formal study for an advanced degree is not normally acceptable as a sabbatical leave project."[60]

Medical or Sick-Leave

One other important leave is medical leave or sick-leave. Two-thirds of the agreements include such a provision (66.3 percent). This includes 71 percent of the public colleges and universities and nearly as many of the private institutions (63 percent). Among these fifty-nine agreements there is considerable variation. In fact, there is more disparity over this contractual provision than any other considered so far.

One consideration is whether there is to be a minimum employment waiting period before a faculty member qualifies for sick-leave benefits, or whether the benefits are available from the first day of employment. On the generous side of this issue is the Minnesota State System Agreement, where a faculty is given fifteen sick-leave days for use immediately upon hiring if they are needed.[61] Among others near the other end of this continuum is the New York Institute of Technology where the agreement states that no sick leave can be earned during the first three months of employment, and only in the twenty-fifth month of employment does one reach the maximum earning power for sick-leave days of one per month.[62]

The range of how many sick-leave days can be accrued per year is from 10 days (9 percent of the agreements) to a full 6 months at full pay available immediately during the first year of service at one institution. Twelve days and fifteen days a year are the most commonly designated (11.9 percent in each case). Other amounts designated are 11 days, 16 days, 18 days, 20 days, and 21 days of sick leave accumulating per year of service.

Regardless of how soon sick-leave is available and how many days accumulate in a given year, there is another numerical consideration: the maximum number of accumulated days that can be used for sick leave.

There is a very extensive range here. The fifty-one agreements that are clear on this issue distribute themselves as summarized in table 8.

TABLE 8
**Frequency of Maximum Amounts of Sick Leave
That Can Be Accrued by Faculty**

MAXIMUM SICK LEAVE AT FULL PAY	NUMBER OF AGREEMENTS
30 days	2
40 days	1
42 days	1
60 days	4
75 days	1
90 days	7
100 days	1
112 days	1
120 days	5
150 days	1
165 days	1
180 days (6 months)	9
195 days	1
200 days	1
275 days	1
280 days	1
No limit	13

What happens to unused sick-leave upon retirement? Can it be cashed in for dollars, or is it to be viewed as protection when needed, but if not needed, then of no monetary value to the individual who earned it? Most institutions and agreements take the latter position. But in ten agreements (16.9 percent of the agreements that have provisions for sick-leave) a final pay-out of from one-quarter of the dollar value of unused sick-leave to full value (number of unused sick days times the rate of pay upon retirement) is provided.

For faculty members who continue to be ill or disabled beyond the period of sick-leave provided in the agreement, slightly over half of the agreements (54 percent) provide some kind of long-term disability coverage that continues payment to the faculty member at 50 to 60 percent of regular salary. Of the substantial minority that do not include long-term disability insurance in the agreement, it is undoubtedly true that some of these institutions actually have some kind of long-term disability coverage either by state mandate or on the basis of long-standing tradition. Nonetheless failure to contractualize the provision of such coverage for faculty could be a serious omission for particular faculty members who might face the specter of long-term disability without specific written guarantees of income protection.

Retirement Programs

That contributions be made to a retirement program on behalf of faculty members probably is second only to salary itself in the list of economic concerns of faculty members. It is somewhat suprising, then, to discover that not all collective-bargaining agreements include the retirement issue. In fact, 30.3 percent of agreements do not speak to the retirement question at all. And, several more agreements speak only to the issue of mandatory age of retirement and omit any reference to the monetary amount contributed to a faculty retirement fund. Twenty-four agreements (38.1 percent of the sixty-three agreement that contractualize anything at all on the subject of retirement) make no mention of the proportion of salary that is to be contributed by the employer to the retirement program of faculty members. Ten of these state explicitly, however, that they shall abide by applicable state statutes where the amounts of employer's contributions are specified. Six others state that current practices will continue.

It is likely that state statutes regulate most, if not all, of the remaining eight institutions, as well as the twenty-six schools that constitute the 29.2 percent of the collective-bargaining agreements that make no mention of retirement. I say this because all of the agreements that lack reference to retirement are state institutions (100 percent of the private schools have incorporated some aspect of retirement in their agreements). Further, most of these state institutions that have not incorporated retirement language currently or formerly are state teachers' colleges where a mandatory state retirement system is likely to be in effect.

There is great variation in the amount of percentage of employer contributions to faculty retirement programs among the thirty-nine institutions where such specification is contractualized. In fact, there is so much variation and there are so many unique arrangements it is difficult to summarize; but a few primary points of contrast can be introduced. First, a majority of agreements specify a fixed percentage of contributions to be made by the employer. Twenty-six agreements establish such a fixed percentage (66.7 percent of the thirty-nine agreements that contractualize percentage contributions to a faculty retirement annuity). The remaining 33.3 percent (thirteen agreements) provide for variable percentages. The variation may be based on years of service (at Adelphi University, for example, the university's contribution increases from 6 to 10 percent after twenty years of service in a series of four steps),[63] or on a faculty member's age (at Stevens Institute of Technology, the proportion contributed by the institute increases in a series of five steps from 6 percent for faculty in the twenty- to thirty-year age bracket to 10 percent for faculty in the 60- to 65-year age bracket),[64] or amount of salary (at Loretto Heights College, the employer contribution is 5 percent of salary up to the FICA maximum, and 10 percent on salary above the FICA maximum).[65]

Second, the range in the proportion of the employer's contribution to the retirement program is wide, starting at 4 percent of annual salary (one agreement) and ranging as high as 13 percent at one institution. Another institution has contractualized a 12.5 percent contribution from the employer, another 12 percent, another 11 percent. Eight agreements (30.8 percent of those that have established a fixed proportion of salary) have established a rate of 10 percent. Two agreements have established 8 percent, and three have set 7 percent. Five percent ties with 10 percent as the most frequently occurring proportion contributed by employers to faculty retirement annuities (eight agreements).

Of those thirteen agreements that have some kind of varying percentage to be contributed by the institution, the maximum proportion specified is 20 percent of earnings in excess of $10,800 after twenty years of service to the institution.[66] Another agreement has set 15.75 as the maximum proportion. One agreement contractualizes 11 percent of monthly income over $400 (5 percent on monthly income up to $400).[67] Nine agreements specify 10 percent as the maximum contribution by the institution. One is at a low of 6 percent. Clearly a 10 percent contribution by the institution is not only most common but tending slightly toward the high side (38.5 percent of institutions with contractual language on the proportion to be contributed by the institution require proportions lower than 10 percent, 17.9 percent require proportions higher than 10 percent, with the remaining 43.5 percent holding to the 10 percent figure either across the board or as a maximum). Clearly any collective-bargaining agreement that has negotiated a contribution by the institution to the faculty retirement program in excess of 10 percent has done well by the faculty, if not necessarily absolutely then certainly relatively.

Third, there is considerable variation in the amount that faculty members are required to contribute to their own retirement programs. The range is from none in 14.5 percent of the agreements, and unknown or unspecified in 44.9 percent of the agreements, up to 5 percent in 29 percent of the agreements. The remaining agreements range from 2 to 4 percent. Two specify that the ratio shall be two-to-one of institution-to-faculty contributions, but they do not specify the maximum amounts. The most common pattern is for a 5 percent faculty contribution.

As we move away from the financial aspects of retirement, we are left with two interlocked issues: whether a mandatory retirement age is specified in the collective bargaining agreement and the age that is then specified. With respect to the first question, 56.2 percent of the agreements do not specify a mandatory retirement age. Presumably they either go along with the conventional age of sixty-five or seventy or rely on state statutes. Of the 43.8 percent that do mandate an age at retirement, we find that the variations in table 9 answer our second question. A clear majority specify a variant of the sixty-five-year age level as that of mandatory retirement.

TABLE 9
Frequencies of Various Mandatory Ages at Retirement

MANDATORY RETIREMENT AGES	FREQUENCY
Age 65 with no modification or extensions beyond that age specified	8
Age 65 with possible annual extensions to age 68	4
Age 65 with possible annual extensions to age 70	14
Age 65 with no upper limits specified	4
Age 68	2
Age 70	3
Age 70 with the possibility of annual extension	3

Other Fringe Benefits

The most common of fringe benefits that is not included under the three major categories of insurance, leaves of absence, and retirement programs is that of tuition waivers for faculty, their dependents, or both. A total of 50.6 percent of the agreements provide some kind of tuition waiver or rebate to faculty members, and more than half (56.2 percent) provide some kind of tuition waiver or reduction for spouses of faculty, their children, or both.

Of the forty-five agreements that provide waivers for faculty, eight (17.8 percent) speak simply of "past practice," "current practice," or "prior arrangements." Another twenty-seven agreements (60 percent) provide their faculty what is essentially unlimited availability of courses at their institution without tuition charge. Only a few set limits: five agreements specify a maximum of two courses per semester, two set a limit of three credit hours a semester, two a limit of four credit hours, and one specifies that only half the tuition for graduate courses shall be refunded (but full tuition for undergraduate courses and credit). In three cases, regardless of whether there are restrictions on the number of credit hours that a faculty member can take, the faculty must be employed for a specified amount of time (three to six months) before the tuition-waiver provision becomes operative. Five agreements specify that the provisions are for full-time faculty only or that there shall be a tuition reduction for part-time faculty that is proportional to the amount of teaching for which they are contracted. One agreement that pays full tuition for courses taken by faculty includes a restriction that tutorial courses such as music lessons shall elicit a tuition rebate of only 50 percent.[68] The difference between public and private institutions is clear: 62.5 percent of the private colleges and universities provide tuition rebates for faculty, but only 41.7 percent of the state institutions do so.

A tuition waiver plan for the spouses and dependent children of faculty is somewhat more common (56.2 percent of all agreements) than the faculty tuition waivers. It is close to being exclusively a provision in agreements at private colleges and universities, however. Ninety percent include a tuition waiver for dependents of faculty, but only 23 percent of the agreements at public institutions do so. Collective-bargaining agreements here simply reflect a long-standing tradition in many private colleges and universities of granting tuition waivers for faculty dependents, a provision not picked up historically by many state-supported schools. These proportions parallel almost perfectly national survey data gathered in the early 1960s by Mark Ingraham. He found that 93 percent of the private institutions waived some or all (most cases) of the tuition for faculty members' children, but this was true at public institutions in only 13 percent of the cases (20 percent of the public universities, 8 percent of the public colleges).[69]

Of these fifty agreements that have some kind of plan, thirty-six (72 percent) provide for a full tuition payment for faculty children at the institution that is participant to the agreement. Another seven agreements stipulate that present policies shall continue. Most of these probably provide a full tuition waiver. Two others provide full tuition waivers but only after the faculty parent has been employed two years. Another specifies three years for the same benefit. Loretto Heights College offers a real bargain: up to eighteen hours per semester for only $100 for the children of faculty employed prior to 1971.[70] Northern Michigan University offers less, paying half the tuition of the children of faculty.[71]

An almost completely parallel practice appears to have been negotiated for spouses of faculty. Only six fewer agreements specify full waiver of tuition for spouses, and the six agreements that specify present policies for children do so for spouses as well. The remaining agreements specify somewhat less generous waiver provisions, set limits on the number of hours, or require a minimum employment period of the faculty member before the spouse can use the tuition waiver fringe benefit.

Eighteen agreements provide a tuition waiver program for the children of faculty members who have become disabled, have died, or have retired from the institution. Although in most cases there are minimum amounts of time the faculty must have been employed by the institution, the time periods do not seem to be long (in no case longer than ten years, usually five years, and in three cases no time requirement at all).

An extension of the tuition waiver concept that is very attractive to faculty and that has been included in some agreements is the provision of reciprocal agreements with other colleges or universities or outright tuition payments to children of faculty to attend other institutions. Two schools are in a tuition exchange program with other institutions; three provide some support (approximately half) for faculty children to attend other schools; two pay the full tuition cost elsewhere; and two note that a joint administrative-faculty committee shall study and try to work out reciprocal arrangements with other institutions.

A somewhat popular fringe benefit that has been included in several agreements (29.2 percent) is that of the availability of parking for faculty. Eight of these twenty-six agreements specify a fee. In the remaining majority, the agreements state that faculty parking shall be free of charge (fourteen agreements). In three others the implication is that of free parking. At one institution the agreement states that the two sides could reach no agreement on the parking issue.

A few other fringe benefits are insignificant in their frequency but interesting nonetheless and show the variety of practices at various colleges and universities with collective bargaining. The availability of faculty discounts on various items is provided by the collective-bargaining agreement at nine institutions. Usually it is a discount (10 to 20 percent) on purchases at the college or university bookstore and discounts on the purchase of athletic tickets or tickets (or free admission) to other university events. Faculty and their immediate families at the University of Dubuque are admitted free of charge to all university events, except those to which students are charged admission.[72] University of San Francisco faculty are entitled by their collective-bargaining contract to purchase books and supplies for their personal use at the university bookstore at a 10 percent discount, to purchase home basketball tickets on a two for the price of one basis, to receive two free tickets for opening night performances by the college players, and to be afforded free admission to all lectures sponsored by the university.[73] Goddard College faculty are entitled by their collective-bargaining agreement to purchase $6.50 worth of meal tickets for $4.00.[74]

Two rare items are the provision of physical examinations for faculty at university expense and the offering of free day-care services to faculty children. The first is a fringe benefit of three institutions. At Saginaw Valley State College, physical examinations that might be required by law or by the board of trustees shall be without charge to the affected faculty member.[75]

At the University of Delaware, physical examinations are mentioned in a list of personal benefits that were past practice and shall be guaranteed by the collective-bargaining agreement but we are not provided the details.[76] In contrast, the Youngstown State University Agreement explicitly states that complete physicals on an annual basis up to a cost of $150 shall be provided for all faculty.[77]

Only one agreement guarantees free day-care services. Another states that both the college and the faculty subscribe to the desirability of establishing an on-campus day-care center for the children of faculty and agree to establish a joint union-administration committee to accomplish same. The one agreement that guarantees day-care services for children of faculty is at Bloomfield College.[78] There the existing day-care facilities shall be available without charge to faculty members with children of preschool age when both spouses are working or when there is a single parent.

Conclusions

Amid a somewhat bewildering array of variety in fringe benefits, our first observation must be simply that there is great variety and a wide range of levels of benefits. Some agreements have very generous fringe benefit packages. Some provide very stingy sets of benefits. Most are somewhere in between. Certainly no agreement has them all.

An area of singular disappointment from the faculty perspective is that of medical insurance. Very few collective-bargaining agents have bargained comprehensive, top-of-the-line medical packages that are fully or even close to fully paid by the employer. Perhaps this reflects as much as anything else a fairly pervasive phenomenon in higher education: relatively low to moderate levels of coverage in the medical-hospitalization insurance area.

An extension of the above is the low frequency and the attendant light coverage of dental insurance in collective-bargaining agreemens in higher education. Further, long-term disability insurance is included explicitly in only slightly more than half (54 percent) of the agreements. The same is true with respect to life insurance. At only 40.4 percent of the colleges and universities with collective bargaining is faculty life insurance at least 50 percent paid by the employer. And at only a quarter of the institutions is the life insurance value equivalent to or greater than a faculty member's annual salary.

Although many short-term leaves of absence are quite routinely expected —leaves for jury duty, expert witnessing in courts of law, attendance at funerals, and so on—fewer than half of the agreements in higher education have included them. Of course, it is likely that precisely because of their routine nature these leaves have been left out of many contracts. However, maternity and child-care leaves are more significant, particularly in their omission in slightly over half of the agreements.

The sabbatical leave is the one most likely to be contractualized, yet nearly a quarter of the agreements are silent here too. With respect to medical leaves, a third are silent.

Thus, it quickly becomes clear that many pairs of bargaining teams can look forward to spending a great deal of time on the subject of leaves of absence. Many faculty are totally unprotected in this area. Many others are protected only by tradition and precedent either within academe generally or in their own institution specifically. Without a doubt, some faculty in such situations will press for something that is possibly implicit now to become explicit in future collective-bargaining agreements.

The subject of retirement is still problematic. There is great variation in the amounts of money contributed by the employer. Of those agreements where proportions of salary for retirement are registered, only seven commit the employer to contribute more than 10 percent toward a retirement annuity for faculty.

All of the fringe benefits discussed in this chapter are bona-fide bargaining issues, and what could be a strong benefit area in many agreements is still a void. The fringe benefit area is one into which bargaining teams can step boldly and expect to cut new paths.

Notes

1. Agreement (1978-79), Marymount College of Virginia, p. 9.
2. Agreement (1979-80), Park College, p. C-3.
3. Agreement (1977-79), University of Delaware, p. 15.
4. Agreement (1975-77), City University of New York, p. 44.
5. Agreement (1976-78), Adelphi University, p. 10.
6. Agreement (1976-79), Oakland University, p. 48.
7. Agreement (1977-80), Central Michigan University, p. 43.
8. Ibid.
9. Agreement (1977-79), University of Detroit, p. 21.
10. Agreement (1976-79), Dyke College, p. 16.
11. Agreement (1977-79), Iowa State Colleges, p. 24.
12. Agreement (1975-78), Quinnipiac College, p. 6.
13. Agreement (1976-78), Wayne State University, p. 21.
14. Agreement (1977-78), University of Dubuque, p. 29.
15. Agreement (1975-78), Ferris State College, p. 20.
16. Agreement (1977-80), Central Michigan University, p. 43.
17. Agreement (1977-80), New York Institute of Technology, p. 8.
18. Agreement (1977-81), Youngstown State University, p. 7.
19. Agreement (1977-79), Minnesota State Colleges, p. 12.
20. Agreement (1977-80), New York Institute of Technology, p. 8.
21. Agreement (1976-79), University of Connecticut, p. 33.
22. Agreement (1977-79), Bryant College of Business, p. 12.
23. Agreement (1976-79), Southeastern Massachusetts University, p. 28.

24. Agreement (1977-79), Southern Oregon State College, p. 14.

25. Agreement (1977-80), Central Michigan University, p. 43.

26. Agreement (1976-80), Temple University, p. 11.

27. Agreement (1977-79), New Jersey State College, p. 28, and Agreement (1979-81), College of Medicine and Dentistry of New Jersey, p. 14.

28. Agreement (1978-81), University of Bridgeport, p. 56.

29. Agreement (1978-82), Detroit College of Business, p. 17.

30. Agreement (1975-77), Northern Michigan University, p. 53.

31. Agreement (1976-78), Wayne State University, p. 22.

32. Agreement (1977-79), D'Youville College, p. 37.

33. Agreement (1978-81), Pratt Institute, p. 44.

34. Agreement (1976-79), Oakland University, p. 50.

35. Agreement (1976-80), Temple University, p. 13.

36. Agreement (1979-81), College of Medicine and Dentistry of New Jersey, p. 13; Agreement (1977-79), New Jersey Institute of Technology, p. 13; Agreement (1977-79), New Jersey State Colleges, p. 28.

37. Agreement (1977-78), University of Dubuque, p. 31.

38. Agreement (1975-77), Rhode Island College, p. 28 (emphasis added).

39. Agreement (1975-77), Northern Michigan University, p. 44.

40. Ibid.

41. Agreement (1976-81), University of San Francisco, p. 21.

42. Agreement (1976-80), Temple University, p. 12.

43. Agreement (1975-78), Emerson College, p. 15.

44. Agreement (1977-79), Illinois Board of Governors State Colleges and Universities, art. 6:1.

45. Agreement (1977-80), Robert Morris College, p. 20.

46. Agreement (1976-78), Wayne State University, p. 30.

47. Agreement (1977-79), University of Detroit, p. 26.

48. Agreement (1975-77), Eastern Montana College, p. 16, and Agreement (1977-79), Northern Montana College, p. 53.

49. Agreement (1976-78), Saginaw Valley State College, p. 110.

50. Agreement (1977-79), Fairleigh Dickinson University, p. 9.

51. Agreement (1976-78), Florida State College and Universities, p. 30.

52. Agreement (1979-81), South Dakota State Colleges and Universities, p. 44.

53. Agreement (1976-78), Stevens Institute of Technology, pp. 15-16.

54. Agreement (1979-80), Vermont State College, p. 45.

55. Agreement (1978-81), Pratt Institute, pp. 49-50.

56. Agreement (1977-80), Wagner College, p. 43.

57. Agreement (1977-79), State Universities of New York, pp. 50-52.

58. Agreement (1975-77), Bloomfield State College, p. 19.

59. Agreement (1975-77), Rhode Island College, p. 25.

60. Agreement (1976-81), University of San Francisco, p. 20.

61. Agreement (1977-79), Minnesota State Universities, p. 15.

62. Agreement (1977-80), New York Institute of Technology, p. 6.

63. Agreement (1976-78), Adelphi University, p. 12.

64. Agreement (1976-78), Stevens Institute of Technology, p. 49.

65. Agreement (1975-80), Loretto Heights College, p. 15.

66. Agreement (1976-79), Hofstra University, p. 20.

67. Agreement (1977-80), Long Island University, C. W. Post Center, p. 68.

68. Agreement (1979-80), Park College, p. C-7.

69. Mark H. Ingraham, *The Outer Fringe: Faculty Benefits Other Than Annuities and Insurance* (Madison: University of Wisconsin Press, 1965), p. 36.

70. Agreement (1975-80), Loretto Heights College, p. 15.

71. Agreement (1975-77), Northern Michigan University, p. 55.

72. Agreement (1977-78), University of Dubuque, p. 30.

73. Agreement (1976-81), University of San Francisco, p. 28.

74. Agreement (1976-78), Goddard College, p. 51.

75. Agreement (1976-78), Saginaw Valley State College, p. 44.

76. Agreement (1977-79), University of Delaware, p. 15.

77. Agreement (1977-81), Youngstown State University, p. 7.

78. Agreement (1975-77), Bloomfield College, p. 24.

6. WORKING CONDITIONS

The concept of working conditions can be defined or categorized variously and can include an almost overwhelming list of details. For the purposes of our analysis of collective-bargaining agreements in higher education and for the sake of simplicity and clarity, I shall subsume these data under only two major headings: academic working conditions and facilities. The first heading includes those working conditions that have an obvious and direct bearing on the performance of faculty members in their teaching functions. In this list are such factors as course load, class size, number of course preparations, and student-faculty ratios. The facilities category includes the provision for faculty offices and their accoutrements, meeting and dining facilities, library hours, and the like.

Academic Working Conditions

Course Load

Probably of paramount concern to faculty is the number of hours that they teach and the number of different course preparations they are expected to handle. Although of great interest and concern to faculty, they have been successful only a little more than half the time in negotiating course load. Specifically, 55.1 percent of the agreements tie down in somewhat precise ways the size of the course load of faculty members. An additional 4.5 percent (four agreements) speak to the subject of teaching load in very general terms but do not specify a precise number of hours. One of these agreements states that the teaching load shall be "not excessive"; in another, "current practice" shall continue; in the third, a task force shall be appointed to make a recommendation; in the fourth, teaching loads shall be "reasonable." If we add these with vague or nonspecific language on teaching loads to the ones that are more precise, 57.3 percent of the collective-bargaining agreements in four-year institutions of higher education address the teaching load of faculty in some manner.

The maximum teaching load that is specified almost universally is a twelve-hour load per semester or, as specified fairly often, a twenty-four annual load that need not necessarily be on a basis of twelve hours per semester but should total twenty-four for the year. Four agreements have contractualized a maximum of three courses per semester for each faculty member, but in at least two of these schools the courses are four-hour ones. In fact, at one school the supplemental comment in the agreement is that the total hours taught shall not exceed thirteen while a faculty member teaches a maximum of three courses.

Others have higher maximums. One specifies a maximum of thirty hours per year, and in four schools on the quarter system are maximums of thirty-six or thirty-seven quarter hours per year. Another school incorporates a range of nine to fifteen hours and specifies more explicitly what several other agreements state shall be left to ad hoc negotiations among faculty members, chairpeople, and deans: a reduction of the twelve-hour load for specific circumstances such as heavy advising duties, active engagement in research, and the like.

The Detroit College of Business Agreement appears to have contractualized the largest normal class load—sixteen hours.[1] One agreement appears to have reached a compromise between an earlier expectation in academe of teaching fifteen credit hours and a more recent one of twelve hours by contractualizing a maximum of twenty-seven hours an academic year—presumably fifteen hours one semester and twelve hours the other.[2] One school has a truly unique approach to teaching loads; its agreement specifies that full professors shall teach twelve hours, associate professors thirteen hours, assistant professors fourteen hours, and instructors fifteen hours.[3] The agreement at Dyke College provides inferential evidence of the effects of collective bargaining. It specifies that although the annual teaching load shall be thirty-three credit hours per faculty member in the first year of the agreement, that number shall be reduced to thirty-one and a half in the second year, and to thirty in the third year of the agreement.[4]

The private colleges and universities are decidedly more likely to have contractualized course load. Although it is true that the most prestigious state universities are far less likely than the private colleges to contractualize course load (40 percent versus 75 percent), the middle-level emerging state colleges and universities are no more likely than their more prestigious counterparts to contractualize course load. Only 38.2 percent of these institutions have contractualized course load, the lowest proportion of all.

Only eight agreements address the issue of number of course preparations. In each case they specify that there shall be required no more than three different preparations or courses for a faculty member in a quarter or semester.

An issue of importance for faculty in the laboratory sciences, foreign languages, the various fields of art and music, and sometimes speech and English as well is the amount of teaching credit accorded the laboratory or studio form of contact with students. Although such courses involve a great many faculty at any college or university, only 23.6 percent of the agreements (twenty-one) address the issue, and among these is considerable diversity. Two agreements say that laboratory or studio is equivalent to a regular lecture or discussion-type class hour, a ratio of one-to-one. Six agreements specify that four laboratory or studio hours shall equate to three lecture-discussion hours, a ratio of four-to-three. Three agreements establish a ratio of three-to-two. Five agreements value laboratory and studio contact time at a straight two-for-one ratio. One agreement says that hours of laboratory teaching shall count at a ratio of three lecture hours counting as two laboratory hours, except in the cases of the sciences (biology, chemistry, physics, and earth science) where laboratory and lecture teaching hours shall be counted as of equal value.[5] Finally, three agreements differentiate among various laboratory-studio teaching hours, rating some at a three-to-two ratio, others at a two-to-one ratio. For example, at Lincoln University each contact hour in physical education, studio art, laboratory science, and English laboratory shall be equal to two-thirds of a teaching hour; in a language laboratory class or a supervised music practice session, each hour shall equate to one-half the regular teaching hour.[6]

The University of Massachusetts Agreement states well what all faculty hope would not only be recognized but be high in the minds of both administrators and boards of trustees when the issue of faculty work loads surfaces. Article XV on faculty work load states:

The Employer recognizes the central fact, common to all institutions of higher education, that, generally, one hour of scheduled instruction by a faculty member requires several hours of instruction related work which takes place outside the classroom. This includes preparation and on-going revision of teaching material, remaining professionally up to date, as well as being available to students both through scheduled office hours and other traditional methods of student-faculty contact. These activities are expected of all faculty members and are taken into account in the assignment of instructional workloads.[7]

Class Size and Student-to-Faculty Ratios

Another working condition that faculty consider as having direct bearing on their academic performance is the size of their classes and the student-to-faculty ratios they or their departments might be required to maintain. The size of the class not only affects how much work the faculty member must perform (the more students, the more examinations and papers to grade, for example) but also the teaching methods one employs—lecture, discussion, laboratory, individual research consultation, and so on. Many faculty would observe further that bigger classes do not only mean more effort in terms of more tests and papers but almost by definition take away energy and time from research, writing, and keeping up with developments in one's field of specialization.

A relatively low proportion of agreements have incorporated these items. Only 27 percent of the agreements speak in any way to class size. Most of these both say little and do little by way of pinning down an institution to anything concrete so far as class size is concerned. In addition, only five agreements (5.6 percent) have contractualized something on student-to-faculty ratios. Four of these specify a maximum ratio: 18 to 1 at the University of Delaware,[8] 20.7 to 1 at Oakland University,[9] 19.5 to 1 at Western Michigan University,[10] and 15 to 1 at the University of Lowell.[11] In all four cases this number is to be a university average. The stated assumption is that ratios will vary from school to school and department to department within the college or university. Such maximum ratios are clearly designed to protect faculty members from the imposition of increased class size requirements. But at two of these institutions, the agreement also can work the other way. At Western Michigan University, the agreement not only specifies a maximum of 19.5 to 1 but also states that should the ratio drop below a specified level (17.5 to 1) the institution may implement layoff proceedings.[12] At Oakland University the agreement speaks of "over ratio layoff."[13] This means that if there are more than ten faculty in excess of the number calculated by the 20.7 to 1 ratio, layoff procedures can be implemented. At Western Michigan University layoff procedures based on the minimum student-to-faculty ratio provision were implemented not long after the agreement was signed. Upon assertion that the student-to-faculty ratio had dropped below 17.5 to 1 the administration announced in the winter of 1977 the intended layoff of from thirteen to sixty-one faculty.[14] The fifth agreement that addresses the question of ratios is at Wagner College. There, the student-to-faculty ratio for each department shall be established by the dean of the faculty following consultation with the faculty council.[15]

Only seven agreements specify class size: a maximum class size of thirty at one institution,[16] a maximum of thirty-five to forty at one;[17] at another any class of forty-six and larger shall yield extra compensation;[18] at two institutions any total teaching load for the semester that exceeds two hundred students shall bring additional compensation;[19] at the C. W. Post Center of Long Island University, for any class over sixty-five students the faculty member shall receive an additional credit of compensation at a rate of one credit for each thirty additional students up to a maximum of six credits.[20] At Wagner College a regular section is defined as constituting thirty-five or fewer students. If there are more than one hundred students in a section, the faculty member shall receive credit for another course or receive $60 a credit hour for each additional twenty or fewer students that exceed forty-five and are still enrolled after the last day in the semester that one can drop a course without penalty.[21] For example, presumably a faculty member teaching a class of forty-eight students in a three-credit-hour course would receive $180 extra compensation. So would a person teaching a class of sixty-four students. But to teach sixty-six students would net $360 by way of additional compensation.

Eight other agreements do not mention numbers but speak simply of determining class size for departments or particular classes within them by consultation between department chairpersons and deans. Two other agreements specify essentially that the department shall establish class size, but with the dean's approval. Two turn the task of working out some kind of class size arrangement to a committee. One lists a maximum class size only for courses at the graduate level or above (maximum of thirty-five). One speaks only of minimum sizes before either the faculty's payment for teaching the course will be reduced or the class will be dropped altogether. One handles the class-size issue by explicitly excluding it from the agreement except with reference to the School of Social Work, where some special arrangements are included as an appendix to the agreement.[22] One agreement says that if a faculty member has taught "extra large" (the description is not defined) sections for two successive semesters, that person shall, where feasible, be given a reduced number (unspecified) of course assignments in the following semester. One agreement states that classroom size will be considered in assigning individual work loads. Another says simply that the college reserves the right to determine class size, though it may consult with the department chairperson on such matters.

Differences do exist with respect to the question of possible variations in class sizes in public and private institutions. The private institutions are decidedly more likely to contractualize something about class size than are the public colleges and universities. The proportions are 45 percent and 10.2 percent, respectively. Further, only one of the prestige institutions (6.7 percent) discusses class size in any form in the agreement.

Three agreements extend the subject of work load by establishing a work-load inequities committee. At Adelphi University the twenty-person (half appointed by the union and half by the administration) Productivity and Workload Inequity Committee shall be created to identify areas of productivity increases and cost savings derived therefrom that could be allocated to faculty salaries and fringe benefits and to identify areas of work-load inequities and recommend their rectification (subject to joint aproval by the bargaining agent and the administration).[23] At Stevens Institute of Technology and at Western Montana College, the committee appears to have authority to resolve the inequities. Failing solution in a particular instance, the president of the college finally shall dispose of the matter.[24] At Stevens Institute the committee reports both to the bargaining agent and the institute itself, with some kind of negotiations (unspecified) presumably to ensue.[25]

One other issue under the heading of academic working conditions that faculty and boards at six institutions have contractualized is that of textbook selection. In all six cases the language is permissive in that freedom of textbook selection is allowed each faculty member. Each agreement, however, also imposes a restriction. At Saginaw Valley State College the requirement is that the selection and assignment of textbooks for classes not "result in an unreasonable financial burden on students."[26] At Youngstown State University the freedom-of-selection principle applies except in multiple section or sequential courses where the department must make a textbook determination.[27] In the Western Montana and Northern Montana agreements, a requirement is appended that whatever texts and course materials a faculty member selects shall conform to published course syllabi or catalog course descriptions.[28] The Agreement for the New Jersey Colleges states that faculty members have the right to selection of textbooks and course materials, but such selection shall be "consistent with the resources, objectives and procedures of the department."[29] The agreement for the University of Massachusetts specifies that all royalties or personal profits accruing from assigning one's own textbook in one's course shall revert to a campus trust fund established to benefit students in ways to be determined by a three-person committee representing the students, administrators, and faculty.[30]

Clearly there have been very few faculty victories so far as the issues of maximum class size, student-to-faculty ratios, and the like are concerned. There is more reliance on mutual goodwill between faculty and administrators and more vague, nonspecific language in this area than in almost any other major topic area in which contract language has been written. Part of the problem is the great disparity among disciplines and departments in terms of the type and size of classes that can be taught at all, let alone taught well. Although it is possible to teach a course in the history of the Civil War to a class of two hundred and, for the sake of argument, perhaps even teach it well, it would be physically impossible, let alone academically feasible, to teach a class of two hundred how to play the organ, throw a pot, or dissect an iguana.

The second reason that contractual language on these issues has tended toward vagueness and generality is apprehension on the part of administrators to tying down the insitution to specific numbers, particularly with the specter of declining enrollments. For this reason faculties press for specific language in this area of academic working conditions, setting the stage for some very heated exchanges during negotiations as faculty call for protection and administrators want flexibility. Faculty will be quick to define administrative behavior as callous and will begin to see or sense potential "atrocities" behind every shrub. Administrators will have to be particularly careful and sensitive to faculty concerns. No doubt this area of academic working conditions is wide open for innovation so far as contractual language and phrasing is concerned.

On the other hand, not to have contractualized work load is not to have lost but perhaps even to have won a battle. We need to look carefully at those institutions (the state colleges and universities, and particularly the more prestigious among them) that have left the work-load issue open, usually not even introducing the topic in any context. Tradition as well as departmental and school autonomy and control over such issues is often strong enough and flexibility is great enough that many of these faculties consider it riskier to include anything in a collective-bargaining agreement on work load. (It should be realized, from the faculty perspective, that to seal up such tradition and precedent, such departmental and school autonomy and control, with appropriate contractual language would make their situation even more secure.)

Facilities

Many agreements speak to the issue of facilities that faculty members need to have available if they are to perform their educative role, by calling out highly specific items that faculty must have. These are elements of working conditions that approximate tools for faculty members: an office with amenities such as desk, chair, file, bookcase, and phone, secretarial assistance, access to a library, perhaps free services of the college computer, and so on.

Contractual specifications in this area are far from universal. In fact, only a few over half (55.1 percent) include such items at all. The private schools are only slightly more likely to have contractualized items along these lines (62.5 percent) than the public institutions (51 percent).

The most commonly contractualized academic service item is that of a faculty office (33.7 percent of the agreements). Most agreements specify something like "suitably equipped" faculty office space, and some provide details concerning furniture. Expectations here are fairly standard—desk, chair, file cabinet, bookcase. A few mention closet space; one even specifies a waste basket. But most are relatively vague and unspecific. For example, the agreement at the C. W. Post Center of Long Island University requires only that "every reasonable effort" shall be made by the administration to provide adequate space for faculty.[31] And the City University of New York Agreement does not speak of office space but a desk, file, and bookshelf for each faculty member. Only when new facilities are to be built shall 120 square feet of office space for each faculty member be included in the planning and design of such facilities.[32]

If elements are specified at all in this area of facilities and services that are available to faculty, secretarial service is next most likely to be named. Nearly one-third (29.2 percent) of the contracts provide some language here—ranging from "adequate clerical help," through the provision of a secretarial pool, or a specified number of secretaries, to one for each department, or, better yet, provided at a one-to-five ratio as at the University of Guam.[33]

In 15 percent of the agreements telephone services are mentioned, though in some of these it is specified that the telephone need only be intracampus. Eleven percent of the agreements mention teaching and/or professional supplies requisite to faculty members carrying out their job. The availability of photocopying and duplicating equipment to faculty on a daily basis, or in each classroom building, or without further specification is required by 10.1 percent of the agreements.

A few agreements (12.4 percent) express concern for safe, healthful working conditions for faculty. The Agreement at Moore College of Art says succinctly, "The College shall provide safe and healthful working and teaching conditions."[34] Western Montana College's agreement adds two ideas: student safety and, somewhat more explicitly, the idea of preventative measures: "Faculty members shall not be required to work under hazardous conditions or to perform tasks which endanger their health or safety, nor will they require their students to do so. Protective devices and first aid equipment shall be provided faculty members who participate in hazardous instructional environments."[35] Related to the above is contractual language at two institutions that deals with the issue of temperature and noise. At the University of New Haven, "The Administration shall try to provide healthful temperature conditions for both classroom and faculty offices."[36] Should temperature control problems arise, they will be reported to the "President's Committee on the Environment" for resolution.[37] Further, "Offices for research and professional activities should not suffer from noise pollution problems."[38] Saginaw Valley State College includes the following statement in the agreement:

If classroom temperatures become so hot or so cold or noise becomes so loud as to preclude the possibility of meaningful academic discourse, the faculty member involved shall first attempt to locate a suitable alternative location for class, and if none is available, the said faculty member may dismiss class.[39]

Occurring rarely (in from one to three agreements depending on the item) are contractual requirements for computer facilities, mail distribution, typewriters, student assistance, laboratory coats for laboratory teachers, access to the university recreational facilities, faculty dining room and lounge facilities, and the provision of motor vehicles when carrying out instructional activities.

Although contractual language so far as faculty services and facilities are concerned is often extremely explicit, most agreements have an administrative escape clause. Qualifying phrases such as "within budget limitations," "subject to availability of funds," or "reasonable" access to secretarial assistance, telephone, or typewriter occur in nearly half of the contracts that have any language in this topic area at all. Although more brief than most, the Agreement from the Illinois Board of Governors' Universities typifies the vague, escape-clause type of language we are referring to here. Article 8 of that agreement states, "To the extent consistent with its responsibility to operate and manage the universities and in accordance with applicable law and policy, the Board will seek to provide adequate equipment and materials and adequate instructional, office, and laboratory facilities."[40]

One final observation with respect to contractual language on faculty facilities, equipment, and assistance is that these seem to be extremely difficult areas for which to provide language. That nearly half of the agreements remain silent about any of the wide variety of topics under this heading likely is indicative of the difficulty of constructing language that is acceptable to both parties to a collective-bargaining agreement. This is not to suggest that administrations and boards of trustees want faculty to get along without offices or without chairs at their desks. But to list generic categories without precise definitions of each is to invite a variety of interpretations, definitions, and expectations. On the other hand, to define all items precisely would be to create a volume of verbiage that would be totally overwhelming. Therefore one of two choices appears to have been made: avoid the subject altogether and hope that past practice, common understandings, and mutual trust will take care of the matter, or list items but define in only general terms.

The Robert Morris College Agreement provides a third alternative. A "side letter" covering all the topics touched upon here is appended describing what the faculty consider to be ideal working conditions, facilities, and services that could be provided by the institution. Although the board of trustees explicitly states it does not necessarily agree on each item, a recommendation will be considered in future planning.[41]

Notes

1. Agreement (1978-82), Detroit College of Business, p. 19.
2. Agreement (1979-80), Park College, p. 21.
3. Agreement (1977-80), New York Institute of Technology, p. 12.
4. Agreement (1976-79), Dyke College, p. 9.
5. Agreement (1974-77), Pennsylvania State Colleges and Universities, p. 40.

6. Agreement (1976-78), Lincoln University, p. 14.

7. Agreement (1977-80), University of Massachusetts, p. 17.

8. Agreement (1977-79), University of Delaware, p. 19.

9. Agreement (1976-79), Oakland University, p. 72.

10. Agreement (1976-77), Western Michigan University, p. 31.

11. Agreement (1976-77), University of Lowell, p. 62.

12. Agreement (1976-77), Western Michigan University, p. 31.

13. Agreement (1976-79), Oakland University, p. 29.

14. "WMU-AAUP Letter," American Association of University Professors, Western Michigan University Chapter, vol. III, no. 17, Feb. 7, 1977, p. 1.

15. Agreement (1977-80), Wagner College, p. 48.

16. Agreement (1975-77), Rhode Island College, p. 29.

17. Agreement (1976-78), Roger Williams College, p. 8.

18. Agreement (1976-79), University of New Haven, p. 13.

19. Agreement (1976-78), Saginaw Valley State College, p. 16, and Agreement (1974-77), St. John's University, p. 16.

20. Agreement (1977-80), Long Island University, C. W. Post Center, p. 46.

21. Agreement (1977-80), Wagner College, p. 67.

22. Agreement (1976-78), Adelphi University, pp. 5, 22-23.

23. Ibid., p. 8.

24. Agreement (1977-79), Western Montana College, p. 15.

25. Agreement (1976-78), Stevens Institute of Technology, p. 12.

26. Agreement (1976-78), Saginaw Valley State College, p. 21.

27. Agreement (1977-81), Youngstown State University, p. 33.

28. Agreement (1977-79), Northern Montana College, p. 15, and Agreement (1977-79), Western Monana College, p. 15.

29. Agreement (1977-79), New Jersey State Colleges, p. 12.

30. Agreement (1977-80), University of Masschusetts, p. 41.

31. Agreement (1977-80), Long Island University, C. W. Post Center, p. 79.

32. Agreement (1975-77), City University of New York, p. 45.

33. Agreement (1977-80), University of Guam, p. 32.

34. Agreement (1976-79), Moore College of Art, p. 11.

35. Agreement (1977-79), Western Montana College, pp. 18-19.

36. Agreement (1976-79), University of New Haven, p. 13.

31. Ibid.

38. Ibid.

39. Agreement (1976-78), Saginaw Valley State College, p. 44.

40. Agreement (1977-79), Illinois Board of Governor's Universities, art. 8.

41. Agreement (1977-80), Robert Morris College, side letter.

7. PROFESSIONAL ROLE AND CONDUCT

Just as collective bargaining provides opportunities for faculty members to negotiate for items that they feel they need and want, management has its lists as well. What the administrations and boards of trustees expect of faculty members by way of minimal performance of their roles and professional behavior generally is the focus of this chapter.

There are two broad categories of expectations around which this discussion will center: general professional conduct and role performance and specific academic duties, such as student advising, participating in commencement, attendance at institutional functions, holding office hours, and the like.

Professional Conduct and Role Performance

Not an overwhelming number of agreements speak at a philosophical or general level about the professional conduct of faculty members. Of the thirty-eight agreements (42.7 percent of the total number of agreements at four year colleges and universities) that address the subject of the professional role and responsibilities of faculty members, only seventeen (19.1 percent of the total number of agreements) do anything more than include a list of specific responsibilities that faculty shall have.

The opening paragraph of section XV, "Professional Duties," in the agreement at Rutgers University says, "The parties recognize that the University accomplishes a variety of academic and professional services including undergraduate, graduate, and professional instruction, research and community service. The professional duties required of the faculty shall be in accordance with the mission of the University."[1] Although the statement mentions the basic criteria by which faculty members tend to be judged—teaching effectiveness, research, and service—the paragraph is hardly specific. The introduction to article V on the faculty in the agreement at Bryant College of Business goes a little further. It not only mentions major categories of the professor's role but makes a positive affirmation of the central role of faculty in the educational process:

The primary function of the faculty is teaching and the discharge of the related responsibilities of undergraduate instruction. The college looks to the faculty for mastery of the subject matter in the respective areas of curriculum, for leadership and maintaining pace with the modern trends in business, and for adaptation to the purposes of the program of studies, new developments in learning theories and instructional techniques. Emphasis is placed on the *student learning experience* and the faculty member shall divide his time between classroom, class preparation, student conferences, and committee work, to the attainment of the end objective of an effective teaching institution.[2]

The University of Dubuque Agreement manages to present faculty in a positive light and yet challenges them to a high level of effectiveness. In article VIII, "Faculty Rights and Responsibilities," the faculty association and the board affirm a joint mission "to provide quality education for students in a learning environment which affirms student development."[3] After detailing certain professional responsibilities such as setting standards of student grading and classroom conduct, degree requirements, course offerings and curricular content, and a few others, that are exclusive prerogatives of the faculty, the agreement states, "Each faculty member shall seek ways of contributing to the life of the college through its various committees, program elements, and student development activities."[4]

The agreement at Eastern Montana College affirms academic excellence when it states that when people accept a faculty position at the college they will "maintain professional competence and keep personal knowledge current by continuous reading, research, etc." They also commit themselves to perform fully and faithfully the duties of a college faculty member.[5]

Perhaps the best general statement that summarizes the broad range of qualities that make the complete faculty person is the introductory paragraph of the article on "Professional Responsibilities of the Faculty and Librarians" in the agreement at the University of San Francisco:

Effectiveness of teaching, professional growth as reflected by creative work, willing acceptance of responsibilities other than teaching, worthy representation of the University in public affairs, participation in the programs of professional societies, and successful maintenance of sound personal and ethical relations with one's colleagues and the Community—these are among the professional responsibilities of the faculty.[6]

Another excellent statement that is not only a commitment by both administrators and faculty to high academic standards and quality in general terms but also a list of some specific expectations so far as faculty responsibilities are concerned is found in the Fairleigh Dickinson University Agreement:

The University and Council each recognize that mutual benefits derive from continual improvement of the University as an institution of higher learning, and that, toward this end, the primary professional responsibility of each member of the bargaining unit is to the University and the University community. The University and the Council concur that each member of the bargaining unit should display a high degree of professionalism. He should therefore:

(a) To the best of his ability, aspire to excellence in teaching his students, promote the learning process, and stimulate the intellectual development of his students. To this end, he shall meet each class as scheduled or provide equivalent instruction outside the classroom (e.g., field trips). Early in the semester he shall clarify course objectives and the evaluative techniques and standards to be used for each class taught. In addition, he shall evaluate assignments submitted by students in an effective manner for the student's development in the course.

(b) Possess knowledge of his subject matter and strive to keep informed of contemporary developments in his field of specialization.

(c) Seek to manifest objectivity and fairness in his relationships with members of the University community and most especially in the conscientious examining, grading, advising, and counselling of students.

(d) Strive conscientiously to improve the methods of instruction and to apply new approaches to teaching which show promise of success or which have been proven successful.

(e) Recognize the diversity of the student body by attempting to adjust to individual differences in the students.

(f) Accept a reasonable number of committee assignments, conscientiously serve on those committees of which he is a member, and fulfill the specific duties of any office to which he has been elected or in which he has volunteered to serve.

(g) Serve as a resource to student organizations on the campus where this is consistent with his interests and other commitments.

(h) Recognize his obligation to the entire University community but most especially to our graduates and their families by making every effort to attend the commencement exercises. The administration shall make every effort to promote a meaningful ceremony with an appropriate recognition of the faculty role in the University.

(i) Adhere to reasonable deadlines and schedules established for the timely reporting of grades and for other matters related to student registration and record keeping.

(j) Assume a fair share of responsibility in department, college and campus registration advisement and in the student academic review process.

(k) Maintain reasonable adherence to course descriptions in accordance with the representations of the University Bulletin and other official University publications, and participate in a continuing review of such course descriptions to keep them current.[7]

Specified Academic Duties

Nearly half (42.7 percent) of the agreements contractualize to some extent specific duties and responsibilities of faculty members. These are in addition to the contractualization of course load and the number of preparations for each faculty member that we discussed in the previous chapter. The specific duties and academic responsibilities are such ancillary tasks to the academic enterprise as advising students while preregistering or at other times, supervising independent study courses for students, serving as thesis advisers, helping with registration, serving on departmental, school, and college committees, holding office hours, attending university functions such as convocations, faculty meetings, and commencement exercises, doing a responsible job of grading and evaluating students' work, and the like.

Office Hours

Although 42.7 percent of the agreements list some specific responsibility, there is little consensus on what set of duties should be contractualized. The greatest consensus is on the duty of being available to students by holding regular office hours, but not all agreements list even this standard academic responsibility. We find 38.2 percent (thirty-four agreements) of all agreements in four-year institutions (89.5 percent of those thirty-eight agreements that provide any listing at all of specific duties) committing to contractual language something about office hours. Of these thirty-four agreements, seven simply speak to the requirement of holding regular office hours but do not specify a minimum number, or say something like "a reasonable number of regularly scheduled office hours." The remaining twenty-seven agreements mention a minimum number. The range is from two a week at Bard College[8] to twelve a week at Northern Michigan University.[9] Aside from two agreements that specify a minimum of ten regularly scheduled office hours a week (Eastern Michigan University[10] and the University of Guam[11]), the majority cluster in the three to six hours a week range. Six agreements specify three office hours a week, five require four hours, nine require five hours, two require six hours, and one requires eight hours a week.

Two agreements require that the office hours be distributed on at least two different days of the week, three require distribution on three days, two specify distribution of the hours over four different days in the week, and one requires at least one office hour every weekday. Two agreements mention that a faculty member shall be expected to provide more office hours during such times as the week of final examinations and the period of preregistration and required fall and winter registration periods. Several agreements mentioned not only that the place where the faculty member would be available for her/his office hours be reasonably convenient for students, but that the list of one's office hours be posted.

The public versus private variable is significant here. As with course load and class size, discussed in the previous chapter, the private colleges and universities are more likely than the public institutions to address the topic. Fifty-two and one-half percent of the private schools do so; only 36.7 percent of the public institutions do so; and the prestigious public universities are least likely of all to require a minimum number of office hours (26.7 percent).

Service on Committees

The next most frequently contractualized specific faculty duty relates to college or university committees. Twenty-seven agreements (30.3 percent of the total number of agreements, or 71.1 percent of the thirty-eight agreements that contractualize specific faculty duties) say something in the agreement about academic committees. What is contractualized is not always the obligation of faculty to participate and serve on committees but that certain committees be established. Nine agreements specify that one or more committees be established or, if they are already in existence, then the agreement specifies how the members shall be selected. Several agreements state not simply that there shall be a faculty component in the process of selecting committees but that faculty operating through their bargaining agent shall either provide a slate of nominees or do the actual selecting. As an example of the former, the agreement at Bryant College of Business requires that the faculty members on all college committees shall be nominated by the board of directors of the faculty federation.[12] An example of the latter is at Moore College of Art where the agreement specifies that faculty members shall be appointed by the faculty union to committees that have been established formally and sanctioned by the agreement.[13]

Ten agreements specify the creation or authentication of certain committees and require faculty members to serve on these and other committees at various levels within the institution's structure. The final eight agreements simply require faculty participation in committee work as part of their normal academic responsibility. When they speak to the requirement that faculty members serve on committees, most agreements do not set either minimum or maximum numbers of committees upon which a faculty member is expected to serve. A few, however, protect faculty by setting maximum numbers of committees that they can be required to participate in. For example, at Wagner College faculty cannot be required to serve on more than two committees simultaneously.[14] At Youngstown State University the maximum is four concurrent committee assignments.[15]

The pattern of differentiation between the private colleges and universities and the public ones obtains here again. Although none of the more prestigious public universities contractualize an obligation by faculty to serve on committees, 17.6 percent of the less prestigious state colleges and universities and a high of 30 percent of the private colleges, have done so.

Student Advising

The next most frequently contractualized item of a faculty duty nature is student advising responsibilities, found in twenty-four agreements (27 percent of the total number of agreements, 63.2 percent of the thirty-eight agreements that contractualize specific faculty duties). All of these agreements say something to the effect that advising is considered part of the normal work load of faculty. Usually no more than that is said. In five cases, maximum numbers or something approaching upper limits are established. At both Rhode Island College[16] and Robert Morris College[17] the maximum is thirty advisees per faculty member. At Dyke College the maximum number of advisees shall be fifty-six students.[18] At Saginaw Valley State College no faculty member is to be assigned more than one advisee more than any other faculty member.[19] At Fairleigh Dickinson University the language of the contract is even less specific; faculty members shall advise a "reasonable number of students as equitably assigned by their department in consultation with the College Dean."[20]

None of the more prestigious public universities contractualize a requirement of faculty to advise students. This contrasts with 37.5 percent of the private institutions. The less prestigious state colleges and universities are intermediate, with 23.5 percent contractualizing advising requirements.

Only two other ideas with respect to advising have been contractualized. One is to request faculty to do a good job in their advising. At Adelphi University the phrasing is, "Faculty members should make every effort to provide full and accurate advisement and academic counseling to students."[21] And at Fairleigh Dickinson University, in addition to the regular advising that takes place during the normal workday and work week, certain faculty members may be designated as college advisers by the appropriate dean in consultation with the College Educational Planning Committee to serve students in the evening program and to be on hand during the intersession and summer session. These advisers shall be remunerated at $12 per hour.[22]

Grading Obligations

Grading is the next most frequently contractualized duty item (in nineteen agreements, 21.3 percent of the total number of agreements, or 50 percent of the thirty-eight agreements that contractualize specific faculty duties).

Usually the instructor must meet deadlines that have been established by the institution in submitting grades. Twelve agreements incorporate the deadline idea, but only two include precise dates or time periods. At the

University of San Francisco final grades are to be turned in within fifteen days from the close of the examination period,[23] and Youngstown State University has the unique contractual requirement that all students shall have been accorded at least one grade by the end of six weeks of the course.[24] Four agreements state unequivocally that grading is the exclusive right of faculty. Four state that faculty shall treat students fairly and impartially. Two state that grading the performance of students is one part of the faculty member's role. And two others require that faculty retain their students' examinations for a specified minimum amount of time. At the University of San Francisco, faculty may retain students' final examinations for one month after the beginning of the next semester.[25] At Northern Michigan University students' written work should be available for their review in their instructor's office for one full year.[26]

None of the more prestigious state university agreements includes such a faculty duty as a contractualized item. In this case, however, the less prestigious state colleges and universities are not in between but are represented in essentially identical proportions with the private colleges (26.5 percent and 25 percent, respectively).

Commencement and Other Functions

Another duty of faculty members that has been contractualized with modest frequency is that of faculty attendance at commencement exercises and/or other institutional functions. Twenty-one agreements (23.6 percent of all agreements, 61.8 percent of those that have any contractual language concerning faculty duties and responsibilities) do so. Seventeen of these specify commencement as an academic function that is either mandatory or very strongly suggested for faculty. Some say only that "each faculty member shall make every effort to attend commencement,"[27] but most do not equivocate. For example, "Faculty attendance is required" is the language used by Monmouth College.[28] Nor does the language in the Moore College of Art Agreement leave doubt:

It is understood that attendance at commencement exercise by the faculty is an accepted tradition that is required; however, under extenuating circumstances where personal hardship or serious illness makes such attendance impossible the administration shall waive required attendance upon advance notification to the College, where possible. Proof of personal hardship and/or illness shall be required upon request by the College.[29]

At the University of New Haven, attendance at one of the two commencements conducted each year is required, though deans can excuse faculty for "appropriate reasons."[30] But if after ordering academic regalia a faculty member fails to attend, that person shall reimburse the university for the rental charges.[31] Both the Detroit College of Business and the Vermont State Colleges agree to furnish academic garb while requiring faculty attendance.[32] The Youngstown State University Agreement requires faculty attendance for one-third of the faculty at a given commencement as the faculty are scheduled by the ceremonials committee.[33] The Saginaw Valley State College Agreement states explicitly that attendance at institutional functions shall be voluntary.[34] The New Jersey State Colleges Agreement poses the most intriguing situation of all; when faculty are required to attend ceremonial functions such as commencements, "the wearing of academic regalia shall be at the option of the employee."[35]

In addition to requirements with regard to commencement, eleven of the twenty-one agreements require attendance at faculty meetings. Usually the referent here is a college- or university-wide faculty meeting commonly held at relatively small institutions. Often included by specific designation are departmental, divisional, and school meetings.

Five agreements list convocations as school functions that faculty are required or at least expected to attend. By way of contrast, however, the Wagner College Agreement lists both convocations and baccalaureate ceremonies as voluntary, while at the same time noting that attendance at regular meetings of the faculty and commencement exercises is expected.[36]

Another responsibility that most faculty at least take a turn at but find actually required by contract at only nine four-year institutions (10.1 percent of all agreements, 23.7 percent of the agreements that contractualize any specific faculty duties) is that of assisting with registration of students. The implication, or direct statement, is that faculty should be available for such duties and can be assigned to some when a dean or chairperson sees need. Of interest is the statement in the Monmouth Agreement that says that the principal function of the faculty during the registration period and process is the counseling of students.[37]

With respect to the public versus private and the institutional prestige variables, the data in table 10 summarize the frequencies with which various functions have been contractualized at the three types of institutions. The pattern is very familiar. There are very few abberations from the patterns already observed with respect to advising students, grading, and service on committees. That is, it is very seldom that the more prestigious state universities contractualize normal faculty duties.

Thesis Advising

Two other duties of faculty that have in common a one-on-one relationship of faculty members with students are serving as a graduate or senior thesis adviser and advising students taking an independent study course. Nine agreements say something about the former; eleven reduce to contract language some aspects of the latter.

TABLE 10
**Frequency of Contractualized Faculty
Duties, by Type of Institution**

	HIGHER PRESTIGE STATE UNIVERSITIES	LOWER PRESTIGE STATE UNIVERSITIES	PRIVATE COLLEGES AND UNIVERSITIES
Attendance at commencement required	5.4%	11.8%	20.0%
Attendance at Faculty meetings required	0	5.9	22.5
Attendance at convocations required	0	2.9	10.0
Participation in registration required	5.4	8.8	12.5
Advising required	0	23.5	37.5
Grading contractualized	0	26.5	25.0
Service on committees required	0	17.6	30.0
Office hours contractualized	26.7	41.2	52.5

With thesis supervision the idea is not that such activity is obligatory; what appears to be at issue is how much teaching credit should derive for faculty from their supervision. There is no consensus except that faculty should receive some kind of credit toward teaching load for supervising theses. That consensus is important because we would assume that most of the agreements that do not specify that thesis supervision counts something toward teaching load reduction do not provide such credit and apparently assume this activity to be part of a faculty member's regular academic load. As such it merits neither extra compensation nor a teaching load reduction.

The only consensus is in the similar though technically distinct contracts at the three branches of Long Island University where each thesis that is accepted merits credit of one hour of teaching.[38] One assumes that a faculty member who has accumulated several of these credits can use them to reduce her or his teaching load in a given semester by one two-hour, three-hour, or four-hour course, as the case may be.

Moving from the statistical mode of one teaching hour of credit per thesis, one encounters a substantial range. It is from one-third and one-half of a credit teaching hour per thesis at Southeastern Massachusetts University[39] and Rhode Island College,[40] respectively, to one and one-half teaching hours credit at Youngstown State University.[41]

Independent study not only shows some diversity in how it is handled, but we see added a monetary dimension that does not occur in the thesis supervision area. The branches of Long Island University are uniform in offering faculty remuneration at $30 per credit hour offered under independent study.[42] Regis College offers $100 per student, only slightly higher than the rate at the Long Island University campuses if we assume that the course credit is commonly three hours.[43] Robert Morris College provides both a monetary and load-overload option. First, compensation shall be one-third of the tuition charged, but never less than $25, or the course load credit can be figured as ten independent study students equivalent to one course.[44] Youngstown State University compensates independent study supervision at one-half credit hour per fifteen s.c.h. of independent study—what amounts to a ratio of ten students per hour of course credit.[45] By way of contrast, Quinnipiac College grants one hour of course credit for a faculty member for every three students,[46] and Rhode Island College grants teaching credit on a one-to-one basis.[47] Saginaw Valley State College takes a distinctive approach. If faculty produce 0 to 300 s.c.h. per year (including any independent study credits), there will be no extra compensation to independent study supervisors. If the faculty members produces 301 to 599 s.c.h., then added remuneration of $10 for each s.c.h. of independent study will accrue. If the faculty member teaches more than 600 s.c.h., the rate of extra compensation for independent study will be $15 per s.c.h.[48]

Course Scheduling

One final area that straddles the concepts of faculty duties and faculty rights is that of course schedule and the scheduling process. With respect to the duty idea, several agreements have included statements to the effect that the faculty's obligation is to schedule a solid core of courses for students.[49] But most of the agreements emphasize the rights of faculty with respect to the scheduling done by the administration. As such, the language is protective in its aim. Frequently the sixteen agreements that speak to scheduling contain phrases such as "with maximum consideration for faculty requests,"[50] faculty shall not be assigned an "unreasonable schedule,"[51] and "no assignment without consultation with faculty members."[52] Occasionally faculty committees are used, and deadlines for notifying the faculty of her or his next semester's schedule are listed. Five of the sixteen agreements restrict the number of consecutive hours for courses a faculty member can be scheduled to teach or the earliness or lateness of the hour that faculty can be expected to teach. For example, at Quinnipiac College a faculty member cannot be assigned more than two courses that begin after 5:00 P.M. or, alternatively, more than one weekend course in any semester.[53] At Robert Morris College the institution shall make reasonable efforts to establish a class schedule so as not to exceed a span of eight clock hours per day and should allow a minimum of twelve hours between the end of a faculty member's class on one day and the beginning of the first class the following day.[54] At Moore College of Art there shall be scheduled no more than two consecutive three-hour studio classes per day unless mutually agreed upon during a consultation at which a union representative is present.[55]

Outside Employment

A final issue relates directly to the question of duties and responsibilities for faculty members. That is the issue of outside employment, particularly insofar as it might interfere with a faculty member's performance of regular duties at the employing college or university. Thirty-eight agreements (42.7 percent) speak specifically to this issue, and all of them are permissive on the issue so long as the person's performance of primary full-time employment is not harmed.

Many are not only permissive with regard to outside employment that does not interfere with one's performance on campus, but they assert that such an application of a faculty member's professional skills is a desirable activity, even to be encouraged. For example, the Adelphi University Agreement says that professonal consultation or services to organizations outside the college for remuneration is to be expected and is valued.[56] The Bryant College of Business Agreement states that a "modest amount" of faculty participation in business is desirable.[57] At Stevens Institute of Technology this idea is expressed as follows: "Consultation with or without additional compensation is recognized as an appropriate professional activity to the extent that it enhances the professional stature and vitalizes the teaching and research capabilities of the institute and the unit member."[58]

Although a few agreements are fairly terse with respect to the outside-employment issue, various combinations of ideas are added to many of the thirty-eight agreements: inform one's department chairman and/or dean, and/or president or academic vice-president in writing and receive official permission (twenty-four agreements); refrain from using any supplies or services of the college or university in the performance of such outside employment (twelve agreements); make clear that one's outside employment is based on one's individual expertise and does not represent the college or university in any way (seven agreements); and be wary of one's employment becoming a conflict-of-interest issue if the goals and activities of the supplemental employment are at odds in some manner with those of the college or university (six agreements).

Five agreements specify the number of days that are generally permissible to use in the performance of supplemental employment. Three agreements allow an average of eight hours (one day) a week; one says two days a month; and one sets the limit at eighteen days during an academic year.

In short, collective bargaining appears not to have placed undue restrictions on outside consultation and other remunerative activities by faculty members. A majority of the agreements do not speak to the issue at all, and of those that do, none is repressive or overly restrictive.

Differences by type of institution are apparent. Whereas only 20 percent of the more prestigious state institutions speak to the subject of outside employment, 41.2 percent of the less prestigious state schools and 45 percent of the private colleges do so.

Conclusion

A clear majority (over 57 percent) list nothing by way of specific tasks and responsibilities that faculty members are to perform. Although it is easy to understand why in some agreements a legalistic approach has been taken (faculty required to attend commencement exercises, obligated to hold a certain number of office hours, and so on) and although some faculty might prefer such a system in which they know rather precisely what is expected of them, most faculty are inclined to feel that to become highly specific in the sphere of faculty duties "cheapens" the professional aspect of the faculty role. Such an approach encourages a legalistic, by-the-book type of perspective that will be more harmful to the relationship of faculty with administration and board and to the overall effectiveness of the educational process than will a more flexible and collegial relationship in which the professional integrity of faculty is assumed and certain commonly accepted practices of faculty members are presumed.

This is clearly the lead that the state universities, the more prestigious among them in particular, are providing. The almost total absence of detailed duties and obligations for faculty in these agreements is truly striking. Although some faculty will disappoint their colleagues, the administration, and the board of trustees by taking advantage of the openness of the situation, the encouragement of collegiality for the majority should more than compensate for the shirkers and the disappointment they generate.

Notes

1. Agreement (1975-77), Rutgers University, p. 17.
2. Agreement (1977-79), Bryant College of Business, p. 21.
3. Agreement (1977-78), University of Dubuque, p. 5.
4. Ibid.
5. Agreement (1976-77), Eastern Montana College, p. 2.
6. Agreement (1976-81), University of San Francisco, p. 10.
7. Agreement (1977-79), Fairleigh Dickinson University, pp. 24-25.
8. Agreement (1977-78), Bard College, p. 5.
9. Agreement (1975-77), Northern Michigan University, p. 28.

10. Agreement (1976-78), Eastern Michigan University, p. 15.

11. Agreement (1977-80), University of Guam, p. 31.

12. Agreement (1977-79), Bryant College of Business, p. 3.

13. Agreement (1976-79), Moore College of Art, p. 23.

14. Agreement (1977-80), Wagner College, p. 67.

15. Agreement (1977-81), Youngstown State University, p. 32.

16. Agreement (1975-77), Rhode Island College, p. 31.

17. Agreement (1977-80), Robert Morris College, p. 24.

18. Agreement (1976-79), Dyke College, p. 9.

19. Agreement (1976-78), Saginaw Valley State College, p. 33.

20. Agreement (1977-79), Fairleigh Dickinson University, p. 18.

21. Agreement (1976-78), Adelphi University, p. 18.

22. Agreement (1977-79), Fairleigh Dickinson University, p. 21.

23. Agreement (1976-81), University of San Francisco, p. 29.

24. Agreement (1977-81), Youngstown State University, p. 33.

25. Agreement (1976-81), University of San Francisco, p. 20.

26. Agreement (1975-77), Northern Michigan University, p. 28.

27. Agreement (1976-78), Adelphi University, p. 17.

28. Agreement (1976-79), Monmouth College, p. 26.

29. Agreement (1976-79), Moore College of Art, p. 9.

30. Agreement (1976-78), University of New Haven, p. 17.,

31. Ibid.

32. Agreement (1978-82), Detroit College of Business, p. 20, and Agreement (1979-80), Vermont State Colleges, p. 43.

33. Agreement (1977-81), Youngstown State University, p. 33.

34. Agreement (1976-78), Saginaw Valley State College, p. 33.

35. Agreement (1977-79), New Jersey State Colleges, p. 14.

36. Agreement (1977-80), Wagner College, p. 54.

37. Agreement (1976-79), Monmouth College, p. 26.

38. Agreement (1976-79), Long Island University, Brooklyn Center, p. 46; Agreement (1977-80), Long Island University, Southampton Center, p. 41; and Agreement (1977-80), Long Island University, C. W. Post Center, p. 46.

39. Agreement (1976-79), Southeastern Massachusetts University, p. 35.

40. Agreement (1975-77), Rhode Island College, p. 30.

41. Agreement (1977-81), Youngstown State University, pp. 29-30.

42. Agreement (1976-79), Long Island University, Brooklyn Center, p. 46; Agreement (1977-80), Long Island University, Southampton Center, p. 41; and Agreement (1977-80), Long Island University, C. W. Post Center, p. 62.

43. Agreement (1977-79), Regis College, p. 5.

44. Agreement (1977-80), Robert Morris College, p. 19.

45. Agreement (1977-81), Youngstown State University, p. 30.

46. Agreement (1975-78), Quinnipiac College, p. 25.

47. Agreement (1975-77), Rhode Island College, p. 31.

48. Agreement (1976-78), Saginaw Valley State College, p. 34.

49. Ibid., pp. 29-31.

50. Agreement (1977-78), Bard College, p. 6.

51. Agreement (1974-76), Fitchburg State College, p. 78.

52. Agreement (1977-79), Board of Governor's State Colleges and Universities (Illinois), art. VII.

53. Agreement (1975-78), Quinnipiac College, p. 25.

54. Agreement (1977-80), Robert Morris College, pp. 24-25.

55. Agreement (1976-79), Moore College of Art, p. 8.

56. Agreement (1976-78), Adelphi University, p. 6.

57. Agreement (1977-79), Bryant College of Business, p. 23.

58. Agreement (1976-78), Stevens Institute of Technology, p. 13.

8.
THE FACULTY AND ACADEMIC GOVERNANCE

When faculty get together to gripe about the institution they serve it does not take long to get on the topic I might call "Why Can't the Administration . . . ?" That is, why can't the administration consult more often and more seriously with faculty? Nothing makes professors angry more quickly than for anyone with an administrative title to imply that professors individually or collectively do not know all there is to know about higher education and what is good for students. Even to suggest, however tentatively, that although the faculty are wise and good and have the best interests of the institution at heart, they are not as informed in certain specialized areas of administration or as aware of selected bodies of information as are certain administrators is to risk their wrath.

A primary reason for higher-education faculties' beginning to flirt with the idea of collective bargaining in the first place has been the trend toward more centralized decision making in administrative offices that are removed from the front lines of the classroom, a trend that almost by definition interferes significantly with the collegial, consultative relationship of administration with faculty that many believe did obtain in many places in the past. Although one would get few arguments from faculty if one said that for all intents and purposes the faculty is the university, many faculty feel the undergirding for such an assertion slipping out from under them.

Therefore, it should come as no surprise when faculty in their collective-bargaining agreements seek to contractualize some principles and procedures designed to prescribe to some extent how the institution is to be governed, with particular attention paid to the involvement of faculty in that governing process. Perhaps somewhat surprising is the discovery that only slightly more than a third of the agreements (37.1 percent) deal at all explicitly, even in passing, with the relationship of faculty and administration in the governnance function at the college or university. An even smaller proportion (25.8 percent) actually devote a specific section or article in their agreement to delineating the relationship.

The Need for Respect

If we could pick one need and expectation that is essentially universal among faculty, probably it would be the need for respect. Thus the most serious mistake an administrator can make is to treat the faculty as just another labor union, or simply as employees, or as people interested solely in improving their own welfare. On the other hand, if faculty sense from the administration that their contributions beyond the classroom and laboratory are sought after and valued, their loyalty and dedication can be boundless, their efforts on behalf of the institution untiring. Thus most faculty would appreciate and feel comfortable with the statement in the University of Cincinnati Agreement that deals with governance; it says that at all levels faculty have the right to aid, advise, and counsel administrators.[1] Such a statement implies the administration's respect for faculty and for their knowledge and judgment. Faculty can in turn then talk about the wisdom of administrators—a wisdom that brings them among other things to look to faculty for counsel.

The statement included in the University of Cincinnati Agreement and similar ones simply describe what most faculty already think is part of their job and responsibility and is a description of what they believe they have traditionally done. Yet it does not commit the administration to very much. The only action prescribed for administrators is that of listening. They do not need to heed the advice or counsel. It is contractual language that is innocent enough as it stands. Yet innocent and essentially noncommittal though it may be, even such a statement is rarely employed in collective-bargaining agreements in higher education.

Exclusive Faculty Prerogatives

More frequent is language that is complimentary to faculty and accords them their special expertise in matters educational—counsel and advice from faculty but on a more specialized, narrow range of topics. For example, the agreement at the University of Dubuque speaks of exclusive faculty rights—rights to set degree requirements, establish grading standards, initially receive and consider new degree programs, recommend earned degree recipients, and approve curriculum content and course offerings.[2] Although the rights are exclusively those of faculty, the range is circumscribed carefully. Another example of restrictive language is in the agreement at the University of Massachusetts, which states that the faculty will exercise primary responsibility in academic matters (such as curriculum, subject matter, and methods of instruction).[3] And the agreement at Moore College of Art states: "In all matters relating to education concerning hiring, promoting, or determining rank, determining curriculum, and evaluating of portfolios for admission of students . . . faculty members shall continue to be involved and participate in the determination of these matters."[4]

Incorporation of Other Documents

A somewhat broader scope is expressed in the collective-bargaining agreement at Bloomfield College, which says that both parties accept the principle of collegial governance as enunciated in the AAUP's 1966 Statement on Governance of Colleges and Universities. Further, both parties recognize and accept the bylaws and standing rules of the Bloomfield College faculty as the basic governing document of the faculty. If either party should object to a proposed change, such change shall not be implemented until good-faith negotiations between the parties have taken place.[5]

Although these provisions do not guarantee as much as one might suppose, they do allow more faculty involvement in decision making than most other agreements do. Probably the Bloomfield College faculty was pleased when both parties approved this section of contractual language.

Several qualities seem important to the agreement: an inherent element of respect for faculty, a commitment to collegial relationships, and a process that forces cool deliberation and discussion of an issue before change is implemented within the institution. Yet such language is rare. In fact, the mention of the AAUP's 1966 statement is unique to the Bloomfield College Agreement.

A few other agreements incorporate another document that delineates the rights of faculty and the extent of faculty participation in the collegial decision-making process. Fifteen agreements (including Bloomfield College) have incorporated either by reference or as a fully intact document a faculty constitution of some sort—a document, which almost always predates the collective-bargaining agreement, setting forth the rights and responsibilities of faculty so far as participation in the governance of the institution is concerned. This step gives significant added weight to such documents in that prior to incoporation into the collective-bargaining agreement, the documents had authority only by tacit agreement in that a board of trustees had final authority. It is unlikely that any of these documents had legal authority to the degree that a federal- or state-regulated collective-bargaining agreement does. What this amounts to is to extend significantly the scope of any particular collective-bargaining agreements. The best examples of such extensions of the collective-bargaining agreement through incorporating in some form other documents and their attendant organizational processes are those at the following institutions: Fairleigh Dickinson University, St. John's University, Lincoln University, and the University of Cincinnati. The Lincoln University Agreement says that the bylaws of the Lincoln University faculty appended as exhibit B are "the legal instrument defining the role of the Faculty in the governance of the University."[6] Cincinnati's agreement says that the parties to the agreement recognize the university senate, the student senate, and the faculty senate and the bylaws that govern their relationship with the university. Further, with respect to faculty priorities in those areas that are not specifically dealt with through the collective-bargaining process, both parties recognize the faculty senate as the primary governing body that represents the faculty and has the right to advise the president. Finally, the intent of both parties is to support the role of existing governing bodies in the affairs of the university.[7] The St. John's agreement states, "During the term of this Agreement, the Administration will not institute changes in the organizational structure and responsibility of the University Senate and/or Faculty Councils, except as otherwise provided in this Agreement."[8] According to the Fairleigh Dickinson Agreement, both faculty and administration share a concern over the potential for conflict between their respective responsibilities in the collective-bargaining relationship and the activities of the senate. Consequently they have contractualized a procedure to resolve such difficulties. It stipulates that if both the association and the administration agree that a subject being considered by the senate is outside its jurisdiction, whether by law or because the subject has been made part of the agreement directly or indirectly, they shall jointly so advise the senate. On the other hand, if the two parties disagree with respect to the propriety of certain senate actions, either party may submit the issue to binding arbitration.[9]

The Process of Change

Faculties fear becoming victim to what they consider arbitrary or capricious action on the part of superiors in the higher education hierarchy. That, of course, is fundamentally what constitutions, sets of procedures, and collective bargaining are all about; they are all parts of an endeavor to avoid precipitous action. All of them slow down the process and introduce a series of steps to be followed. Consultation with more than one person is required. In an endeavor to avoid arbitrary action, the faculty attempt to anticipate possible situations and constellations of events in advance and establish some principles from which to proceed and against which to compare, as well as what criteria of judgment are to be employed. In other words, change that may be necessary should proceed in an orderly, measured manner and involve principles and procedures that the parties have accepted ahead of time. The intent is not necessarily to impede change but to establish an orderly and principled set of procedures to be followed.

In this connection two agreements stand out: those at Kent State University and Central Michigan University. The 1977-80 agreement at Central Michigan University includes a requirement that the issue of changing university policies with respect to tenure, promotion, and reappointment shall be referred to the academic senate for deliberation and recommendation; however, any method developed by the academic senate must be accepted by *both* the faculty association and the university. Any method—whether through a committee structure, senate process, faculty association action, negotiations with Central Michigan University, or administrative fiat—is acceptable *so long as* all three parties agree.[10]

The Kent State University process involving faculty contributions to the governance process is far from air-tight, but at least it has built-in pauses during which faculty have opportunity to consider issues and make recommendations to the administration concerning them. This occurs at several levels. At the primary level the agreement establishes a faculty advisory committee for each department; it may be an entire departmental membership as a committee of the whole. This group shall be an advisory and recommendatory body to the department chairperson on such academic matters as tenure and promotion, appointment and reappointment, evaluations relating to salaries and merit increases, budget priorities and guidelines, selecting and structuring committees, teaching assignments and class schedules, research and other leaves, student advisement, and the like.[11]

At the next level is a collegial advisory committee composed of the elected representatives of each departmental faculty advisory committee within each college. This committee shall be advisory to the dean. Each collegial advisory committee in turn should elect a representative to the faculty advisory council, which will be advisory to the vice-president for academic affairs. Each of these units shall establish handbooks to implement university policy and include such other subjects as are reasonably related to the mission of the unit.[12]

The agreement at Fairleigh Dickinson University also provides for a very careful, orderly, and deliberate processs of adopting changes in policies and procedures. It enumerates the procedures to be undertaken before a senate recommendation is implemented. (1) The administration shall forward any senate recommendations to the faculty association within two weeks and state whether the recommendations conflict with the agreement or the university's obligation to bargain. (2) If the faculty association believes that the senate recommendations conflict with the agreement or obligations by the university to bargain, within two weeks it must object in writing to the president of the university. (3) The two parties shall confer to resolve differences. (4) If they are not resolved within two weeks, the faculty association may inform the president of the university of its decision to go to binding arbitration. As a further requirement, the administration shall consult with the AAUP with regard to any proposed amendment of the senate bylaws before transmitting it to the board of trustees.[13]

These and a few other agreements provide a fairly effective way of assuring faculty that their role in governance and their contributions shall be no less than in the past as future developments unfold. Particularly as changes are proposed, the collective-bargaining agreement ensures that no matter what erosion of faculty participation might occur elsewhere, no matter what administrative changes there might be concocted to skirt established procedures, no matter how arbitrary or capricious any one individual might want to be, no action following upon such conditions or attitudes is without challenge and redress as an alleged violation of the legally constituted collective-bargaining agreement.

Departmental Organization, Procedures, and Bylaws

The tradition at many colleges and universities, especially the larger ones, is to have much of the basic decision making, particularly in the personnel area (hiring, tenuring, and promoting) carried out at the departmental level. Thus, although technically the ultimate, penultimate, and antepenultimate decisions are made by the board, the president, and the vice-president for academic affairs, respectively, these later decisions are firmly rooted in the recommendations at the preceding level and seldom contradict the department's original recommendation, particularly if it was overwhelmingly consensual.

Therefore, what is contractualized concerning a department's rights and role within the institution is important, especially to faculty members. Yet far fewer than a majority of the agreements include any language about departmental organization and role. In fact, only 36 percent of the agreements address the topic. And among these thirty-two agreements there is considerable diversity. For example, although the principle of democratic participation is implicit in all agreements that speak to the role of the department in university governance, six add the idea of democratic participation of all faculty in developing and implementing departmental policies and procedures. As an example, the agreement at the University of Dubuque says, "Each academic department shall deliberate as a participating group of all members in formulating its own policies and decisions in accordance with basic democratic procedures of open discussion and voting on propositions."[14]

It is clear that decision making, or, rather, recommending, in the personal area is one of the prime concerns of faculty at the departmental level. Sixteen agreements feature the establishment, structuring, and functioning of either a departmental personnel committee (eight agreements) or a departmental evaluation committee (eight agreements), the function of which is to aid the department in making its standard personnel recommendations. The agreement at Long Island University (Brooklyn Center) states this function in a classic manner: "Each department and the Library shall elect annually, . . . by secret ballot of all full-time members . . . one or more committees to recommend appointment, reappointment, promotion, and tenure."[15] The agreement at Fitchburg State College is even more explicit; it stipulates that the role of the departmental evaluation committee shall be to evaluate each faculty member at least annually on the basis of standard criteria. They should use the faculty evaluation form and in addition shall obtain student evaluations using the standard student evaluation form. They also may arrange a visitation of classes.[16]

Seven agreements require that departments shall establish departmental bylaws. The 1977-80 agreement of Central Michigan University requires that departments establish criteria and procedures for personnel decisions, as well as create bylaws concerning a variety of other issues, such as retrenchment, allocation of travel funds, and teaching assignments.[17] The University of Dubuque Agreement is very clear on this matter:

> Each academic department shall deliberate as a participating group of all members in formulating its own policies and decisions in accordance with basic democratic procedures of open discussion, and voting on propositions such as course offerings, curriculum matters, teaching assignments, budget requests, personnel recruitment, and annual appraisal of department operations.[18]

Along the same lines, the agreement at Western Michigan University requires each department to appoint a committee to develop a departmental policy statement. Although this policy statement must be reviewed by the dean and the vice-president for academic affairs in light of the agreement, the department chooses what it wants to include.[19]

Other Faculty Involvement

The issue of faculty involvement in the academic planning process is introduced in only a few agreements. At a very general level is the Western Michigan University Agreement, which says in article 45 that in order to "provide for the continuous assessment of the status and direction of the University, it is the intention of Western to establish an advisory committee on long range planning which shall include representatives from a variety of university constituencies including the Board of Trustees, administration, faculty, students and professional staff."[20] At D'Youville College, faculty will be provided a "reasonable opportunity for consultation, input and advice regarding the development of the annual academic budget."[21] At the University of Cincinnati the time for budget review by the faculty through the senate will be a minimum of ninety days.[22] The Hofstra University Agreement devotes nearly three pages to academic planning. Faculty are integrally involved at several levels: department, college, and total university.[23]

Another area is curriculum revision. Eight agreements devote space to explicit treatment of curricula. In most cases curriculum is simply included in a list of primary or exclusive rights of faculty decisions and/or recommendations. In one case, however, faculty contributions to the decision of proposed additions to or revision of a curricular program are clearly only advisory. At the University of San Francisco the university shall fully disclose curriculum changes to the president of the faculty association, who has forty-five days within which to submit consultative remarks to the vice-president for academic affairs. The agreement notes that these consultative comments are not binding on the university and are not grievable except in the alleged case of the university's not consulting with the faculty.[24]

Another topic that is at least peripheral to the topic of governance is that of calendar. Although starting and ending dates of semesters and the scheduling of vacation periods generally continue in a fairly uniform manner year after year, nonetheless it remains important to know precise dates. That this item has been included in collective-bargaining agreements more frequently than many others probably attests not so much to its controversial nature or even its importance as to the perception by faculty that calendar is a term and condition of employment. In all, 42.7 percent of the agreements under consideration have included some language on the subject of calendar. But beyond the idea of approximately nine months within the span of September 1 to June 1 and involving two semesters or three trimesters, the precise days, number of days or weeks, and precedures for arriving at an official calendar each year become almost unique to each agreement. The greatest degree of consensus is on the procedure that the academic calendar is recommended by a special calendar committee to the president of the institution, who then makes a final determination. This is what happens at Adrian College, the University of Guam, Rhode Island College, St. John's University, and Southeastern Massachusetts University. In the process contractualized at Wagner College and in the Minnesota State College system, the president sets the calendar following some kind of consultation with faculty that does not involve a standing committee for that purpose. Three agreements (City College of New York, Lincoln University, and Southeastern Massachusetts University) specify that regardless of the manner of the routine year-by-year setting of an academic calendar, if any significant change is proposed or contemplated, the issue shall be negotiated to determine whether what is proposed would have an effect on what has already been contractualized.

Most of the other agreements comprising the 42.8 percent that have contractualized something on calendar have contractualized dates, number of days, number of weeks, and the like that generally add up to what everyone assumes an academic year to be. It is common to require faculty to be on campus one week prior to the beginning of classes in the fall.

Two agreements are noteworthy for the extent to which faculty are involved in the establishment of the academic calendar. At the C. W. Post Center of Long Island University a presidential calendar committee shall prepare a calendar, but it must be forwarded to the faculty for approval.[25] Even more democratic is the agreement for the Vermont State Colleges, where the academic calendar for each college "shall be *negotiated* with the Federation Chapter."[26] These contrast with the statement included in the Northern Montana College Agreement: "The Commissioners and the Administration reserve the right to determine the academic calendar."[27]

One final item also fits here. The item, unique to the agreement at Western Michigan University, concerns the evaluation of administrators by the faculty. Article XIX of the Western Michigan University Agreement says that faculty members and/or the AAUP bargaining agent may conduct evaluations of administrators at or above the level of department chairperson up to and including the vice-president of academic affairs, apparently stopping short only of the president. The results are not to become public knowledge, however. Rather, the results should go to the person being evaluated and to those charged with making personnel decisions concerning such administrators.[28]

Relationship of the Faculty Senate and the Collective-Bargaining Agent

We turn now to a topic that is raised as a serious question about as many times as any other when a faculty starts to consider the possibility of collective bargaining for their campus: how the existing faculty senate will fare as it relates to a new organization calling itself the association, the federation, the coalition, and chapter—a faculty union by any other name. While some observers of the campus scene have viewed the coexistence of an academic senate and a collective-bargaining organizations as impossible, most, even those who view the two organizations as fundamentally compatible, recognize that some problems of relationship and function can arise. In anticipation of certain problems and trying to forestall them, some agreements have included language on the senate, its role, and its relationship to the union.

A total of 19.1 percent (seventeen agreements) have included their academic or faculty senate in the collective-bargaining agreement. This is done with slight modification in four basic ways. First, the faculty association may be defined as essentially an equal to the faculty senate, but each with specialized functions, both in turn dividing a larger body of labor and responsibilities with another specialized unit, the administration. The result is a type of troika form of government. Second, the faculty association recognizes or even creates a faculty senate through the collective-bargaining agreement, but as such the senate is a specialized subunit within the faculty association. The senate cannot act autonomously but must recommend action to the faculty association for its recommendation to or negotiation with the administration and board of trustees. Third, the relationship may be essentially the reverse of the previous method: the senate remains the stronger of the two, with the faculty association relegated to highly specific functions. Fourth, there may be no senate. That may mean eliminating a preexisting senate or simply not creating one.

Faculty Association and Senate as Equal Partners

Variations on this approach constitute the most common resolution of what to do with the senate when a collective-bargaining agent has begun to operate on campus under the terms of a negotiated agreement with the board of trustees. This approach in a classic form is seen in the Emerson College Agreement:

> The presently constituted organizations, committees and governance structure i.e., the Faculty Assembly, the Faculty Council, Academic Policy Committee, All-College Advisory Council or any other similar body composed, in whole or in part of the faculty may continue to function at the College provided that the actions thereof may not directly or indirectly repeal, rescind, or otherwise modify the terms and conditions of this agreement.[29]

This phraseology seems to include a typical and legitimate concern of faculty that their traditional academic functions and procedures not be compromised, let alone usurped, by what in other contexts would be called a labor organization or union. The paragraph sounds as if it were written by faculty who do not want to lose or even modify what authority, influence, and prerogatives they had before, even though they are supplementing all of that with a collective-bargaining agent and agreement.

Although the paragraph starts at the opposite end, a similar statement of a tripartite decision-making process is included in the University of Connecticut Agreement:

> Although the A.A.U.P., as the elected bargaining agent, retains the exclusive right to negotiate and reach agreement on terms and conditions of employment for

the members of the bargaining unit, and the board of trustees retains its rights, under law, to manage and direct the university, the parties recognize the necessity of a collegial governance system for faculty in areas of academic concern. It is mutually desirable that the collegial system of shared governance be maintained and strengthened so that faculty will have a mechanism and procedure, independent of the collective bargaining process, for making recommendations to appropriate administrative officials and to the board of trustees, and for resolving academic matters, through the organizational divisions of the University, the University Senate, and Administration and the Board of Trustees.[30]

Still another way of contractualizing the same relationship is illustrated by the agreement at the University of Delaware, in which the parties agree that the board of trustees, the university administration, and the university faculty senate "have undiminished power and authority to establish, change, or eliminate policies."[31] In the same spirit the agreement at Fairleigh Dickinson University expresses concern over the potential for conflict among the three parties (senate, administration, union) and describes the following procedures that become policy upon approval of the agreement by the board of trustees and the faculty:

a) If the A.A.U.P. and the Administration agree that a matter under consideration by the Senate is an appropriate subject for collective bargaining either by law or by virtue of being encompassed directly or indirectly within this Agreement, they shall jointly so advise the Senate.

b) If the two parties to the Agreement disagree, either party may submit the issue to an arbitrator whose decision shall be final and binding on all parties.[32]

Senate as a Subunit of the Bargaining Agent

What many faculty have feared would be on outcome of approving a collective bargaining agent is that the academic senate would become weak. The closest example to this senate subordination pattern is that of the specifications of the agreement at Northern Michigan University. Here the legitimation of the academic senate is established only as the agreement states its raison d'être very succinctly as follows: "There shall be an Academic Senate whose membership shall be limited to members of the bargaining unit and whose function shall be to advise the Association on matters of faculty-wide concern."[33] The senate shall be governed by bylaws as approved by the association and will concern itself with the following matters that are delegated in the agreement to the senate: recommendations for minor curriculum or program changes, recommendations for programs that do not involve the reallocation or reduction of existing academic positions or programs, endorsement by the faculty of the awarding of degrees, and review and ranking of faculty proposals for academic study and research.[34] This list is not characterized by a high level of inherent significance in its execution. Further, the agreement itself says that although the association agrees to be bound by senate action in these matters, senate recommendations in even these matters go to the administration through the association.[35] On the other hand, the academic senate may take recommendations to the faculty association on any such matters of academic policy or general faculty concern as the senate chooses.[36] That, of course, makes eminent sense since it is faculty to faculty either way, yet there is an important subtlety here. In fact, it gets at the essence and genius of academic collective bargaining and the fundamental difference between what it does and what a senate can do: what the collective-bargaining agent contractualizes with the board of trustees or its representatives is a legally binding contract, while what a senate does is recommendatory to the board and not binding upon anyone.

The only other agreement that appears to approach the Northern Michigan pattern is that for the Connecticut State Colleges. As subheadings under the general topic of "Faculty Participation Procedures," the agreement defines the constituency of the college senate and asserts that the senate shall adopt a written constitution and bylaws and a faculty handbook.[37] It appears that much of the legitimacy for the college senate comes from the collective-bargaining agreement.

Senate in a Superordinate Position

By way of contrast with the Northern Michigan University pattern of faculty association superordination, one might expect its opposite to appear somewhere. Actually there is no instance of this opposite type in pure form, but there is some indication that a number of faculties regard the senate as a superior body, perhaps because of its scope of interest in all areas of the institution's life, while the faculty association is viewed as a specialized group dealing with a narrower range of activities and issues in the institution's academic life. Quite naturally such a view is one that boards of trustees and administrations would prefer because the less broad the scope of bargaining, the greater flexibility they have insofar as decision making and policy implementation are concerned. The closest to this pattern are a few agreements where the phraseology seems to be at some pains to keep the faculty association subordinate and see it as pertaining to a somewhat narrower range of concerns and issues. The University of Cincinnati Agreement (a generally well-executed agreement) states, for example, "With respect to faculty priorities in those areas not specifically dealt with through the collective bargaining process both parties to this agreement recognize the Faculty Senate as the primary governing body representing the faculty which shall have the right to advise the President and the Vice Presidents."[38] Although there is no question that such language is meant to strengthen and reinforce the faculty senate, one cannot be certain that the intent is to superordinate and subordinate the faculty senate and the faculty association, respectively. The language may be designed to appease some who chafe in the face of power shifts to the faculty association. Or it may be an innocent statement designed simply to cover all the bases, not just those included in the collective-bargaining agreement.

The No-Senate Option

The final option is to have no academic or faculty senate and to rely solely on the collective-bargaining agent. This could occur as a faculty association simply replaces a senate by conscious, deliberate determination, or as a senate atrophies over time as a faculty association takes over the senate's former functions. Or conceivably this could come about as a faculty association fills a vacuum that existed because no senate or comparable organization had been in place before.

A considerable amount of speculation has emerged around this issue. The specter of a dying faculty senate under the heel of a triumphant, greedy faculty union commonly is employed by opponents of a move to unionize a faculty. Others, trying to take a more objective view, nonetheless raise doubts about the long-term viability of an arrangement of a faculty association and senate working in tandem. It is worth noting that the imagery used becomes important. To speak of the two-headed faculty governance model suggests a "monster"; but to speak of two arms on the faculty body is to suggest something normal and functional. Most of the scholarly literature has come down somewhere between these two. Correspondingly so has the historical record, brief though its time span may be. To my knowledge a faculty association has not yet destroyed a faculty senate anywhere.

After noting important differences between single-campus and multi-campus institutions, Frank Kemerer and J. Victor Baldridge observe that at single-campus institutions, "the prospects for effective dual-track bargaining of senate and union are reasonably optimistic, but faculty bodies will probably face a difficult struggle in relation to multi-campus unions."[39] Joseph Garbarino reaches a similar conclusion when he observes that predictions of a displacement of faculty senates by faculty unions has been exaggerated and the variety of relationships between senates and unions has been underestimated.[40] He goes on to say that an "integration of union and senate functions is at least a possible outcome, with the unions as dominant partners but with senate-style collegiality surviving in important areas of academic decision making."[41] My data support such a conclusion as well. When the subject is broached at all in collective-bargaining agreements, a specialization of function is described and a division of labor is prescribed.

Student Involvement in Decision Making

Provisions for students to participate in institutional decision making are made in relatively few agreements. Only ten agreements (13.9 percent) say anything at all about the subject. And what is said usually is not much. The ten agreements are in clusters: three Montana state colleges (Eastern Montana College, Western Montana College, and Northern Montana College), two branches of Long Island University (Brooklyn and Southampton), and five state colleges in Massachusetss (Fitchburg, Framingham, Salem, Worcester, and Massachusetts College of Art).

The three Montana agreements state that the commissioner of higher education, the administration and the union coalition all recognize that students are a vital factor in efforts to maintain and improve the quality of education available at the institution.[42] The agreements go on to say that the "inclusion of students in the decision-making process is both necessary and desirable."[43] To this end there shall be student representatives on all standing committees. Western Montana adds, "Students shall be permitted to provide input concerning pertinent matters to the Academic Dean on tenure and promotion matters, and the Administration shall give consideration to student evaluations when making its determination."[44] The Northern Montana Agreement requires that all search committees and committees appointed by the faculty senate include voting student members; there must be at·least one per committee but not more than 25 percent of the total membership of the committee.[45]

At the five state institutions from Massachusetts, after a positive referendum vote by students, there would be established a mechanism for student participation in decision making by adding them to existing college committees.

A new dimension is incorporated in the agreements at two of the branches of Long Island University: the legitimation and continuance of students' being able to observe the bargaining process, "provided they continue to observe comprehensive confidentiality."[46]

The turmoil that surrounded the student movements in the late 1960s and early 1970s and the response of higher education to that movement is reflected almost not at all in higher education collective-bargaining agreements. Granted, at many campuses student participation is significant at the departmental level, but such arrangements have not been contractualized. Therefore, students have no legal base from which to build. Their opportunities for participation in academic decision making are likely to be dropped almost as quickly as they were added a few years ago. Apparently neither faculties nor administrations and boards of trustees have been eager to incorporate students into the collective-bargaining process.

Conclusion

Although this chapter hardly has been a chronicle of a host of faculty and union success stories so far as their securing a more influential role in institutional governance and decision making, it is full of examples of what might be gained. Within the sphere of academic collective bargaining are clear precedents for considerable democratization so far as academic governance is concerned. Some faculties may view such changes as so revolutionary on their campus as to be virtually impossible. Some administrators may feel apprehension at the potential effect of such innovations on their campuses. Certainly the historical context of an institution will set some limits that will be a challenge to extend, and some institutions already have more faculty involvement and proceed under a more democratic mode than do others. Yet with the approval of collective bargaining and by actual bargaining, administrators and boards of trustees will expect the faculty to make proposals designed to lead to greater democratization and sharing of decision making.

From the perspective of faculty who fear loss of a traditional faculty role through a senate, there is ongoing concern that faculty unions will try to seize too much power. Such aggressive behavior by faculty unions is possible theoretically and an empirical reality here and there, but it is by no means a foregone conclusion. Again, precedents are available in collective bargaining in higher education for a sharing of authority and for more than one forum of deliberation to exist. It is possible for union and senate to coexist amicably and to supplement and enhance one another. Only a minority of agreements address the relationship of union and senate (19.1 percent). To uncover the relationship of senate and union at the 80 percent majority of schools (minus, of course, those institutions that do not have a senate), requires a separate study in itself that is beyond the purview and scope of my analysis here. Nonetheless, sufficient precedents of an amicable, supplemental relationship exist to encourage faculties to attempt to make such applications to their particular situation.

Notes

1. Agreement (1977-79), University of Cincinnati, p. 31.
2. Agreement (1977-78), University of Dubuque, p. 5.
3. Agreement (1977-80), University of Massachusetts, p. 14.
4. Agreement (1976-79), Moore College of Art, p. 23.
5. Agreement (1975-77), Bloomfield College, p. 6.
6. Agreement (1976-78), Lincoln University, p. 5.
7. Agreement (1977-79), University of Cincinnati, pp. 31-32.
8. Agreement (1974-77), St. John's University, pp. 3-4.

9. Agreement (1974-77), Fairleigh Dickinson University, pp. 75-76.

10. Agreement (1977-80), Central Michigan University, p. 26.

11. Agreement (1978-80), Kent State University, p. 6.

12. Ibid., pp. 11-12.

13. Agreement (1977-79), Fairleigh Dickinson University, p. 51.

14. Agreement (1977-78), University of Dubuque, p. 36.

15. Agreement (1976-79), Long Island University, Brooklyn Center, p. 10.

16. Agreement (1974-76), Fitchburg State College, pp. 54-55.

17. Agreement (1977-80), Central Michigan University, pp. 17-18.

18. Agreement (1977-78), University of Dubuque, p. 6.

19. Agreement (1976-77), Western Michigan University, pp. 30-31.

20. Ibid., p. 61.

21. Agreement (1977-79), D'Youville College, p. 11.

22. Agreement (1977-79), University of Cincinnati, p. 32.

23. Agreement (1976-79), Hofstra University, pp. 6-9.

24. Agreement (1976-81), University of San Francisco, pp. 4-5.

25. Agreement (1977-80), Long Island University, C. W. Post Center, p. 39.

26. Agreement (1979-80), Vermont State Colleges, pp. 43-44.

27. Agreement (1977-79), Northern Montana College, p. 39.

28. Agreement (1976-77), Western Michigan University, p. 29.

29. Agreement (1975-78), Emerson College, p. 8.

30. Agreement (1977-79), University of Connecticut, p. 2.

31. Agreement (1977-79), University of Delaware, p. 24.

32. Agreement (1977-79), Fairleigh Dickinson University, p. 75.

33. Agreement (1975-77), Northern Michigan University, p. 10.

34. Ibid.

35. Ibid., p. 11.

36. Ibid., p. 13.

37. Agreement (1976-79), Connecticut State Colleges, pp. 13-14.

38. Agreement (1977-79), University of Cincinnati, p. 32.

39. Frank R. Kemerer and J. Victor Baldridge, *Unions on Campus* (San Francisco: Jossey-Bass Publishing, 1975), pp. 164-65.

40. Joseph Garbarino, *Faculty Bargaining* (New York: McGraw-Hill Book Company, 1975), p. 150.

41. Ibid., p. 151.

42. Agreement (1975-77), Eastern Montana College, p. 19; Agreement (1977-79), Western Montana College, p. 9; Agreement (1977-79), Northern Montana College, p. 9.

43. Agreement (1975-77), Eastern Montana College, p. 20; Agreement (1977-79), Western Montana College, p. 10; Agreement (1977-1979), Northern Montana College, p. 9.

44. Agreement (1977-79), Western Montana College, p. 10.

45. Agreement (1977-79), Northern Montana College, p. 9.

46. Agreements (1976-79), Long Island Universities, Brooklyn and Southampton campuses, pp. 65, and 62, respectively.

9. THE RELATIONSHIP OF THE FACULTY UNION WITH THE COLLEGE OR UNIVERSITY

It is certainly no secret that it is with uncertainty and anxiety that both the faculty and the administration of a college or university enter a collective-bargaining agreement for the first time. Regardless of what the feelings of each side toward the other might be, regardless of the nature of the factors that precipitated the faculty's approval of collective bargaining, regardless of the level of mutual distrust and antagonism that might exist, both parties want to be optimistic about the future. Either they look to collective bargaining to help bring about a more stable and predictable relationship, or they hope that collective bargaining will not erode what they feel has been a positive relationship in the past. Therefore many agreements speak to the subject of the relationship of faculty and their union with administrations and governing boards and then specify each other's rights and obligations. In part this is to identify a tenor of the relationship, in part to anticipate some of the specifics of this new legal relationship of two parties to a contractual relationship. Here there are questions about the sharing of data and information, who shall be responsible for printing and distributing copies of the agreement, under what circumstances both parties should meet, who among the many subgroups in the institution should be parties to the agreement, what should happen if one or both parties wish to bargain other items during the life of the agreement, and so on.

A Context for the Relationship

There are two places where this concern is most likely to be observed: at or very near the beginning of the document as an expression of the purpose of the collective-bargaining agreement being entered into and, in connection with a no-strike, no lockout clause that can come almost any place in the agreement but usually near the end.

A good example of the early statement of joint purpose appears in the agreement at Bloomfield College:

The purpose of this agreement is to promote the welfare of the college and further its educational aims by defining the principle of shared responsibility in the governance of the college, a purpose to be pursued through collective bargaining in good faith and through careful observance of both the letter and the spirit of this agreement, to which the parties intend to be legally bound.[1]

It would be a rare faculty member, whether deeply committed to collective bargaining or not, who would object to such a statement. The featured ideas of shared responsibility, good-faith bargaining, careful observance of both the letter and the spirit of the agreement, and recognition of the legally binding nature of the document would be desirable to most bargaining unit faculty. As part of its preamble, the agreement at the University of New Haven expresses similar ideas very succinctly: "This contract will be carried out by both parties within the spirit of collegiality, mutual respect, confidence and good faith."[2]

Although worded quite differently, the agreement at the University of Cincinnati attempts to express many of the same ideas in a preamble. It precedes even the statement of "Recognition and Description [definition] of the Bargaining Unit" that constitutes article 1 in the University of Cincinnati Agreement and most others as well:

The intent of this Agreement entered into by and between the Board of Trustees of the University of Cincinnati and the University of Cincinnati Chapter of the American Association of University Professors is to provide the members of the Bargaining Unit and the University of Cincinnati with a collective bargaining agreement which will contribute to a healthy and a viable institution of higher learning capable of supporting a quality program of teaching, research and public service. This Agreement seeks to maintain educational excellence, facilitate effective faculty participation, assure fair and reasonable conditions of employment and provide techniques and procedures for the peaceable adjustment of disputes should they arise.[3]

Also in a preamble the agreement for the City University of New York states in part, "The Board and the PSC [Professional Staff Congress of CUNY] affirm collective bargaining as a process to be used for the improvement of the University."[4] The agreement then speaks of their joint subscription to the principles of academic freedom.

In article II, "Purpose," the agreement at the University of Delaware speaks of its purpose as that of promoting "harmonious relationships between the faculty and the administration . . . and to improve the quality of education and to maintain the high standards of excellence at the University of Delaware."[5] In addition, "It is agreed and understood that that intent and purpose at all times shall be improvement and maintenance of the educational, research and related programs of the University, and the welfare of the student body."[6]

The agreement at the University of Dubuque has a preface before article I, which says:

The University of Dubuque and the Faculty Association of the College of Liberal Arts are agreed on the basis for our professional service together. We are agreed that our institution exists to provide our students with an environment and a process which stimulates intellectual growth, facilitates career preparation, promotes self-development, and encourages world citizenship. We are agreed that our College should provide a context within which faculty can pursue their scholarly goals, carry on their classroom teaching with dignity, and receive the support of their fellow professionals.[7]

In a more lengthy preamble than most, the agreement at Robert Morris College makes much of the attitudinal stance of both parties:

The officers of both the College and Federation recognize and realize that this school depends on more than words in a labor agreement, that it depends primarily on attitudes between people in their respective organizations and at all levels of responsibility and authority. The parties believe that proper attitudes must be based on a full understanding of and regard for the respective rights and responsibilities of both the College and the Federation. The parties believe also that proper attitudes are of major importance where day-to-day operations and administration of this *Agreement* demand fairness and understanding. The parties believe that these attitudes can be encouraged best when it is made clear that the College and Federation representatives and officials, whose duties involve negotiation of this *Agreement*, are sincerely concerned with the best interests and well being of both the College and its employees.[8]

Other agreements are not as explicit in stating joint purposes. For example, article I of the agreement at Bryant College of Business states, "The College and the Federation agree to maintain the academic character of the College as an institution of higher education for business and administrative leadership in both the private and public sectors."[9]

The introduction to the agreement at the University of San Francisco is unique in that it includes "educational aims" and also a "credo" that expresses a variety of commitments, such as the "inviolable dignity" of each person and the "sanctity of that human love which forms and protects the family," and a belief in God and Jesus Christ. Also this agreement makes explicit what is only implicit in other agreements: "The Preamble, Credo, and statement on educational aims as written here shall not be deemed part of this agreement."[10]

Several agreements that have a preamble or a statement of purpose or introduction restrict their remarks to the formal, legal purposes of collective bargaining. For example, the first article of the University of Massachusetts Agreement reads:

Pursuant to the provision of M.G.L. Chapter 150 E and rules and regulations promulgated thereunder, the parties clearly recognize their statutory obligations to negotiate in good faith with respect to wages, hours, standards of productivity and performance, and any other terms and conditions of employment.[11]

Others build a contextual framework around the minimum statements regarding wages, hours, and conditions of employment. For example, the Western Montana College Agreement reads:

This Agreement . . . has as its goals the furtherance of quality education, the establishment of an equitable procedure for the resolution of grievances and a formal understanding with regard to salary, hours, and conditions of employment.

The parties recognize that good faith in collective bargaining is a means of achieving these goals through a process which gives legitimate expression to the concerns of the faculty members as represented by the Association and of the Western Montana College Administration and the Board of Regents as represented by the Commissioner of Higher Education.[12]

Nearly a third of the agreements at four-year institutions of higher education do not include a preamble or introduction of any of these types. Although this lack does not suggest that these institutions are marked by more acrimony and less cooperation than one observes at institutions that have tried to establish a written context of collegiality, partnership, and respect, and although such expressions may be little more than pro forma, it would seem to be harder for either side to act precipitously or with no thought to the other party after they have pledged to work together in developing and maintaining an institution of excellence.

Another point where the mutual commitment of the parties to collegial relationships is expressed occasionally is in connection with contractual language on the no-strike, no lockout issue. For example, the opening sentence in the no-strike, no lockout article in the New York Institute of Technology Agreement says, "The Council and the Institute subscribe to the principle that any and all differences under this agreement be resolved by peaceful and appropriate means without interruption of the Institute's programs."[13]

The agreement at Hofstra University speaks similarly when it states by ways of introducing its no-strike provision, "The A.A.U.P. and the University subscribe to the principle that any and all differences under this Agreement be resolved by peaceful and appropriate means without interruption of the University's program."[14]

The agreement at Roger Williams College prefaces its prohibition against strikes and lockouts with a reference to a grievance procedure and a statement that such procedures shall be followed in the resolution of all disputes that arise during the period covered by the agreement.[15]

Defining the Bargaining Unit

One of the first articles in agreements sets out in detail a definition of the bargaining unit, stating who is to be included (and often who is not included) in the union. This point covers both who is eligible to join the unit and who is to be covered or governed by the provisions of the agreement.

There is great variety in terms of the definition and limitation of who can or shall be included in the bargaining unit. Often the persons or roles that one agreement specifically includes, the next agreement specifically excludes. For example, forty agreements (44.9 percent) state that only full-time faculty shall be eligible, and twenty-nine (32.6 percent) explicitly include part-time faculty (most of these, however, set limits on how little one can teach and still be considered a part-time faculty member for purposes of inclusion in the bargaining unit). The remaining agreements simply speak of "faculty" without making any distinction between full- and part-time status. Similarly nineteen agreements (21.3 percent) explicitly include members of the counseling staff (usually mentioning that they must also have faculty status), and five agreements just as explicitly exclude such staff. Five agreements include, and three exclude, athletic coaches. Four agreements include certain kinds of administrative-professional persons such as registrars, laboratory technicians, business managers, college or university physicians, computer programmers, and the like, and one explicitly excludes such persons (most agreements implicitly exclude such persons by making reference to faculty status and rank as a criterion for membership in the union). One of the four agreements to include such academic professionals is the Temple University Agreement, which defines them as a category. The agreement states that an academic professional "is a full-time employee of the University whose work is necessary or adjunct to the teaching of students or to research functions of the university." The work shall:

A. 1. be predominantly intellectual and varied in character; and
    2. require consistent exercise of discretion and judgment; and
    3. require knowledge of an advanced nature customarily acquired by specialized study in an institution of higher learning or its equivalent; and
    4. be of such character that the output or result accomplished cannot be standardized in relation to a given period of time; or
B. be original and creative in character in a recognized field of artistic endeavor and the result of which depends primarily on the invention, imagination, or talent of the employee.[16]

One significant difference related to the prestige and/or private versus public nature of the institution is clear-cut. The more prestigious state institutions are far more likely explicitly to include part-time faculty in the bargaining unit (60 percent), while the less prestigious state colleges and universities are very unlikely to do so (only 18.2 percent), with the proportion of private colleges in between (34.1 percent). Differences with respect to other employment categories are not significant.

In order of importance next to the full-time, part-time issue is that of whether departmental chairpersons (heads) should be included in the bargaining unit. The evidence, although far from unanimous, leans in favor of including them. Thirty-three agreements (37.1 percent) explicitly place them in the bargaining unit, while only 24.7 percent (twenty-two) explicitly exclude them. Most of the remaining agreements speak only of "faculty" and therefore by not explicitly excluding chairpersons in the bargaining unit implicitly include them. Nine agreements, however, do not define the bargaining unit within the agreement. They reference a public law, another document, or the original certification papers as containing the definition. For these nine agreements, then, I have no information at hand to answer the question of whether chairpersons are inside or outside the bargaining unit. In one additional instance (University of Massachusetts), at the time of ratification of the agreement the decision with regard to chairpersons and the bargaining unit was before the courts.[17] A decision has since been handed down that excludes them. There are no differences by type of institution on the issue of whether department chairpersons should be included or excluded from the bargaining unit (see table 11).

TABLE 11

Agreements Explicitly Including or Excluding Department Chairpersons from Bargaining Unit, by Type of Institution

	MORE PRESTIGIOUS STATE INSTITUTIONS	LESS PRESTIGIOUS STATE INSTITUTIONS	PRIVATE COLLEGES
Department chairpersons included	33.3%	36.4%	36.6%
Department chairpersons excluded	26.7%	18.2%	29.3%

Collective-bargaining agreements at four-year colleges and universities are far more likely to include than to exclude department chairpersons in the bargaining unit. Although this is frequently a point at serious issue when bargaining units are determined, in only one-quarter of the agreements are they excluded.

The next most common issue appears to be whether professional librarians are to be included in the unit. Part of the answer rests with whether they have faculty status. If so, in many agreements they would automatically be included, and well over half of the agreements (fifty-one) specifically include them. Only five agreements explicitly exclude them. The sentiment to include librarians in the unit is reinforced by the inclusion in four institutions of the director of libraries as a member of the bargaining unit. There are no differences with respect to the inclusion of librarians by type of institution.

The question of graduate students' being included in the unit in their role as a graduate assistant or teaching assistant is not common, though six agreements speak explicitly to the subject. Of these, only two specifically list teaching assistants as members of the bargaining unit. The remaining four specifically exclude graduate assistants of any kind.

Although relatively few of the colleges and universities that have approved collective bargaining have professional schools of medicine, law, and dentistry, five that do have such schools have explicitly excluded the faculty teaching in them from the bargaining unit. Both the University of Connecticut[18] and Temple University[19] exclude faculty in all three fields. So does the University of Detroit,[20] which also adds faculty in military science and all members of the campus ministry (a unique reference). At Hostra University[21] and the University of San Francisco[22] the law faculties are excluded from the bargaining unit. At Fairleigh Dickinson University, however, the faculty in the School of Dentistry are included in the bargaining unit, but with a separate salary schedule.[23]

Such exclusions or separate treatment is undoubtedly because faculty in such professional schools and units invariably (save the clergy at the University of Detroit) command higher salaries than colleagues in other units and do not want to be limited by what is negotiated for the rest by way of salary increments. We would speculate further that they may be more entrepreneurially oriented than other faculty, want to negotiate their salaries individually, and are unable to abide collective bargaining in the first place. I do know that whether to include faculty in such professional schools has been a serious issue, even a temporary blockage, on all campuses with such schools when collective bargaining for faculty has been considered.

Adjunct faculty are included in the bargaining unit in five agreements and excluded in four. Visiting faculty are excluded in six agreements and explicitly included in nine. Temporary faculty specifically are included in one agreement and excluded in two and excluded by inference in all the others because they refer to "regular faculty" or some other synonymous designation of faculty in a tenure track position.

Variations in the definition of the degree to which a faculty member can be part time and still be considered a member of the bargaining unit are evident. Eight agreements speak only of part-time faculty, with no minimum or maximum so far as teaching hours specified. Twelve include in the unit those who are at least one-half time. One requires a fraction of at least six-thirteenths. Another requires at least one-quarter time. Still another specifies teaching one or more courses. The University of Cincinnati uses the proportion of 65 percent as the cutting point. One school (Saginaw Valley State College) includes in the bargaining unit all faculty who are teaching at least two-thirds time. Two agreements specify three-fourths time or more.

Recognition Clause

One feature that every agreement must have and that can evidence relatively little variation is a recognition clause: official recognition and affirmation that the faculty are represented authentically by the organization (bargaining agent) that is the second party to the agreement.

The statement of recognition in the agreement at St. John's University is typical:

> The Administration hereby recognizes the AAUP-FA as the exclusive bargaining representative for all full and regular part-time members of the faculty presently or hereafter employed by the University in the bargaining set forth in the certification issued by the New York State Labor Relations Board, dated April 22, 1970.[24]

Some, such as the agreement at Youngstown State University, elaborate a bit more and spell out in some detail what the concept of exclusivity means. The Youngstown article on "Recognition" states:

> The Administration recognizes the Association as the exclusive bargaining agent for the members of the bargaining unit described below. Exclusive recognition means that the Administration will not deal with any other organization, or any individual, in a manner or for a purpose inconsistent with the terms of the Agreement. Individual contracts of employment with members of the bargaining unit shall in all respects be consistent with this Agreement, which shall be deemed incorporated by a reference in such individual contracts. In recognizing the Association as the exclusive bargaining agent for the members of the bargaining unit, the Administration shall cooperate with the Association in enforcement of this Agreement.[25]

Agency Shop-Agency Fee Issue

An issue that has more potential for divisiveness among the faculty than any other is the question of agency shop. Yet despite its divisiveness and the potential unpleasant explosiveness of its introduction to faculty discussion, this issue must be faced at the very beginning. Once the vote has taken place and the collective democratic selection of a collective-bargaining agent has been made by the faculty, the next question is whether to require that all faculty either join the faculty union and pay its dues or pay a fee approximately equal to dues to the union for services rendered.

In classic labor-relations terminology, there are three primary options available to faculty once the decision to approve a bargaining agent has been made. First, the open-shop pattern makes a union membership truly voluntary. Faculty who are represented by the collective-bargaining agent on campus (the AAUP chapter, the faculty association, the faculty federation, or whatever the local unit calls itself) and ultimately protected by and benefiting from the agreement that eventuates from bargaining are free to join or not to join the organization and to pay or not to pay the dues that are assessed. By law the bargaining agent is required to represent each faculty member (however the bargaining unit has been defined) equally and without prejudice or discrimination regardless of whether said faculty member has become a dues-paying member. Second, the agency-shop option requires eligible faculty either to join the union and pay the dues established by the organization or pay an agency fee, an amount that may be exactly equivalent to dues or slightly more or less than dues and is regarded as paying for services rendered but involves no obligation for the individual faculty member to join the union organization. Third is the union shop (sometimes called closed shop), which requires every member of the bargaining unit (in this case the faculty) to join the union and pay dues as a condition of employment, subject to dismissal from the institution after a defined period of grace if a given faculty member refuses to join.

Examples of all three options are found among the four-year institutions of higher education that have negotiated collective-bargaining agreements, but the open shop is by far the most common; 73 percent (sixty-five of eighty-nine) of the agreements provide for open shop. Nevertheless only five of these deal at all explicitly with the issue. Two of them (the large multiunit State University of New York and City University of New York systems)[26] include in the agreement the provision to reopen negotiations upon ten days' notice on the subject of agency shop should legislation be enacted within the state of New York that would permit public employees and public employers to enter into an agency-shop agreement. By inference, then, these institutions shall operate under open-shop conditions until such time as appropriate legislation would be enacted. Similarly, the New Jersey State Colleges Agreement states that upon thirty days' notice following the enaction into state law of an agency-shop provision, the state shall enter negotiations with the bargaining agent.[27]

The most direct statements on the subject of open shop do not actually use the phrase *open shop* but affirm it quite emphatically nonetheless. The Regis College Amendment says, "This Chapter does not request, and there is no provision in the Agreement for an 'agency shop' (payment of dues to the Chapter by faculty members who do not join the Chapter)."[28] The agreement for the civilian faculty at the U.S. Coast Guard Academy says, "Nothing in this Agreement shall require an employee to become or remain a member of a labor organization or to pay money to the organization except pursuant to a voluntary written authorization by a member for payment of dues."[29]

The remaining agreements that comprise the 73 percent do not mention the open- versus closed- or agency-shop issue. Therefore, in a sense by default in not contractualizing either an agency shop or a union shop, an open shop is what obtains.

The next most common choice among the three options is that of agency shop. All but three of the remaining agreements (23.6 percent) provide for some form of this option, though two distinct patterns have been contractualized. In the first case (involving fifteen of the twenty-one agreements with some form of agency shop) are straightforward statements that faculty shall either join the union or pay a service fee. The agreement at the University of Detroit is typical:

All employees shall be required, as a condition of continued employment, within 60 days after the date of their employment, to do one of the following: a) Tender payment in full to the union of the dues and initiation fees uniformly required for the acquisition and retention of membership in the UDPU [University of Detroit Professors' Union]. b) To tender payment in full to the union of the service fees uniformly assessed against bargaining unit members who are not members of the UDPU. c) To sign an authorization form for the payroll deduction of such dues or fees required by (a) or (b) above.[30]

Most of the agreements with the agency-shop provision require faculty to join the union or pay dues as a condition of employment or continued employment. In most cases (as in the Detroit example) a specified time period (thirty or sixty days) is provided faculty to join or pay the fee, with notice of termination then being served in the event of noncompliance. Then a grace period of thirty days, or occasionally until the end of the semester, is provided before the dismissal becomes effective.

One agreement has a unique solution to the problem of watching time limits and needing to go through the trauma of dismissal proceedings in the event of noncompliance by one or more faculty members. The agreement at Rhode Island College states that "the State Controller shall deduct union dues or the service charge each pay period from the wages of all the employees in the bargaining unit.''[31] These dues are forwarded promptly to the union treasurer. This procedure is simple and appears to be airtight as well. The agreement at Bryant College of Business is not airtight. Here it is specified that the college will deduct either federation dues or an agency service fee provided that each faculty member submits a written authorization to the college for such deductions.[32] Clearly faculty members can ignore the requirement to pay either dues or service fee. As such, although the agreement at Bryant College of Business appears to be an agency-shop agreement, in reality it belongs in the category of open shop.

The second pattern of agency-shop provision has been chosen by six institutions and involves allowing a third alternative to the payment of dues or the payment of the service fee. If for reason of conscience or religious dictum or conviction, a person wishes to pay neither dues nor service fee, that person may apply for an exemption. At Bloomfield College the exemption appears to be full and complete. So long as an affidavit that provides reasons for requesting the exemption is submitted by the individual and subsequently is approved by a three-person review board selected from and by the negotiating team for the agreement, then the individual owes no one any dues or fees relative to collective bargaining.[33] At four of the remaining institutions, however, those who claim an exemption for reason of conscience or religion must contribute an amount equivalent to dues or service fees to a campus student scholarship trust fund (University of Massachusetts and Central Michigan University) or to a nonreligious charity in accordance with the applicable procedures in Oregon State Law at Southern Oregon State College,[34] or to any campus use such as scholarships or library but not to modify salaries (Hofstra University).[35] In the Massachusetts case the union makes the judgment on the individual's request for a waiver.[36] In Central Michigan University's agreement two steps are required for exemption. First, the individual must be a contributing member of "a bonafide religious body or sect whose established tenets prohibit financial support to a union organization." Second, the individual must send written notification of such objection to the faculty association together with supporting evidence within sixty days of the beginning of an academic semester.[37] The agreement at the sixth institution with a conscientious-objection provision documents the existence of such a provision but does not provide detail, referencing the prior agreement.[38]

The dollar amount of the service or agency fee is usually equivalent to dues. However, a few agreements specify a different amount. At Quinnipiac College the agency fee is set in the agreement at two-thirds the amount of dues.[39] In the Massachusetts State College system, the agency service fee is set at 93 percent of current dues.[40] At Southern Oregon State College the agency fee is 100 percent of local dues and 90 percent of the state (Oregon

Education Association) and national (National Education Association) dues.[41] At Massachusetts and Central Michigan University there are procedures for the service fee payer to get a rebate for that portion of fees that would go for political or ideological causes (at Central Michigan University this process applies also to dues-paying members).[42] Such differences in dollar amounts between membership and service fee reflect in most cases differences in services. For example, some journal subscriptions may accompany membership; access to discounts on automobile insurance through group rates may be available only to members; and the privilege of voting for union officers and on contract proposals are reserved for members.

The factor of whether the institution is public or private or of greater or lesser prestige is relevant with respect to agency shop. The less prestigious state institutions are significantly more likely than either their more prestigious counterparts or the private colleges to have negotiated the agency-shop provision. A third of the less prestigious state institutions have included the agency shop (eleven of thirty-three), but only 13.3 percent of the more prestigious state schools and 17.1 percent of the private institutions have done so. (Overall the proportion of agreements with the agency-shop provision is 22.5 percent.)

The most extreme form of union membership options is that of union shop. This option, which speaks of actual dues-paying membership as a condition of employment, has been contractualized at only four institutions —the University of San Francisco, Detroit College of Business, Hofstra University, and the New York Institute of Technology—none of them a public or state institution yet representing only 9.8 percent of the private schools (four of forty-one).

The first two instances are classic, pure cases of union shop. The relevant language in the agreement at the University of San Francisco is direct, unequivocal, and allowing of no exceptions:

All employees shall become members of the Association in good standing (31) days after the effective date of this Agreement or thirty one (31) days after the beginning of their employment, whichever is later, and shall, as a condition of continued employment with the university, remain members of the Association in good standing by the payment of the periodic Association dues, special assessments, and initiation and/or reinstatement fees uniformly required of all such members. If any member of the Association is certified, in writing, by the Association to the University as not in good standing by reason of the failure of the employee to tender said payments, he shall be dismissed by the University within two (2) weeks after such notice, unless the employee has offered or tendered said payments within that period.[43]

The Detroit College of Business Agreement is equally clear:

Any new member of the bargaining unit shall become a member of the Association within thirty (30) days of employment with the College and shall remain a member of the Association to the extent of paying dues as a condition to continued employment with the College. Failure to comply with the above provision is reasonable or just cause for dismissal.[44]

New York Institute of Technology requires union membership as a condition of employment, but if for "reasons of conscience," anyone objects to union membership, that person may inform the chapter president in writing on or before the thirtieth day following the effective date of the agreement or commencement of employment, whichever is later.[45] This agreement makes no mention either of a service-fee option or the requirement to contribute an amount equal to dues or service fees to a scholarship fund or charity.

One agreement's treatment of the union-shop issue is likely to leave readers confused. The agreement at Utica College specifies that as a condition of their employment, the members of the union will continue their membership for the life of the agreement; however, bargaining unit members who are not union members can, "on date of contract signing, elect to join or not join."[46] If they decide to join, they will be treated like those who joined earlier and must remain members as a condition of employment for the life of the agreement. New faculty shall have a similar opportunity to join or decline membership upon hiring. What seems to have been bargained is a truly unique blend of open shop and union shop—open until the individual might choose to close it. The agreement for the Pennsylvania State College and University faculties is similar, at least for current members of the faculty union. As a condition of continued employment, they shall maintain their membership, being allowed to withdraw only during a window period of fifteen days prior to the date of expiration of the agreement.[47] In both cases a more appropriate term than *union shop* would be a *maintenance-of-membership* provision.

Rights of the Faculty Union

Access to Information

One of the prime needs of a collective-bargaining agent on campus is information and data. Certainly the union will want as much detailed information as it can get concerning the financial base and operations of the institution as it prepares for negotiations. It will want statistical data on enrollment patterns and projections. For its day-to-day operations, it needs information on the faculty concerning name, address, rank, department, tenure status, and salary. Therefore it is no surprise that the issue of access to information is a commonly negotiated term (negotiated in fifty-four agreements, 60.7 percent of the total).

Essentially all of these agreements that have negotiated an access-to-information component in the agreement have language to the effect that the college or university shall provide such information as is necessary to implement the agreement and later to negotiate a successor agreement. Typical is the language in the Goddard College Agreement, where reference is made to "such statistics and financial reports related to the collective bargaining unit and in possession of the college as are necessary for negotiations and implementation of the agreement."[48] Many of these same agreements are quick to specify further that the institution shall not be required to compile new information or present it in a form different from that in which it normally appears.

To speak of "information necessary to implement and later to renegotiate an agreement" is to be less than specific, with the nature of that information subject to a variety of interpretations when particular pieces of information are at issue. In attempting, among other things, to forestall confrontation and debate over the question of specifically what information could be so classified and to maintain a harmonious relationship between union and administration, several agreements leave the union with even less than what the Goddard Agreement specifies. These require only that each party shall "acknowledge" one another's requests for information. Such is the case in the Wagner College Agreement[49] and at the New York Institute of Technology, whose agreement specifies, "The Institute and the Council agree to consider and to answer questions for information properly submitted by one to the other. This does not obligate either the Institute or the Council to provide the requested information."[50] Another way to accomplish essentially the same end and protect administrative prerogatives is to speak of "reasonable" requests for information. In any event, it is clear that the faculty have really gained nothing as a consequence of such phraseology.

A number of other items are sometimes included. Following the essentially universal (among the 60.7 percent that have included an access to information component in the agreement) pair of ideas mentioned above (information for implementation and negotiation of an agreement, and no new compilation of data) are the official, public minutes of the board, public agendas of the board, and either the proposed or adopted annual budget of the college or university. These specifications occur in fifteen, fourteen, and ten agreements, respectively. Only Hofstra's agreement goes so far as to specify that the collective-bargaining agent shall be supplied with a line-by-line budget of any academic or administrative department it requests.[51]

The agreement for the New Jersey State Colleges is most explicit and clear in terms of identifying information to be supplied by the institution. It requires a number of items. (1) The Union shall receive a copy of the tentative agenda of all board of higher education and college board of trustees meetings at least one week prior to such meetings. (2) A copy of the adopted minutes of the public meetings of the boards shall be forwarded to the union within one week of adoption. (3) The union shall have the right to designate a representative from each college to participate in any public budget hearing. (4) The union shall have the right to speak at all public sessions of the boards of trustees. (5) The union shall have the right to appoint one employee representative to each college-wide committee of each state college and one to each "master plan" advisory committee. (6) The union shall be kept advised of any advisory committees that are established to study aspects of higher education in New Jersey.[52]

Several other items negotiated concerning information deserve mention. Only five agreements specifically call out individual faculty salary information as something that shall be required by the agreement to be sent to the bargaining agent. Although it is common (in fact, usually considered part of the information that is necessary to implement an agreement and negotiate a new one) for salary information by category of rank, gender, years of service, department, school, and so on to be provided the bargaining agent by the administration, usually the identities of the individual faculty members are removed from the data.

Five agreements require that demographic data, including salaries, be provided the union for all new faculty joining the institution. Three require a full listing of fringe benefits paid to each faculty member. Five require that notification be sent to the union of any termination that occurs. Three require notification of any other change of status of faculty members that might occur (promotion and tenure decisions, most likely). Two require that the union be supplied with a list of all full- and part-time administrators. One requires that the administration provide an organizational chart on an annual basis. Finally, four agreements specifically state that the administration shall provide all information necessary to process a grievance that is filed by a faculty member.

Access to Facilities

With respect to the rights of the collective-bargaining agent to various services and facilities that are available on the college campus (meeting rooms, campus mail distribution, use of bulletin boards, office space, duplicating machinery, and the like), not all agreements have negotiated items along these lines; however, 68.5 percent have. This does not automatically mean, of course, that in 31.5 percent of all campuses that have a collective-bargaining agreement with the faculty, the faculty union is denied access to such facilities. Nevertheless what is assumed to obtain in a collective-bargaining relationship or what may have been past practice is ensured only when the idea is actually included in the collective-bargaining agreement.

The prestige and nature of the institution is an important variable. Both the less prestigious state institutions and the private colleges are equally more likely than the more prestigious state institutions to have negotiated facility items: less prestigious state institutions, 72.7 percent; private colleges, 70.7 percent; more prestigious state universities, 46.7 percent.

Of the various items and privileges included in those sixty-one agreements that have bargained something under the broad topic of facilities and services, by far the more common are meeting rooms, access to bulletin boards, and free access to the intracampus mail service (table 12). The

TABLE 12

Frequency with Which Various Facilities and Services Are Provided the Bargaining Agent and Unit

FACILITY OR SERVICE	FREQUENCY	% OF TOTAL AGREEMENTS	% OF AGREEMENTS WITH LANGUAGE ON FACILITIES AND SERVICES
Meeting rooms on campus	49	55.1	80.3
Access to bulletin boards	43	48.3	70.5
Access to intracampus free mail service	42	47.2	68.9
Access to auxiliary services such as photo-copying at campus organi-zational rates	37	41.6	60.7
Free office for the faculty union and its president	29	32.6	47.5
Listing in the campus tele-phone directory	5	5.6	8.2

meeting rooms almost invariably are free of charge, though frequently the proviso "if available" or "upon prior reservation" is part of the agreement. There are almost as many variants on the use of bulletin boards as there are agreements with language on this topic. Universal among these agreements is the availability of a minimum number of bulletin board locations where the faculty union can post notices and inform the faculty of its activities. These may be established as one per campus office and classroom building, one per department and academic unit, one in each of specifically named buildings, or a minimum number at locations yet to be specified and agreed upon. Mail service is to be provided as to any other legitimate campus organization that wishes to convey information to faculty and staff.

Such auxiliary services as access to central duplicating facilities, food services, computer facilities, audiovisual equipment, and the like generally are available to the faculty union either without charge or at whatever rate is normal for any other faculty, staff, or student organization on campus.

Probably most of these facilities and services are extended to the union by the college or university without being listed in the agreement. But the next most frequently mentioned item—on-campus office space for the union and its president that is provided free of charge—is found in thirty agreements (33.7 percent).[53] Unless called out specifically, it is not likely that such a service will be provided. Thus it appears that two-thirds of the local faculty unions do not have on-campus office space; at least not free of charge.

The prestige and public versus private factors are relevant. Whereas 42.4 percent of the less prestigious state institutions and 34.1 percent of the private colleges have negotiated some kind of office arrangements for the faculty union, only 13.3 percent of the more prestigious universities have done so.

A few specific provisions in some agreements with respect to office space are of some interest. Although most probably assume so, a few agreements actually specify that the office that is provided shall be furnished. One (Saginaw Valley State College) specifies that the office must be a minimum of 144 square feet in size.[54] Another (Bryant College of Business) requires that the office be large enough or be some kind of suite so that there is room for a secretary to work and answer the telephone (secretarial services beyond those of student help are not provided, however).[55]

That a majority of faculty unions are not provided office space by the institution is not automatically an implicit signal of failure by the faculty bargaining representative. Some (perhaps most) faculty unions do not seek free office space on campus out of fear of becoming too beholden to the institution and looking too much like a company union.

Discussion of a few more items, though essentially unique, will demonstrate some of the diversity of ideas that are contractualized. At Monmouth College, the president of the union is granted permission to use the services of his or her home department secretary for union matters.[56] At Hofstra University any faculty member may utilize department secretaries for union business so long as the chairperson consents and so long as the union activities will not interfere with the operation of the department.[57] At Western Montana College the faculty union shall be granted time during college faculty meetings for brief reports and announcements.[58] The University of Detroit agreement guarantees $500 of computer time for the faculty association during each year of the agreement.[59] And at Wayne State University, the union shall be granted the privilege of two "master parking cards" (at the regular fee).[60] These provide privileged parking at lots located strategically across campus.

Dues Checkoff

Probably of primary interest with respect to the contractual arrangement of a dues checkoff system whereby the employer deducts dues from employees who are members of the union on a regular basis and remits those to the union in a timely manner is the discovery of such a high proportion of agreements—87.6 percent—that have adopted that system. Although there is considerable variation on this rather straightforward issue, much of the variation is tied to the pay schedule of the college or university. Usually paychecks are distributed on a monthly or biweekly basis, and deduction of dues follows the same schedule. Another variable is the date when the deduction of dues should commence (that is, how far into the fall semester?). Still a third variable is the number of pay periods in which the deduction should be made. The range is from three equal first-of-the-month paychecks at Bard College to twenty installments extending over nine months at six colleges and universities. The most common is a once-a-month deduction.

Because of the legalities of the matter, most colleges and universities with collective bargaining require some kind of written authorization by the individual faculty member before deduction of dues can be made. Some agreements specify a certain form to be filed by the faculty member and include a copy of it either in the body of the agreement or in an appendix. But once authorized, how revocable is that decision? Any such decision is, of course, revocable by some sort of procedure, but revocation is more easily made at some places than others. For example, at the University of Delaware,[61] Moore College of Art,[62] and the University of San Francisco,[63] revocation can be made by a faculty member only during a fifteen-day period that extends from thirty to fifteen days prior to the end of the period that had been authorized earlier. At Lincoln University the period is the final fifteen days of the agreement.[64] At the University of Detroit the period is for thirty days each year (April 1-30).[65]

Rutgers University and Temple University have an unusual provision in that their agreements allow revocation only during the period of October 14-31 (Rutgers) and October 15-November 1 (Temple), to be effective on January 1 of the following year.[66] A few agreements, including Fairleigh Dickinson University, Polytechnic Institute of New York, Stevens Institute of Technology, Utica College, and Wagner College, states that the decision is irrevocable for a minimum period such as a year (stated in the Utica Agreement as "for the life of the Agreement").[67] The Pennsylvania Agreement makes the faculty member's authorization irrevocable for the term of the agreement or any extension thereof or successor thereto, except during the fifteen days prior to an expiration date.[68] By far the majority allow revocation at any time but only upon a minimum number of days notice (usually thirty, occasionally sixty, never more). Five agreements (Bard College, Illinois Governor's Universities, Northern Michigan University, Saginaw Valley State College, and Wentworth College) simply say "at any time." The Monmouth College Agreement is almost as open as these in its specifying that a faculty member can revoke the dues authorization fifteen days before any payday.[69]

Distribution of the Agreement

Basically there are three issues here. First is the question of whether the distribution of the agreement to faculty members and others is contractualized at all. Second, how shall the cost of printing it be divided? Third, how many copies shall be produced?

The answer to the first question is 31 percent. The remaining agreements are totally silent on the subject of production and distribution of the agreement, relying apparently on informal agreements. With respect to the second question, the preponderance of agreements state that the cost of printing shall be totally borne by the college or university (78.6 percent of the twenty-eight agreements that speak to the issue at all). The remaining six institutions state that the costs of printing shall be borne equally by the institution and the union. Such specification often is qualified by placing an upper limit on the number of copies produced and paid for by the institution. Answering the third question: ten include a specific number that shall be printed and paid for by the institution. For example, the agreement at the University of Dubuque states that the university shall print and distribute one copy per faculty member, plus ten for the union. Any beyond that shall be distributed at "a reasonable cost."[70] Eastern Michigan University says the same thing, but the number to the association is twenty.[71] Similarly at Ferris State College, but the number provided the faculty association is set at one hundred.[72] At Wayne State University the number to the union organization is two hundred.[73]

Released Time for Union Officers

Another item, is the possibility of some released time from teaching and other faculty responsibilities for union officers, particularly the president and perhaps the chief negotiator or chairperson of the faculty grievance committee. In all, 33.7 percent of the agreements present some kind of released time arrangement for those representing the faculty union, even if it is only on a day-by-day basis such as in the State University of New York system where union representatives from the many campuses must travel some distance for meetings of the entire unit. I have not included one institution that speaks to released time in its agreement because the union must reimburse the university in full for the amount of time released. The same is true of the South Dakota State Colleges and Universities' Agreement, which provides for released time for two statewide officers but at union expense.[74]

Four other agreements speak of released time but not from teaching, implying release only from committee work, and I do not include these agreements as providing released time in the primary sense of released time from teaching responsibilities. An example is the Southern Oregon State College Agreement, which specifies that up to six members of the negotiating team shall be released from all assignments other than teaching their regular load, advising students, and keeping office hours for one month prior to the beginning of negotiations and during the course of active negotiations.[75] The agreement at Pratt Institute provides both kinds of release: one-quarter released time for three persons to handle grievances, and release from all nonclassroom activities for the union president, and during the last semester of the agreement a similar release for up to six other persons to serve on the negotiation team.[76]

The range of the amount of released time that has been negotiated for union representatives is considerable. At the low end is Adelphi University, where the president of the union is released from teaching one three-credit course per year. At the other end is St. John's University, where the number of three-hour courses that union representatives can be released from is eighteen. The number of eighteen, however, is reached only during the last semester of the agreement when six members of the faculty bargaining team shall receive a one-course reduction. These six courses are added to the twelve-course reduction offered six members of the university grievance committee, apportioned at the rate of one course for each person per semester.[77]

Other institutions with fairly substantial blocks of released time to union representatives are the University of Cincinnati where twelve courses (thirty-six quarter hours) are released, but with the proviso that released time per person cannot exceed one course per quarter.[78] Hofstra University has a nine-course released time allocation that is divided among the president of the union and the chairperson of the university faculty personnel board—each with one course reduction per semester—as well as fifteen credit hours per year that can be divided among faculty serving on committees as the union and the university provost agree.[79] The University of Delaware and Framingham College designate eight courses as released time per year with the common proviso that there shall be no more than one released course per person at a time. At Framingham State College four of the eight courses are reserved for release only at the college president's discretion.[80]

Two agreements specify six courses (Eastern Michigan University and Eastern Montana State College); two other agreements grant fifteen credits (five courses) to the faculty union (in the case of Ferris State College)[81] for the discretionary use of the faculty association; and at Rider College one course each semester for both the president of the union and the faculty grievance officer, with the remaining one course reserved for the faculty chief negotiator during the final semester the current agreement is in effect.[82] At the University of Bridgeport twelve hours are released for union service but with the stipulation that the hours be allocated at a rate of no more than three per person.[83] Finally, in one school and two schools, respectively, released time is apportioned at the rate of three courses and two courses.

Some agreements specify clearly what office carries with it what amount of released time; others leave the allocation to the union, in part at least; in a couple of cases the institutional president or provost is included in deciding who the recipients of released time shall be. Slightly under half (48.5 percent of the agreements that speak to the subject of released time) specify precisely who shall be released. An additional 24.2 percent specify, at least in part, who shall be released. The remaining 27.3 percent leave the allocation of released time entirely up to the faculty union's discretion.

The variables of prestige and type of institution have no effect so far as whether released time for union activities is negotiated in an agreement.

Faculty unions have a long way to go in this area. Only a third of the agreements provide any kind of released time for union activities, and only a few of these approach a generous provision. The issue, however, is difficult to resolve. If departments can absorb such released time either by having faculty members teach just a few more students each in other classes to compensate or if the section is not offered and there is no conscious attempt to compensate for the loss of students to the department, then there is no direct dollar cost. On the other hand, if part-time persons are hired to replace those faculty who have released time for union activities, then the salary payments must come from somewhere, perhaps the total amount of money available for faculty salary increases. If so, the salary settlement to the faculty may be slightly less as a consequence. Often the choice is to obtain as big a financial settlement for the faculty as a whole that the union decides is possible or to bargain some released time for union officers. With such a dilemma, perhaps it is not so surprising that only a third of the agreements include some amount of released time for union officers, grievance committee members, members of the negotiating team, and the like.

Rights of Management

Management (in this case the administration and/or board of trustees of four-year colleges and universities) has also demanded rights when it enters into collective-bargaining agreements with faculty. The percentage of agreements with a management-rights section is 85.4 percent. As such, this provision becomes one of the more nearly universal items in higher education contracts.

Management rights probably are expressed no more explicitly and in no plainer language than in article III of the agreement at Stevens Institute of Technology:

It is recognized that there are certain functions, responsibilities and management rights reserved to the Board of Trustees among which are, but not limited to: the direction and operation of the Institute; the determination of the number and location of its facilities; the number and size of the departments, including the merger or elimination of departments and progams and layoff of bargaining members; the curriculums to be offered; the research to be conducted under Stevens auspices; the quality of instruction and research; the facilities and equipment to be provided and their location, relocation and removal; the academic calendar; the assignment of faculty; and the making and enforcing of reasonable rules and regulations necessary to the fulfillment of the Board's functions and responsibilities.

The Institute shall have the right to: employ its faculty and staff from any source it desires; grant tenure, promote or demote; assign, transfer, layoff or recall; dismiss or discipline for cause.

These rights are reserved to management except as may herein otherwise by provided or limited by any provision of this Agreement.[84]

Somewhat in contrast, if not in content or message, then with a more legalistic tone and tendency, is article II from the Kent State University Agreement:

Recognizing that Ohio law vests full authority and responsibility for the operation of the University in the Board of Trustees and restricts the power of the Board to delegate its authority and responsibility, the University acting by and through its duly constituted authorities, retains and reserves exclusively to itself all rights, powers, prerogatives, responsibilities, and authority vested in it, whether exercised or not, none of which are in any way, except as expressly set forth elsewhere in this Agreement, directly or indirectly subject to the Grievance Procedure set forth in Article IV of this Agreement. Without limiting the generality of the foregoing, it is understood and agreed that except where expressly stated in this Agreement, nothing contained herein shall in any way limit the Board's right to adopt new or modify or terminate existing policies, rules, regulations and procedures in furtherance and accomplishment of its statutorily mandated authorities and responsibilities.[85]

One of the briefest statements is found in the Long Island University agreements (Brooklyn Center, Southampton Center, and C. W. Post Center). For example, the Southampton Center Agreement reads: "Nothing in this Agreement shall derogate from or impair any power, right, or duty heretofore possessed by the Board or the Administration except where such right, power, or duty is specifically limited by this contract."[86]

All of the agreements with a management-rights clause say that all traditional rights and obligations of the legally responsible portion of the institution (the board and the administration) continue as before, and that only what is explicit in the agreement by way of rights, privileges, and involvement on the part of faculty can modify the rights of management. The wording varies, however. The management-rights clause of the Loretto Heights College Agreement first talks about the rights of faculty to continue to participate in the process of determining policy in educational matters. Only then does it discuss the college's "ultimate responsibility for all matters concerning the College."[87] At St. John's University amid a lengthy statement of faculty rights, the rights of management are introduced in an almost offhand manner, but the Agreement does include an explicit and fairly standard statement of management rights at that point.[88]

Somewhat in contrast are the many agreements where the statement of management rights is set off in a separate article and straight to the point. The agreement for the Florida State College and University system is typical of most of these: "The Board retains and reserves to itself all rights, powers, and authority vested in it, whether exercised or not, including but not limited to the right to plan, manage, and control the State University System and in all respects carry out the ordinary and customary functions of management."[89] The agreement at Goddard College adds the following directive: "The exercise of such management rights shall not be arbitrary or capricious."[90]

In a similar vein the agreement at the University of Dubuque follows its statement of management rights by saying, "These rights and responsibilities shall properly involve ethical relationships with students, colleagues, administrators, and faculty."[91] The agreement for the Minnesota State College System includes a statement on management responsibilities, not just rights: "The parties also recognize the right and obligation of the employer efficiently to manage and conduct the operations of the System within its legal limitations and with its primary obligation to provide educational support."[92]

The Strike-Lockout Issue

Eighteen percent of the agreements at four-year colleges and universities lack a no-strike clause or section. Even more lack the no-lockout stipulation. Nine agreements that forbid strikes by faculty do not forbid lockouts of faculty by the institution itself.

The articles that treat the strike and lockout issues use a variety of terms. Only five agreements are satisfied with a single term. Four of these use *strike* (the agreements at the University of Connecticut, the Florida State College and University system, the Illinois Board of Governor's Universities, and the Minnesota State College system), and one uses an alternative single term *workstoppage* (Roger Williams College).[93]

Among the agreements, a whole host of synonymous terms, phrases, and clauses is used. I counted fifty ways to describe prohibited activities by faculty that can be subsumed under the concept of the strike. (See table 13.) Most agreements simply line up a series of various combinations of the nouns and verbs in table 13, but a few provide a formal definition of the proscribed behavior. For example, the Ashland College Agreement defines a strike as follows: "For purposes of the Agreement a strike is defined as any concerted intentional slowdown or curtailment in or interference with or picketing of or any suspension or interruption of any or all of the college's opeations and/or the work of any employee or employees."[94]

Occasionally an agreement takes a positive approach in addition to a negative or prohibitory one. The Hofstra Agreement says, "The AAUP and the University subscribe to the principle that any and all differences under this Agreement be resolved by peaceful and appropriate means without interruption of the university program."[95]

Seven agreements include the explicit right of the institution to discharge faculty members for participation in a strike. For example, the Agreement at the University of Detroit states that "the employer will have the absolute and unreviewable right to discharge or otherwise discipline any employee who violates any of the prohibitions set forth in this paragraph."[96] And the Ashland College Agreement says, "Any faculty involved shall be subject to disciplinary action up to and including discharge."[97] The D'Youville College Agreement states its right very categorically:

The Association shall not question the College's right to discipline or discharge employees engaging in, participating in or encouraging such action. It is understood that such action on the part of the College shall be final and binding upon the Association . . . and shall not be subject to the grievance procedure herein.[98]

TABLE 13
Synonyms for Strikes

NOUNS	VERBS
Walkout	Engage in
Slowdown	Incite
Refusal to report to work	Participate in
Mass absenteeism	Aid
Interruptions of work	Condone
Picketing	Counsel
Stay-away	Induce
Boycott of a primary nature	Call
Boycott of a secondary nature	Authorize
Sit-down	Ratify
Stay-in	Threaten
Workstoppage	Support
Withholding of services	Sanction
Interference with the delivery	Cause
of services	Permit
Job action	Take part in
Patrolling	Countenance
Organizational primary picketing	Encourage
Sympathetic walkout	Instigate
General walkout	Direct
Any kind of walkout	Boycott
Sick-out	Prohibit business
Cessation of work	Hinder business
Curtailment	
Interference	
Interruption	
Concerted effort not to meet classes	
Interference with the normal	
operation of the university	
Concerted refusal to perform	
Mass resignations	

A small number of agreements prescribe behavior by the faculty union should some of its members engage in unauthorized workstoppages. One of these is the Ashland College Agreement:

In the event that any breach of the no-strike clause in Section One of this Article occurs, the Association's officers shall publicly declare that the strike is unauthorized, shall promptly make earnest efforts to bring about a prompt termination of the strike, and shall continue such efforts until the employees return to work.[99]

The University of Massachusetts Agreement is even stronger: the "Union agrees to indemnify the Employer for all expenses and damages that occur as a result of any strike, workstoppage, slowdown, or withholding of services when such action is publically condoned by the Union."[100] Similarly the faculty association at Eastern Michigan University shall be liable for damages unless it takes immediate action upon notification by Eastern Michigan University that a violation of the no-strike provision has occurred. Such immediate action shall involve discussion with those faculty members responsible for the violation and informing them that the action is in violation of the agreement, subjecting them to discharge, that the association has not authorized the faculty's action, and that they must return immediately to their jobs.[101]

The agreement at Quinnipiac College contains a unique item. The institution shall not discipline any faculty member or file any claim against the faculty union for any faculty member's refusal to cross a picket line that has been set up by any collective-bargaining agent at the college other than the faculty union; however, neither shall the faculty member be paid for the period of such refusal.[102]

A final point on the no-strike, lockout provisions in collective-bargaining agreements in higher education is the note in three agreements that being absent from work on the day of the strike shall be defined by the institution as participation in the strike on the part of the absent faculty member.[103] The agreements at Robert Morris College and Youngstown State University, however, do provide for bona-fide absences.

Final Technicalities of the Relationship

Here we are concerned with some of the more technical and sometimes almost automatic features of the legal relationship of the bargaining agent to the employer.

Zipper Clause

A *zipper clause* is a section in a collective-bargaining agreement which says that the two parties to the agreement have discussed all that they want to discuss and that the resulting collection of items is complete. No new matters can be brought up during the life of the contract by either party with an expectation that the other party would be obliged to bargain the issue. The agreement is complete as it stands for the time duration specified. The open door through which the parties walked to engage in negotiations is now zippered shut.

Such a clause is included in nearly half (49.4 percent) of the agreements in four-year colleges and universities with collective bargaining. The language of the Detroit College of Business Agreement is typical: "The

Articles and Appendices contained herein constitute the entire agreement between the Detroit College of Business and the College of Business Faculty Association."[104] The phrase *entire agreement* or *entire understanding* is common. Frequently the article will elaborate along the lines of the agreement for the four colleges in the Vermont College system:

Each party had the unlimited right and opportunity to make demands with respect to any subject or matter not removed by law from the area of collective bargaining, and the understandings and agreements arrived at by the parties after the exercise of that right and the opportunity are set forth in this agreement. Therefore, the Vermont State Colleges and the Federation for the life of this agreement, each voluntarily and unqualifiedly waives the right, and each agrees that the other shall not be obliged, to bargain collectively with respect to any subject or matter referred to, or covered by this Agreement, or with respect to any subject or matter not specifically referred to or covered in this Agreement except as provided in Article XLIII.[105]

A few agreements mention that if both parties agree to open negotiations on a particular item or issue during the life of the agreement, they can do so. The negative affirmation of this possibility as included in the agreement at Cooper Union is typical: "Unless otherwise agreed to by both parties, negotiations will not be reopened on any item contained herein during the life of this agreement."[106]

Savings and Separability Clauses

Another item of a legal nature that is included in most agreements (82.8 percent) is referred to as either a savings or a separability clause. Should one or more items or portions of an agreement be declared invalid through subsequent legislation or court decree, the remaining parts of the agreement continue unaffected and in force.

A typical example of an agreement that uses the separability idea is that of the University of Bridgeport: "In the event that any provision of the Agreement in whole or in part, is declared to be illegal, void, or invalid by any court of competent jurisdiction, all of the other terms, conditions and provisions of this Agreement shall remain in full force and effect."[107] The language of the savings clause is almost identical; for example, the agreement for the New Jersey State Colleges states:

If any provision of this Agreement or any application of this Agreement to any employee or group of employees is held to be contrary to the law, or has the effect of making the State ineligible for Federal funds, then such provision or application shall not be deemed valid and subsisting, except to the extent permitted by law, but all other provisions or applications shall continue in full force and effect.[108]

Nearly half of the agreements that have contractualized a savings or separability clause have specified further that in the event a portion is declared illegal, void, or invalid, the two parties shall meet to renogotiate a section that will be compatible with legal opinion or dictate. Thirty-seven agreements (51.4 percent of those with a savings or separability clause) require that negotiations be reopened upon such an event. The time specifications vary considerably. Eight agreements state that negotiations shall be reopened "immediately." One sets a limit of a week. Four say ten days; one says two weeks; one says 15 days; seven set a limit of thirty days. Another refers only to "reasonable period of time." Still another says "as soon as possible." The greatest number (thirteen) state only that negotations shall be reopened but do not set any time frame.

Interest Succession

A few agreements incorporate the provision that should there be a change of ownership or control of the institution, the agreement shall continue to be binding on all parties. The language of Long Island University (C. W. Post Center) is typical. It says that any "employer who purchases or otherwise acquires the operation of the Center (College, School, or constituent part) shall be bound to honor this Agreement and all terms and conditions set forth herein."[109] The language employed in the Cooper Union Agreement is slightly more technical and illustrates the origin of the successor-clause terminology. It states that the "terms and conditions of this Agreement shall be binding on any successor, assignee, transferee, etc. of Cooper Union, or any part thereof, and Cooper Union shall give advanced notice of the existence of this Agreement to any said successor, assignee, transferee, etc. of Cooper Union or any part thereof."[110] Two other agreements (Wagner College and the University of Connecticut) add to the typical interest succession idea by stating that if the institution acquires any othr educational institution or portion thereof, the full-time faculty members in the newly acquired unit or portion shall automatically become members of the bargaining unit of the acquiring institution.[111] Only 16.9 percent (fifteen agreements) of the four-year college and university agreements have incorporated the idea of interest succession in any form.

New Matters and Reopening Provisions

Reopening provisions constitutes the remaining issue of a technical or legal nature. Although all agreements implicitly speak to the reopening provision by stating beginning and ending dates between which the agreement shall be in force, some add specific provisions and limitations. There are three major routes that agreements have followed in this regard. One is to assert that the agreement shall remain in force unless during a special period set aside for that purpose either party to the agreement requests to reopen negotiations for purposes of developing a new agreement. Such a window during which one or both parties request a reopening of negotiations is usually one to three months prior to the expiration of the current agreement. A variant on this theme is to specify one or more items that can become a subject of renegotiations prior to the expiration of the full agreement. The primary specific topic is the issue of salaries. Usually the agreement will specify that at any time after one year the agreement may be reopened for negotiations for salary or, more commonly, that at a specified time each year the agreement may be reopened on salary issues. The third option is to state that negotiations can be reopened on any issue so long as both parties agree. An accompanying zipper clause would simply reinforce the provision of a reopening clause in affirming the necessary mutuality of the consent to renegotiate during the life of an existing agreement.

Conclusion

Clearly there is a lack of consensus so far as identifying the rights of faculty unions. Nothing is universally identified as a right of academic unions. The closest to a universal is a dues checkoff system of some kind (in 87.6 percent of the agreements), but even here details vary. Next in frequency are the union rights to information and access to facilities. Approximately two-thirds of the agreements speak to these issues, but the details are widely diverse. All other union rights are of even less consensus.

Not even management rights are included universally in these collective-bargaining agreements. And when they are stated, the formulations vary. Some are strong on the management rights side; others are more sensitive to faculty feelings. The diversity is as impressive as the similarities.

The most highly controversial and potentially divisive element in faculty collective-bargaining agreements is the open shop-union shop issue. Inasmuch as both poles have been contractualized, it is clear that there is nothing automatic, nothing inevitable with respect to the issue of union membership being required upon approval by faculty of collective bargaining for their campus. The individual faculty unit must make its own decision, and these decisions vary widely.

A fourth observation must be made: despite the diversity and the wide range of options, a highly significant majority of faculty unions have chosen the most open and noncoercive alternative—that of open shop. Although such an arrangement does not preclude a variety of efforts such as moral suasion and cajolery, as well as standard academic arguments on the basis of data and evidence, the faculty members themselves have the right of choice and individual decision.

Negotiating teams appear often to reinvent the wheel. Many have started essentially from scratch so far as determining what might be included in their collective-bargaining agreement. Part of this probably has been somewhat deliberate in the sense that there is a tendency for faculty to define their situation at their institution as unique, demanding unique treatment that only they can devise.

Finally, although we have looked in some detail at many issues that are purely technical or required by law and, as such, tend toward sterility and formality, there is room even here to emphasize elements of collegiality, of partnership, of common goals shared by the faculty, the administration, and the board. Almost all agreements can improve on the ways they incorporate the element of collegiality into expressions of the formal, legal, and technical relationships that need to be identified in a collective-bargaining agreement.

Notes

1. Agreement (1975-77), Bloomfield College, p. 1.
2. Agreement (1976-79), University of New Haven, p. 1.
3. Agreement (1977-79), University of Cincinnati, p. 1.
4. Agreement (1975-77), State University of New York, p. 1.
5. Agreement (1977-79), University of Delaware, p. 1.
6. Ibid.
7. Agreement (1977-78), University of Dubuque, p. 1.
8. Agreement (1977-80), Robert Morris College, p. 2.
9. Agreement (1977-79), Bryant College of Business, p. 1.
10. Agreement (1976-81), University of San Francisco, p. 2.
11. Agreement (1977-80), University of Massachusetts, p. 1.
12. Agreement (1977-79), Western Montana College, p. 1.
13. Agreement (1977-80), New York Institute of Technology, p. 31.
14. Agreement (1976-79), Hofstra University, p. 32.
15. Agreement (1976-78), Roger Williams College, p. 23.
16. Agreement (1976-80), Temple University, pp. 37-38.
17. Agreement (1977-80), University of Massachusetts, p. 2.
18. Agreement (1977-79), University of Connecticut, p. 1.
19. Agreement (1976-80), Temple University, p. 3.
20. Agreement (1977-79), University of Detroit, p. 2.
21. Agreement (1976-79), Hofstra University, p. 3.
22. Agreement (1976-81), University of San Francisco, p. 2.
23. Agreement (1977-79), Fairleigh Dickinson University, p. 4.
24. Agreement (1974-77), St. John's University, p. 1.
25. Agreement (1977-81), Youngstown State University, p. 1.
26. Agreement (1977-79), State University of New York, p. 88, and Agreement (1975-77), City University of New York, p. 6.
27. Agreement (1977-79), New Jersey State Colleges, p. 4.
28. Agreement (1977-79), Regis College, p. 1.
29. Agreement (1978-79), U.S. Coast Guard Academy, p. 2.
30. Agreement (1977-79), University of Detroit, p. 3.
31. Agreement (1975-77), Rhode Island College, p. 4.

32. Agreement (1977-79), Bryant College of Business, p. 2.

33. Agreement (1975-77), Bloomfield College, p. 4.

34. Agreement (1977-79), Southern Oregon State College, p. 5.

35. Agreement (1976-79), Hofstra University, p. 36.

36. Agreement (1977-80), University of Massachusetts, p. 7.

37. Agreement (1977-80), Central Michigan University, p. 6.

38. Agreement (1978-81), University of Bridgeport, pp. 4-5.

39. Agreement (1975-78), Quinnipiac College, p. 1.

40. For example, Agreement (1977), Westfield State College, p. 145.

41. Agreement (1977-79), Southern Oregon State College, p. 5.

42. Agreement (1977-80), Central Michigan University, pp. 57-58, and Agreement (1977-80), University of Massachusetts, pp. 7-8.

43. Agreement (1977-81), University of San Francisco, p. 3.

44. Agreement (1978-82), Detroit College of Business, p. 10.

45. Agreement (1977-80), New York Institute of Technology, p. 4.

46. Agreement (1977-78), Utica College, p. 26.

47. Agreement (1974-77), Pennsylvania State College and University Faculties, p. 43.

48. Agreement (1976-78), Goddard College, p. 20.

49. Agreement (1977-80), Wagner College, p. 31.

50. Agreement (1977-80), New York Institute of Technology, p. 31.

51. Agreement (1976-79), Hofstra University, p. 39.

52. Agreement (1977-79), New Jersey State Colleges, pp. 9-10.

53. There is one exception to the fee requirement (Southern Oregon State College), but there the charge is nominal and requires a reimbursement to the college only for the cost of utilities and janitorial services for the union office. Agreement (1977-80), Long Island University, C. W. Post Center, p. 87, speaks of office space for the union but at an annual fee of $2,000. (This agreement is of course not included in the thirty agreements that provide free office space for the union.)

54. Agreement (1976-78), Saginaw Valley State College, p. 11-12.

55. Agreement (1977-79), Bryant College of Business, p. 2.

56. Agreement (1976-79), Monmouth College, pp. 41-42.

57. Agreement (1976-79), Hofstra University, pp. 5-6.

58. Agreement (1977-79), Western Montana College, p. 11.

59. Agreement (1977-79), University of Detroit, p. 11.

60. Agreement (1976-78), Wayne State University, pp. 5-6.

61. Agreement (1977-79), University of Delaware, p. 4.

62. Agreement (1976-79), Moore College of Art, p. 1.

63. Agreement (1976-81), University of San Francisco, p. 3.

64. Agreement (1976-78), Lincoln University, p. 4.

65. Agreement (1977-79), University of Detroit, p. 4.

66. Agreement (1975-77), Rugers University, p. 3; Agreement (1976-80), Temple University, p. 3.

67. Agreement (1977-78), Utica College, p. 26.

68. Agreement (1974-77), Pennsylvania State Colleges and Universities, p. 43.

69. Agreement (1976-79), Monmouth College, p. 40.

70. Agreement (1977-78), University of Dubuque, p. 3.

71. Agreement (1976-78), Eastern Michigan University, p. 5.

72. Agreement (1975-78), Ferris State College, p. 2.

73. Agreement (1976-78), Wayne State University, p. 6.

74. Agreement (1979-81), South Dakota State Colleges and Universities, p. 6.

75. Agreement (1977-79), Southern Oregon State College, p. 5.

76. Agreement (1978-81), Pratt Institute, p. 14.

77. Agreement (1974-77), St. John's University, p. 18.

78. Agreement (1977-79), University of Cincinnati, p. 26.

79. Agreement (1976-79), Hofstra University, pp. 35-36.

80. Agreement (1977), Framingham College, p. 142.

81. Agreement (1975-78), Ferris State College, p. 5.

82. Agreement (1976-79), Rider College, p. 46.

83. Agreement (1978-81), University of Bridgeport, p. 51.

84. Agreement (1976-78), Stevens Institute of Technology, p. 4.

85. Agreement (1978-80), Kent State University, p. 4.

86. Agreement (1974-77), Long Island University, Southampton Center, p. 60.

87. Agreement (1975-80), Loretto Heights College, p. 29.

88. Agreement (1974-77), St. John's University, p. 3.

89. Agreement (1976-78), State University System of Florida, p. 3.

90. Agreement (1976-78), Goddard College, p. 8.

91. Agreement (1977-78), University of Dubuque, p. 2.

92. Agreement (1977-79), Minnesota State Colleges and Universities, p. 5.

93. Agreement (1976-78), Roger Williams College, p. 23.

94. Agreement (1972-74), Ashland College, p. 2.

95. Agreement (1976-79), Hofstra University, p. 32.

96. Agreement (1977-79), University of Detroit, p. 28.

97. Agreement (1972-74), Ashland College, p. 2.

98. Agreement (1977-79), D'Youville College, p. 7.

99. Agreement (1972-74), Ashland College, p. 2.

100. Agreement (1977-80), University of Massachusetts, p. 25.

101. Agreement (1976-78), Eastern Michigan University, p. 56.

102. Agreement (1975-78), Quinnipiac College, p. 33.

103. Agreement (1977-81), Robert Morris College, p. 28; Agreement (1977-81), Youngstown State University, p. 41; Agreement (1978-79), Marymount College of Virginia, p. 30.

104. Agreement (1978-82), Detroit College of Business, pp. 20-21.

105. Agreement (1979-80), Vermont State Colleges, pp. 49-50.

106. Agreement (1978-80), Cooper Union, p. 45.

107. Agreement (1978-81), University of Bridgeport, p. 62.

108. Agreement (1977-79), New Jersey State Colleges, p. 40.

109. Agreement (1977-80), Long Island University, C. W. Post Center, p. 89.

110. Agreement (1978-80), Cooper Union, p. 45.

111. Agreement (1977-80), Wagner College, p. 58; Agreement (1977-79), University of Connecticut, p. 11.

10. SUMMARY AND ASSESSMENT

When I first conceived of this book, I envisioned three major components. First and foremost would be a presentation of the data on the scope of bargaining—that is, what has been bargained, how often, with what variety, and where. Second would be an assessment component—that is, how I might evaluate the accomplishments of collective bargaining at four-year institutions of higher education particularly during these very recent years that are covered by the agreements under study. The third focus would be the presentation of a sample, model contract. But early in the stages of data analysis I determined not to provide a sample contract. The primary reason was that it quickly became apparent that each agreement arises out of such a unique set of circumstances and speaks to such a unique constellation of problems that there can be no ideal contract. Although some items are certainly central to an adequate agreement, each campus must make its own judgment of what is needed and possible in its particular situation.

The second component, that of assessment, has been visible at various points through the study. But now I plan to assess both where collective bargaining has taken faculties and the governing bodies of the institutions under study and where might (should) collective bargaining proceed in the future.

Major Findings

Faculty Rights

Surprisingly affirmative-action commitments seldom are included in collective-bargaining agreements, although it is likely that such commitments will be included more frequently as agreements are renegotiated. Nevertheless many administrations and governing boards will resist—not because of opposition to affirmative action but because with federal and state laws already providing redress procedures, to add another set through the collective-bargaining agreement may not only appear redundant but might make administration that much more complex.

Although it seems natural for all agreements to include phrasing on nondiscrimination, academic freedom, and professional responsibilities because of their standard acceptability within academe and their inclusion in AAUP principles that have been adopted formally by most academic institutions, approximately a fourth of the agreements do not include such items. Probably administrative personnel at institutions lacking such provisions prefer such an omission. And it is likely that the absence of phrasing on nondiscrimination may be accidental in some instances because no one thought to include it during bargaining sessions.

It seems both reasonable and fair to provide faculty access to their own personnel file, particularly to guard against inaccuracies or accusations that the individual faculty member cannot speak to without such access and the knowledge it would provide. The slightly more than one-quarter of the agreements that lack language on personnel files certainly have a clear agenda item here. Access to one's personnel file with appropriate safe-guards is a reasonable request and probably will be granted fairly graciously in most instances. Another comment with respect to the personnel file issue is that the 38 percent that have not provided a mechanism for the faculty to respond to the contents of the file with explanations, clarifications, or rebuttals need to think these issues through and formulate appropriate contractual language. Further, the majority of agreements that fail to speak to the issue of removing false and purely defamatory materials need to have that issue addressed by their bargaining teams as well.

Another issue that both parties to an agreement must discuss is the scope of grievability through the contractual grievance system. If an academic or faculty senate or other alternative grievance system exists, what does it cover and where does the scope of one grievance system end and the other begin? Normally faculty will strive to expand the scope, while the administration will attempt to keep the scope as narrow as possible. Both sides need to negotiate over this issue and arrive at a conclusion so that faculty can determine the appropriate vehicle for examining the need for redress.

It is important to build in faculty involvement at one or more levels of the grievance system, not only for the benefit of the faculty but for the administration as well. The outcome of a grievance case will be fairer and represent a broader perspective if faculty are involved, and it will be more acceptable to the entire academic community if faculty are involved in meaningful ways.

That binding arbitration is provided as a final recourse in the grievance process in nearly three-quarters of the agreements probably is to be credited largely to the efforts of faculty bargaining teams. Yet one-quarter lack the binding arbitration provision. This will likely become an immediate goal for faculty bargaining teams at those institutions.

Another broad area in which few faculties have made any notable progress so far as producing meaningful contractual language is concerned is that of faculty involvement in personnel decisions—hiring, reappointment, granting tenure, and promotion. In the first two areas, fewer than half of the agreements have contractualized anything on the subject; regarding tenure and promotion, the percentages with language on the subjects are higher—69 percent and 75 percent, respectively—but not universal. Further, in many agreements the language is essentially non-commital. Very few go so far as the Central Michigan University Agreement which says, "Departmental colleagues are best informed and are in the best position to arrive at specific criteria or objectives to satisfy contributions in teaching, research, and related supplemental activities."[1] Further, this same agreement says that the primary responsibility of judging the extent to which departmental members have pursued their professional obligations and have disseminated knowledge rests with the department.[2]

Retrenchment will become increasingly common in the 1980s. Because of a substantially lower birthrate in the 1960s, many say that the pool from which the vast majority of college enrollees is drawn will be contracted by as much as a third. With fewer students to teach and with less money flowing through the system of higher education, not so many faculty will be needed, and various forms of retrenchment will take place as a consequence. Of course, some institutions will maintain stable enrollments; some will even grow and add faculty. Normal attrition will absorb some displaced faculty; and new academic markets will be developed. But the fact remains that scores of campuses will face some level of retrenchment at some time during this decade.

While it is this specter on the horizon that has stimulated the interest of some faculty in unionization in the first place, the record of faculty unions in the area of retrenchment has not been outstanding to date. Approximately 40 percent of the collective-bargaining agreements at four-year institutions leave faculty reduction decisions to the president or other administrators at the institution and require no or very little faculty involvement. Nor is the institution required to justify conclusively the need for such reduction, despite the fact that the AAUP has recommended clearly and unambiguously that when faculty reductions are proposed because of financial exigency, there should be faculty involvement in the recommendations. Among other considerations, the AAUP insists that some faculty body participate in the discussion and determination that a financial exigency either exists or is near; faculty should have primary responsibility for determining the criteria to be used in identifying which faculty shall be retrenched; faculty should identify those persons; and any faculty member who is terminated as a result of these procedures shall have the right to a full hearing before a faculty committee.[3]

Administrators are extremely sensitive on the topic of faculty reduction. Theirs is, after all, the legal responsibility for administering a very large and complex organization and meeting a faculty payroll that constitutes about half of the budget, with total personnel costs absorbing from 70 to 80 percent of the institution's budget.[4] They want and need flexibility and authority and are wary of tying themselves to a single set of considerations and an explicit set of procedures that must be followed, especially if the procedures involve significant faculty participation. For one thing, faculty are not known for the speed with which they reach decisions and make recommendations, especially when a committee or task force of more than three people is involved. Further, faculty behave no differently from other people when they feel threatened.

Yet by the same token, administrators are neither omniscient nor without bias, neither clairvoyant not incapable of precipitous knee-jerk reactions. Thus contractual language that would get both principals together with sufficient time to discuss and explore a variety of options, thereby almost by definition reducing the possibility of arbitrary, capricious, or precipitous action, would seem to be desirable. Yet few pairs of bargaining teams have negotiated such a structure; few agreements provide such measured steps to problem solving.

Compensation

With regard to compensation items, there is wide diversity among agreements in terms of the level of success. Although most agreements have done reasonably well by faculty so far as base salary considerations are concerned, several questions or issues bear restating. First is the question of how many of the various areas in which some form of compensation could be negotiated have been included in actual faculty agreements. It is clear that every faculty has some new compensation items it can strive for; most have several. Second, even when a compensation item is included, there is wide variation in its value. In some agreements, the negotiated value of the item is low enough to have made it hardly worth the effort. Third, some agreements have done well in a multiple of compensation areas, and they will serve as models to emulate. Fourth, the area of compensation that is not only most visible but certainly also most valuable in the long run is that of salary. Here the record of collective bargaining in higher education leaves the faculty fairly well off—significantly better off, I believe, because of collective bargaining.

Fringe Benefits

Despite the fact that the right of faculty members to negotiate with their employer on the subject of fringe benefits is seldom debated, this is an area in which faculty, through their unions, have often failed to do particularly well. An area of major importance to faculty is that of medical and hospitalization insurance, but 20 percent have bargained nothing different from the plan established by the state for its employees (some of these plans, of course, may be very good; the information with which to judge is simply not provided); 22 percent simply reference and reaffirm existing plans; 29 percent include coverage only for the employee, not dependents; an additional 29 percent may shift a large share of the premium for family coverage directly to the employee. In short, although a few agreements have negotiated excellent medical and hospitalization programs and provide for the complete, or nearly so, premium payment to be made by the employer, most agreements have settled for less.

Dental insurance, now almost taken for granted in most trade and industrial union contracts, is found in only 19 percent of the academic agreements, and few of these provide more than token benefits and partial payments.

Although the record with respect to long-term disability insurance is better than for dental insurance, such coverage is far from automatic or universal. Only 55 percent include it. And some (16.2 percent) require that part of the cost be borne by the faculty members themselves.

Although 65 percent of the agreements include a life insurance feature, frequently the cost, at least in part, must be assumed by faculty. Thus the insurance issue is wide open for innovation and improvement from the faculty perspective.

Leaves of absence generally are included in fewer than half of the agreements. And even when they are included, the leaves frequently are quite restricted with respect to availability to faculty. For example, approximately a third of all agreements require more than the normal interval of six years between sabbatical leaves. Another third either do not mention sabbatical leaves or fail to specify the time interval between them. With respect to medical or sick leave, again there is great variation. Over a third have not contractualized such leaves, and of the two-thirds that have, many are not generous. For example, a third of them do not contractualize a long-term disability plan; a third provide twelve or fewer sick days per year; nearly a quarter provide a time period of fewer than six months as the maxium number of days one can draw full pay while on extended sick leave.

On the central subject of retirement, about half of the agreements do not contractualize the amount or proportion of salary that the faculty members shall contribute to a retirement program. To this can be added the slightly over one-half of those that do contractualize an amount but specify a retirement contribution of 10 percent or less. Actually fewer than one-quarter of all agreements contractualize a retirement program that could be considered generous (in excess of 10 percent).

Some form of tuition waiver for family members of faculty is contractualized in slightly more than half of the agreements. Although faculty members are well aware that tuition waivers for relatives of faculty are not universal in academe, the average outsider probably would assume the availability of such a fringe benefit. That nearly half of the agreements do not include this provision therefore seems significant.

With respect to working conditions, collective-bargaining agreements appear in the main to have reaffirmed the status quo ante. For example, most of the agreements specify at least a twelve-hour per semester teaching load. Only three agreements limit the number of different course preparations a faculty member can be expected to shoulder. Only 27.1 percent of the agreements address the issue of class size. So far as facilities are concerned, relatively few agreements are explicit. Even if they are, it is likely that an administrative escape clause has been included specifying that the facilities and accoutrements shall be provided only if the institution can afford to do so.

For faculty not to have fared particularly well in bargaining creature comforts is not to have failed so far as collective bargaining is concerned. This is true particularly if significant gains have been made in rights of due process, participation of faculty in decision making, and various forms of job protection. Actually I suspect that the contractualization in any agreements of details such as office accoutrements and parking privileges marks the end of a long series of bargaining stalemates over issues more central to the educational process than those. A few creature comforts might have been included by way of face-saving compromises. A faculty bargaining team perhaps would have been bargaining hard for a better grievance procedure or an improved retirement plan but had to settle for free parking. Next time they might make more progress in fundamental areas. Without a perfect one-for-one relationship, there is a tendency for the agreements with creature comforts included not to be the ones with the more substantial salary settlements.

Professional Role and Conduct of Faculty

An area under the purview of collective-bargaining agreements that historically probably has been more of administration and governing board origin rather than faculty is that of the duties and responsibilities of faculty in performing their jobs. A list of what is expected of faculty members by the institution is of great interest to faculty; certainly many faculty prefer to know what is expected of them by way of minimum performance. They would then know when and where they were exceeding expectations and would also be able to determine when and at what points they might have performed only minimally or even slipped below expectations. On the other hand, one can understand their apprehension that listing specific responsibilities and duties could be used as an administrative device with which to harass or discipline particular faculty who might be found to have missed some office hours or failed to attend the spring commencement exercises.

This perspective of uneasiness and apprehension has prevailed. Or perhaps the formulations of faculty duties simply have not been put forth by the board of trustees' teams. I do not know because we have, after all, only the end product of bargaining, not the proposals that were put forth by either party that subsequently were rejected or modified in the course of bargaining.

The obvious problem with any specific listing of duties or responsibilities is that it quickly breeds legalism on both sides, equally subversive of sound educational process in either case. No one is helped; many may be harmed.

I suspect that some of the contractualizaton of highly specific duties for faculty stems from an attitude on the part of administrations and governing boards that is just a little vindictive. But to the credit of all parties, very few of the detailed requirements that some have feared would be outcomes of collective bargaining has occurred. The almost classic specter of time clocks, stop watches, and all kinds of numerical measures of productivity reminiscent of the factory setting has remained in the arsenal of opponents to faculty collective bargaining but has nowhere occurred.

Faculty Involvement in Governance

With respect to what is to faculty second only to salary—involvement in and responsibility for the academic program of the institution—collective bargaining agreements on the whole provide very little. Only about a third of the agreements at four-year institutions provide anything explicit about faculty involvement in and responsibility for governance and the policymaking functions of the institution. Granted, such involvement may well be guaranteed or at least included in other documents, but such documents seldom carry the legally binding force of a collective-bargaining agreement.

In only one agreement are any exclusive rights granted to faculty. The University of Dubuque Agreement grants the faculty the exclusive rights of setting degree requirements and approving curriculum contents and courses offered.[5] To this must be added the distinct possibility that the fifteen agreements that incorporate by reference other documents such as faculty constitutions also grant exclusive rights in a few areas. Truly exclusive rights, however, will be rare, if only because a board of trustees-regents-governors holds the ultimate legal responsibility for decision making at the institution.

What many faculty would be happy with and what would seem reasonable to expect is to be guaranteed not only that they will be involved in the decision-making process so far as academic program is concerned but that decisions and actions will not be precipitous. Few agreements have dealt at all seriously with this issue. Yet these few provide models to work from and make specific applications to each institution's unique situation.

An area of great concern to most faculty is the mode of operation and the level of effectiveness of their academic senate or assembly. This concern is heightened when collective bargaining arrives. Of the four possible relationships—bargaining agent an equal partner with the senate, the senate relegated to subunit status vis-à-vis the faculty union, the senate superordinate, with the bargaining agent relegated to highly specific and specialized functions, senate eliminated—the first is by far the most common. That this should be so is a signal of fairly early maturity on the part of the collective-bargaining movement on many campuses. Certainly it is possible for a faculty union and a faculty senate not only to coexist but to work together.

The question of what happens to a cherished senate continues to be very near the top of the list of questions faculty who are beginning to consider collective bargaining will ask. But the answer is clear; examples of successful coexistence between a senate and the faculty union and the complementary nature of their functions are numerous. Although there are no solid data, I suspect that in addition to dedication to sound educational principles as well as principles of cooperation and goodwill, an important ingredient for a successful relationship between an academic senate and a faculty union is that the composition of both groups not be identical. That is, if some college or university administrators, some students, and perhaps some professional staff people join the faculty in the senate but not in the union, chances for successful coexistence and a complementary relationship are improved. Their constituencies are different; their tasks and functions different. On the other hand, if both organizations are limited solely to faculty, then one will become weaker unless there is extraordinary effort to maintain it. Inasmuch as the union has the legally binding responsibility and therefore ultimately more authority, probably it will outlast the senate—but to everyone's loss inasmuch as the principal forum for debate over academic programs and mission will be gone. I believe that both organizations not only can but should complement one another. But to do this, attention will need to be paid to the structure and construction of each organization, particularly that of the senate.

*Issues of Definition and Relationship of the Faculty Union
with the Institution at Large*

An important concern on the part of both the faculty and the administration is how a collective-bargaining agreement will affect their relationship—either not to harm it if deemed currently positive or to improve it is such is needed. Approximately two-thirds of the agreements say something about producing or maintaining a positive relationship between the two parties. Inasmuch as after making such affirmations it becomes somewhat more difficult to engage in nagging, spiteful, and harassing behavior, the inclusion of such affirmations can be recommended to both faculty and governing boards at the remaining institutions.

With respect to defining the bargaining unit, the primary issue seems to be whether to include departmental and divisional chairpersons. This is probably the issue most often used by boards of trustees when they have attempted to stall the implementation of collective bargaining on their campuses by going to court for a determination of eligible membership. Although there is clear support for including and excluding chairpeople from the bargaining unit, twice as many agreements include them as exclude them. Most of the time the decision has hinged on how chairpersons at a particular institution have been identified in the past—whether as a departmental head or a chairperson. As a head, one is viewed more as a representative of the administration; as a chairperson, one is first the representative of one's colleagues and second a representative of the administration to those faculty. My view is that to exclude chairpersons from the bargaining unit is to dip too deeply into the faculty ranks and to suggest a proportion of chairpersons' commitment and time disproportionate to actual allocation. That is, few chairpersons are relieved of teaching duties greater than two courses, usually only one. Therefore, they are faculty primarily and belong in the bargaining unit.

Although a bargaining unit once defined by the appropriate governmental agencies is difficult to redefine, some faculties might well consider pursuing such a change. Faculty who are about to adopt collective bargaining and must define the bargaining unit would be well advised to look very closely at the function of chairpersons at their institution and pursue the goal of including them in the bargaining unit. Such would be consistent with their self-perception, the perceptions of their colleagues, and the allocation of their time.

One of the greatest unresolved issues so far as faculty collective bargaining is concerned is that of open-shop, agency-shop, or union-shop alternatives. Although most agreements have contractualized an open shop, which makes individual membership in the faculty union optional, I recommend starting with the agency shop as a compromise between the other two alternatives. If an agency shop—an arrangement whereby all faculty served by the collective-bargaining agent pay equally or nearly so for those services as dues, a fee, or by way of making an equivalent contribution to a worthy cause or organization—is part of the package upon which faculty vote in that first decision of whether to approve of collective bargaining, then from the very beginning an affirmative vote includes the selection of the agency-shop option and no one later can be accused of deception or false pretenses. Faculty will be more unified, and there will likely be a broader range of participation as faculty members deliberately involve themselves in something they are already supporting financially. There will be one less source of contention and divisiveness, and the faculty can concentrate on substantive issues. Even from the administrative point of view an agency-shop provision would seem to be preferable. None of the choices is foolproof, however. At Central Michigan University, for example, an agency-shop provision not included in the original consideration of the union or the first few contracts, but approved by a technically proper vote in 1974 has been challenged in the courts ever since. By way of further example, a closed-shop provision that seems clear and airtight has resulted in litigation at Temple University because the university (it is alleged by the faculty bargaining agent) did not deal appropriately with a few faculty (by dismissing them) who had not paid their dues by the date specified by the agreement. A similar case has been in process at the C. W. Post Center of Long Island University. There a labor arbitrator in early September 1979 ordered the suspension of five tenured and three nontenured faculty members because they had declined to pay their agency-shop fees. The faculty union had asked that the university enforce the appropriate clause in their collective-bargaining agreement and dismiss the faculty. The administration declined, and the union filed a grievance, which lead to the arbitrator's decision.[6]

A faculty union may have other expectations, some rather mundane, such as access to the means of communication at the institution (bulletin boards, intracampus mail services, a telephone, and so on). About half of the agreements have negotiated such basics. Such items are no-cost or very low-cost items so far as the institution is concerned, but they are extremely helpful services for the faculty's bargaining agent. Therefore these are services that faculty should include in their next agreement proposal and should likely be consented to by the administration and board that are party to the agreement.

The faculty union fringe benefit of some released time for union officers and/or major committee chairpersons has been negotiated in only a third of the agreements. Even in those, the number of credit hours of released time varies greatly. Although a case certainly can be made by faculty for some release from teaching responsibilities in the face of substantial time demands inherent in various union offices and committees, there are definite advantages to being beholden to no one as in the case where no released time is provided by the institution. Couple that advantage with the likelihood that the cost for such released time will come out of faculty salary packages, and released time becomes harder to justify. It is an excellent initial proposal that is expendable and can be traded off as bargaining gets closer to settlement.

Final Assessment

Despite collective bargaining, despite the formalization of relationships, despite the heated exchanges that have occurred during bargaining, despite tendencies to an adversarial relationship, I have been tremendously impressed by how much mutual trust and assumed goodwill is implicit in the collective-bargaining agreements. Collegiality has not been destroyed. True, to go further and say that collegiality has been strengthened might be fanciful, but despite great care in formulating agreements, there remain great opportunities in all of them for administrations to be autocratic and arbitrary and still live up to the letter of the agreement. True, a federal or state law might be broken in the process; the administration might need first to have a meeting with some faculty and consult with or at least inform them. However, subsequent to such requirements the field is open. By way of example, the Long Island University (Southampton Branch) Agreement provides for the faculty union to convene a committee to make recommendations to the administration regarding class size. Rejection of such recommendations by the administration shall be only made for good and compelling reasons.[7] But one can hardly help but ask, Who is to decide if reasons are "good and compelling" and what recourse is there if the bargaining agent disagrees with the rejection of recommendations on the part of the administration? Although it would be foolish and although I have no reason to think that the administration at Southampton College of Long Island University would wish to walk roughshod over the faculty with respect to this issue, the opportunity to do so is certainly there.

A great deal of contractual language in higher education agreements is "meet and confer" language; that is, the administration is required to meet with representatives of the faculty and inform, discuss, and possibly strive to reach some consensus. Should a consensus not develop, the administration remains free to carry out whatever action it wishes. Although it would be ill advised to flaunt such a right, the right is there nonetheless. At the very least though, even such language increases the time span between an administration-board decision and its implementation, so we would expect less precipitous action and more reflection. And there is even the possibility that faculty can affect and shape the subsequent administrative action. Even to agree to meet and confer seems to suggest that some measue of worth is attached to the interaction.

A collective-bargaining agreement is no panacea; it will not turn any party around 180 degrees. If there is not a concerted willingness by all parties to work together to avoid creating problems for one another, then arriving at a collective-bargaining agreement will accomplish relatively little except exacerbation of an already contentious, combative relationship of faculty and administration-board. The route of collective bargaining will not create collegiality where none existed before. On the other hand, collective bargaining will not destroy collegiality that existed before. Collective bargaining still is only one of the vehicles through which an academic community conducts its business and fulfills its mission and objectives. All parts of the academic community need to keep that in mind as they consider collective bargaining. Faculties in particular should not expect too much of collective bargaining. Of course, the other side of that coin is to note that it is easy to expect too little of collective bargaining. Clearly through their collective-bargaining contracts faculties can make substantial gains concerning participation in academic governance, in protection of faculty rights and academic freedom, and in the areas of salary and fringe benefits. The precedents are there.

An overall conclusion that calls itself out so very clearly is the uniqueness of each agreement. Although my attempt in this book has been to summarize and to codify, the uniqueness of each agreement is obvious. Although we have reduced the variability among institutions considerably by excluding from our research universe the many two-year junior and community colleges that have collective bargaining, we still have liberal arts colleges on the one hand and graduate universities on the other; large state universities and small private colleges; single campus institutions and huge multicampus units; and there are Roman Catholic, private, and public institutions. Yet all have collective bargaining.

And here I must affirm once again two themes that have coursed through this book—one explicit, one more subtle. Many times I have explicated diversity in the treatment of the many topics in this book. But a more subtle message has been that such diversity (or at least much of it) should be expected and should not pose a surprise.

Yet despite the diversity of character and despite the unique history of each institution, there are both universal problems or challenges and universal needs. The challenges of tightening budgets, declining enrollments, increasing governmenal strictures, and the like are beyond the purview of this book. But the needs constitute another story. There are universal needs of faculty. And it is those needs that have become the subjects of bargaining: needs for insurance and redress procedures in the face of capricious and arbitrary action by superiors, for a fair and living wage, for meaningful participation in institutional planning and decision making, and for freedom and encouragement to pursue knowledge. Amid the pursuit of such universals faculties and the institutions themselves can learn from one another.

There is, of course, another side. Although there is little risk of its occurrence, I do feel compelled to say that I hope the learning from one another that this book would encourage does not produce standardization and homogeneity. Actually, I do expect changes in collective-bargaining agreements coming about as a consequence of one party or the other seeing items in this book that they want to incorporate in their next proposal and their next agreement, or noting turns of phrase or ways of handling a particular issue that would be an improvement on what they already have. But I do not expect a standardization. For one thing, it is almost characteristic of academicians to believe that generalizations that may apply elsewhere are not likely to apply to their own unique situation. But I do expect that consciousness will be raised as both parties on a particular campus see what is possible and what can be adapted as goals.

Collegiality probably is the primary enduring issue that concerns all parties involved in collective bargaining in higher education. Much of the concern centers around the fact that the laws that regulate collective bargaining have been designed primarily for the industrial sector and reflect an industrial model of collective bargaining. As such there is an underlying assumption of an adversarial relationship between employee and employer. If such a relationship is not perceived and defined in the full Marxian sense of total conflict of interest between the haves and have-nots, the relationship, at least implicitly, is defined as conflicting and adversarial as faculty try to wrest an increased share of the institution's wealth and resources from the administration and the board of trustees. The laws, of course, understand that in an industrial situation there are two clearly definable classes of persons—the workers and the managers. The workers almost never participate in management decision making. And the managers who make decisions and policy only rarely have any among their number who rose from the ranks of the workers. The lines dividing the two parties to a collective-bargaining endeavor are clear and rarely breached.

But not so in higher education. The managers (the administration) almost invariably did rise through the ranks there or at a similar institution and began as faculty, perhaps still preserving as part of their self-concept the idea that they remain academicians at heart. Further, faculty as faculty have participated and continued to participate much more broadly in institutional decision making than do workers in industry.

I do not argue that there is no problem here—a disjuncture of the model and the assumptions that go with it when put in the context and arena of higher education. But the question is how to deal with it. One response made by administrations and boards of trustees in some cases is to follow the industrial adversarial model of two opposing parties—one trying to keep intact as much of the resource hoard as possible, the other trying to grasp bigger handfuls for itself. This approach will not work in academe. It will only exacerbate a situation and lead to total frustration on the part of faculty in particular. It will create battle lines and trenches that were not there before and need not be there at all.

But the agreements that have been reached indicate that bargaining representatives at a majority of the institutions of higher education that have adopted collective bargaining have worked to shape a new model that plays down the adversarial relationship and emphasizes the collegial one. There is no doubt that to do so necessitates the psychological mechanism of compartmentalization. At times, as the two teams haggle over specific issues at the bargaining table or as faculty committees meet with higher-ranking officers of the institution to make joint policy recommendations on academic matters to the board of trustees, both parties will be compartmentalizing and trying not to think about or remember the other situation. Yet it remains true that while an adversary one day, it is colleague the next. Such switches rarely occur in the industrial sector.

This situation suggests the need for a new model, but none has yet been developed to obviate the academic and bargaining schizophrenia that both parties to the collective-bargaining process in higher education must experience and live with.

Now we have come full circle. Just as I said earlier, "It all begins with respect," now I can say, "It all ends with respect." The elements of mutual trust and integrity must both undergird and transcend a collective-bargaining agreement. Both parties rely on much more than is included in the literal language of a collective-bargaining agreement. They rely also on one another's integrity and on coinciding commitments to producing the highest quality education of which they are mutually capable. In the absence of either or both of these qualities, collective bargaining will be little more than a diversionary sideshow of posturing pretenders. With integrity on both sides and with mutual commitments to the highest quality education they can muster, however, collective bargaining in higher education can be a complement to the educational process and a contributor to institutional well-being. History, however, cannot be rewritten. The circumstances that brought about collective bargaining at a particular institution in the first place were real then and are certainly real now in their consequences. Both parties will always live with ambiguity, and collegiality will wax and wane.

Notes

1. Agreement (1977-80), Central Michigan University, p. 25.
2. Ibid.
3. American Association of University Professors, "Recommended Institutional

Regulations on Academic Freedom and Tenure," *AAUP Policy Documents and Reports*, section 5, Washington, D.C., 1977.

4. Kenneth P. Mortimer and Michael L. Tierney, *The Three "R's" of the Eighties: Reduction, Reallocation and Retrenchment* (Washington, D.C.: American Association for Higher Education, 1979), p. 35.

5. Agreement (1977-78), University of Dubuque, p. 5.

6. Chronicle of Higher Education, September 4, 1979, p. 2.

7. Agreement (1974-77), Long Island University, Southampton Branch, p. 47.

APPENDIX: COLLECTIVE-BARGAINING AGREEMENTS USED IN THIS STUDY

Adelphi University, 1976-1978.
Adrian College, 1976-1979.
Ashland College, 1972.
Bard College, 1977-1978.
Bloomfield College, 1975-1977.
Bryant College of Business, 1977-1979.
Central Michigan University, 1977-1980.
City University of New York, 1975-1977.
College of Medicine and Dentistry of New Jersey, 1979-1981.
Connecticut State College system, 1976-1979.
Cooper Union, 1978-1980.
Detroit College of Business, 1978-1982.
Dyke College, 1976-1979.
D'Youville College, 1977-1979.
Eastern Michigan University, 1976-1978.
Eastern Montana College, 1975-1977.
Emerson College, 1975-1978.
Fairleigh Dickinson University, 1977-1979.
Ferris State College, 1975-1978.
Fitchburg State College, 1974-1976.
Florida State University system, 1976-1978.
Framingham State College, 1977.
Goddard College, 1976-1978.
Hofstra University, 1976-1979.
Illinois Board of Governors' State Colleges and Universities, 1977-1979.
Iowa State Board of Regents' Colleges and Universities, 1977-1979.
Kent State University, 1978-1980.
Lincoln University, 1976-1978.
Long Island University, Brooklyn Center, 1976-1979.
Long Island University, C. W. Post Center, 1977-1980.
Long Island University, Southampton College, 1974-1977.

Loretto Heights College, 1975-1980.
Marymount College of Virginia, 1978-1979.
Massachusetts College of Art, 1973-1975.
Minnesota State Colleges and Universities, 1977-1979.
Monmouth College, 1976-1979.
Moore College of Art, 1976-1979.
New Jersey Institute of Technology, 1977-1979.
New Jersey State Colleges, 1977-1979.
New York Institute of Technology, 1977-1980.
Northern Michigan University, 1975-1977.
Northern Montana College, 1977-1979.
Oakland University, 1976-1979.
Park College, 1979-1980.
Pennsylvania State Colleges and Universities, 1976-1979.
Polytechnic Institute of New York, 1975-1976.
Pratt Institute, 1978-1981.
Quinnipiac College, 1975-1978.
Regis College, 1977-1979.
Rhode Island College, 1975-1977.
Rider College, 1976-1979.
Robert Morris College, 1977-1980.
Roger Williams College, 1976-1978.
Rutgers, the State University of New Jersey, 1975-1977.
Saginaw Valley State College, 1976-1978.
St. John's University, 1974-1977.
Salem State College, 1977.
South Dakota State College and University system, 1979-1981.
Southeastern Massachusetts University, 1976-1979.
Southern Oregon State College, 1977-1979.
State University of New York, 1977-1979.
Stevens Institute of Technology, 1976-1978.
Temple University, 1976-1980.
U.S. Coast Guard Academy, 1978-1979.
U.S. Merchant Marine Academy, c. 1977.
University of Bridgeport, 1978-1981.
University of Cincinnati, 1977-1979.
University of Connecticut, 1977-1979.
University of Delaware, 1977-1979.
University of Detroit, 1977-1979.
University of Dubuque, 1977-1978.
University of Guam, 1976-1979.
University of Hawaii, 1977-1979.
University of Lowell, 1976-1977.
University of Massachusetts, 1977-1980.
University of New Haven, 1976-1979.
University of Rhode Island, 1977-1979.
University of San Francisco, 1976-1981.

University of Scranton, 1976-indefinite.
Utica College of Syracuse University, 1977-1978.
Vermont State Colleges, 1979-1980.
Wagner College, 1977-1980.
Wayne State University, 1976-1978.
Wentworth Institute of Technology, 1978-1980.
Western Michigan University, 1976-1977.
Western Montana College, 1977-1979.
Westfield State College, 1977.
Worcester State College, 1977.
Youngstown State University, 1977-1981.

BIBLIOGRAPHY

Aaron, Benjamin, et al., eds. *Public-Sector Bargaining*. Madsion, Wis.: Industrial Relations Research Association, 1979.

Adler, D. *Governance and Collective Bargaining in Four-Year Institutions, 1970-77*. Monograph no. 3. Washington, D.C.: Academic Collective Bargaining Information Service, 1979.

Angell, George W. *Impact of Faculty Collective Bargaining on College and University Trustees*. Washington, D.C.: Association of Governing Boards of Universities and Colleges, 1977.

———. *Management Prerogatives and Faculty Rights*. Special Report no. 29. Washington, D.C.: Collective Bargaining Information Service, 1977.

———, et al., eds. *Handbook of Faculty Bargaining*. San Francisco: Jossey-Bass, 1977.

Bain, Trevor. "Collective Bargaining and Wages in Public Higher Education: The Case of CUNY." *Journal of Collective Negotiations in the Public Sector* 5 (1976): 207-14.

Begin, James P. *Academic Bargaining: Origins and Growth*. New Brunswick, N.J.: Institute of Management and Labor Relations, Rutgers-The State University of New Jersey, 1977.

———. "Statutory Definitions of the Scope of Negotiations: The Implications for Traditional Faculty Governance." *Journal of Higher Education* 49 (May-June 1978): 247-60.

———, et al. *Academics on Strike*. Washington, D.C.: Rutgers-The State University of New Jersey and Academic Collective Bargaining Information Service, 1975.

Bernhardt, R. G. "Why Collective Bargaining in Higher Education?" *Research in Higher Education* 7 (August 1977): 79-85.

Birnbaum, Robert. "Unionization and Faculty Compensation." *Educational Record* 55 (Winter 1974): 29-33.

———. "Unionization and Faculty Compensation: Part II." *Educational Record* 57 (Spring 1976): 116-18.

Borland, David T. "Collective Bargaining: Prospectus for the South." *Southern Journal of Educational Research* 10 (Spring 1976): 75-85.

Brooks, Thomas R. *Toil and Trouble: A History of American Labor*. New York: Delacorte Press, 1971.

Brown, Ronald C. "Tenure Rights in Contractual and Constitutional Context." *Journal of Law and Education* 9 (July 1977): 299-318.

Brown, William W., and Stone, Courtenay C. "Academic Unions in Higher Education: Impacts on Faculty, Salary, Compensation and Promotions." *Economic Inquiry* 15 (July 1977): 385-96.

_____. "Faculty Compensation under Unionization: An Analysis of Current Research and Findings." In *NCSCBHE Proceedings of Fifth Annual Conference*. New York: National Center for the Study of Collective Bargaining in Higher Education, 1977.

Bryant, Anne L. "Faculty Collective Bargaining in Higher Education: A Case Study of the University of Massachusetts, Amherst Election, November 1973." Ed.D. dissertation, University of Massachusetts, 1978.

Bullis, Bruce R. "Trust and Inclination of Faculty toward Collective Bargaining at Northeastern Illinois University." Ph.D. dissertation, Southern Illinois University, 1977.

Carr, Robert K., and Van Eyck, Daniel K. *Collective Bargaining Comes to the Campus*. Washington, D.C.: American Council on Education, 1973.

Chandler, Margaret, and Julius, Daniel. *Faculty vs. Administration: Rights Issues in Academic Collective Bargaining*. New York: National Center for the Study of Collective Bargaining in Higher Education, Baruch College, City University of New York, 1979.

Chandler, Margaret K., et al. *Is Institutional Prestige the Key Variable in Faculty Collective Bargaining?* Washington, D.C.: Academic Collective Bargaining Information Service, 1977.

Chichura, Andrew D. "Change from Strife to Accommodation in Organizational Behavior as Affected by Collective Bargaining: A Case Study." Ed.D. dissertation, Pennsylvania State University, 1977.

Cresswell, Anthony M., and Murphy, Michael J. *Education and Collective Bargaining*. Berkeley, Calif.: McCutchan Publishing Corporation, 1976.

Davis, Barbara C. "The Legal Aspects of Unit Determinations in Faculty Collective Bargaining at Public Institutions of Higher Education." Ph.D. dissertation, Georgia State University, 1976.

Dougherty, J. E. "Collegiality, Governance and Collective Bargaining in the Multi-Campus State University of New York." *Labor Law Journal* 28 (October 1977): 645-50.

Douglas, Joel M., and Garfin, Molly. *Contract Development in Higher Education Faculty Collective Bargaining*. New York: National Center for the Study of Collective Bargaining in Higher Education, Baruch College, City University of New York, 1980.

Dunlop, John T., and Chamberlain, Neil W. *Frontiers of Collective Bargaining*. New York: Harper & Row, 1967.

Duryea, E. D., and Neddy, J. C. *Collective Bargaining: Impact on Governance*. Washington, D.C.: Association of Governing Boards of Universities and Colleges, 1977.

Duryea, E. D., and Fisk, R. S. *Faculty Unions and Collective Bargaining*. San Francisco: Jossey-Bass, 1973.

Ehrle, Edward B., and Earley, Jane F. "Effect of Collective Bargaining on Department Chairpersons and Deans." *Educational Record* 57 (1976): 149-54.

Elam, Stanley, and Moskow, Michael H., eds. *Employment Relations in Higher Education*. Bloomington, Ind.: Phi Delta Kappa, 1969.

Feuille, Peter, and Blandin, James. *Faculty Job Satisfaction and Bargaining Sentiments: A Case Study*. Berkeley: Institute of Business and Economic Research, University of California, 1974.

_____. "University Faculty and Attitudinal Militancy toward the Employment Relationship." *Sociology of Education* 49 (April 1975): 139-45.

Garbarino, Joseph W. *Collegiality, Consensus and Collective Bargaining*. Berkeley: Institute of Business and Economic Research, University of California, 1975.

_____. *Faculty Bargaining*. New York: McGraw-Hill Book Company, 1975.

_____, et al. *Faculty Bargaining in Public Higher Education*. San Francisco: Jossey-Bass, 1977.

Gerry, Frank C. "Reflections on Faculty Unionization: Academic Implications." *Liberal Education* 64 (May 1978): 71-81.

Gold, Lois. "Measuring Faculty Unionism: Quantity and Quality." *Industrial Relations* 13 (October 1974): 325-31.

Golden, Allan J. "A Study of the Effects of the First Faculty Collective Bargaining Agreements on Faculty and Administration Relationships at the City University of New York." Ph.D. dissertation, New York University, 1976.

Hardigan, James E. "An Analysis of Institutional Variables Leading to the Election of a Collective Bargaining Agent at Private Colleges and Universities." Ph.D. dissertation, Cornell University, 1975.

Hedgepeth, Royster C. "An Exploratory Analysis of the Consequences of Collective Bargaining in Higher Education." Ph.D. dissertation, Cornell University, 1974.

Hodgkinson, Harold L. *The Campus Senate, Experiment in Democracy*. Berkeley: Center for Research and Development in Higher Education, University of California, 1974.

Humphrey, Neil D. "An Analysis of Collectively Bargained Contracts in Senior Colleges and Universities in 1973." Ph.D. dissertation, Brigham Young University, 1974.

Ingraham, Mark H. *The Outer Fringe: Faculty Benefits Other Than Annuities and Insurance*. Madison: University of Wisconsin Press, 1965.

Katz, Ellis. "Faculty Stakes in Collective Bargaining: Expectations and Realities." *New Directions for Higher Education* 2 (Spring 1974).

Kemerer, Frank R. "The Impact of Faculty Collective Bargaining on College and University Governance." Ph.D. dissertation, Stanford University, 1975.

_____, and Balridge, J. Victor. "Myth of the Collegial Bargaining Model." *Journal of the College and University Personnel Association* 28 (Winter 1977): 18-22.

_____. *Unions on Campus*. San Francisco: Jossey-Bass, 1975.

Klotz, Neil, ed. *Students, Collective Bargaining and Unionization*. Washington, D.C.: U.S. National Student Association, 1975.

Kraft, Richard J. "The Community of Scholars and Faculty Union." *North Central Association Quarterly* 51 (Winter 1977): 321-30.

Ladd, Everett Carll, Jr., and Lipset, Seymour M. *The Divided Academy: Professors and Politics*. New York: McGraw-Hill Book Company, 1975.

_____. *Professors, Unions, and American Higher Education.* Berkeley, Calif.: Carnegie Foundation, 1973.

Levenstein, Aaron, ed. *Collective Bargaining and the Future of Higher Education.* New York: National Center for the Study of Collective Bargaining in Higher Education, Baruch College, City University of New York, 1977.

Lewis, Lional S., and Ryan, Michael N. "The American Professoriate and the Movement toward Unionization." *Higher Educagion* 6 (May 1977): 139-64.

Lindeman, Lynn W. "The Five Most Cited Reasons for Faculty Unionization." *Intellect* 102 (November 1973): 85-88.

Matlin, Norman. *The Educational Enclave: Coercive Bargaining in Colleges and Universities.* New York: Funk & Wagnalls, 1969.

Merz, Robert P. "Impact of Collective Bargaining on Organizational Characteristics of Higher Education." Ed.D. dissertation, University of Northern Colorado, 1978.

Meskill, L. Drewe, and Meskill, Victor P. "The Effect of Collective Bargaining on the Role of Department Chairman." *College Student Journal* 10 (Winter 1976): 380-87.

Milliken, Marie M. "The Influence of National Faculty Professional Organizations on Collective Bargaining in Small Private Liberal Arts Colleges." Ph.D. dissertation, University of Denver, 1976.

Mintz, Bernard. *Living with Collective Bargaining: A Case Study of the City University of New York.* New York: National Center for the Study of Collective Bargaining in Higher Education, Baruch College, City University of New York, 1979.

Morgan, David R., and Kearney, Richard C. "Collective Bargaining and Faculty Compensation: A Comparative Analysis." *Sociology of Education* 50 (January 1977): 28-39.

Mortimer, Kenneth P. "Academic Decision-Making Processes and Faculty Bargaining." *Liberal Education* 64 (March 1978): 84-89.

_____, and Lozier, G. G. *Collective Bargaining: Implications for Governance.* University Park: Center for the Study of Higher Education, Pennsylvania State University, 1972.

Mortimer, Kenneth P., and Richardson, Richard C., Jr. *Governance in Institutions with Faculty Unions: Six Case Studies.* University Park, Pa.: Pennsylvania State University, 1977.

Mortimer, Kenneth P., and Ross, Naomi V. *Faculty Voting Behavior in the Temple University Collective Bargaining Elections.* University Park: Center for the Study of Higher Education, Pennsylvania State University, 1975.

Nielsen, Robert. *Role of Faculty Unions in Governance.* New York: National Center for the Study of Collective Bargaining in Higher Education, 1977.

Pfnister, Allan O. "Collective Bargaining and Decision-Making in the Four-Year College: Emerging Patterns of a Decade." *North Central Associaton Quarterly* 51 (Winter 1977): 311-20.

Pollitt, Daniel H., and Thompson, Frank, Jr. "Collective Bargaining on the Campus: A Survey Five Years after Cornell." *Industrial Relations Law Journal* 1 (Summer 1976): 191-248.

Polowy, C. *Collective Bargaining and Discrimination Issues in Higher Education*

Institutions. Washington, D.C.: Academic Collective Bargaining Information Service, 1975.

Puffer, William C. "The Faculty Senate and Collective Bargaining: A Case Study of the SUNY Faculty Senate." Ph.D. dissertation, State University of New York, 1975.

Rhodes, A. Lewis. "Some Characteristics of Faculty Union Memberships and Their Implications." *Social Problems* 24 (April 1977): 463-68.

Rhodes, Eric F., and Smith, Robert A. *Collective Bargaining Problems in Colleges and Universities.* Washington, D.C.: Educational Service Bureau, 1977.

Ross, Murray G. *The University: The Anatomy of Academe.* New York: McGraw-Hill Book Company, 1976.

Selden, David. "Faculty Bargaining and Merit Pay: Can They Co-Exist?" *The Chronicle of Higher Education*, October 30, 1978, p. 72.

Serediak, Martin S. "Collective Bargaining and Academic Governance at Five Michigan Universities." Ph.D. dissertation, University of Michigan, 1978.

Shuster, Jack N. "Faculty Unions and Academic Decision-Making: The Governance Experience on Six Campuses." Ph.D. dissertation, University of California, Berkeley, 1977.

Simpson, Stephen T. "Faculty Professionalism in Academic Collective Bargaining Agreements." Ed.D. dissertation, Indiana University, 1973.

Skarpen, Erling. "Professoriate and Faculty Unions." *Educational Forum* 42 (May 1978): 395-410.

Sommers, Alexis N. "Collective Bargaining: Issues and Complexities of the Campus Environment." *Journal of the College and University Personnel Association* 29 (Summer 1978): 16-24.

Sturmthal, Adolf, ed. *White Collar Trade Unions.* Urbana: University of Illinois Press, 1966.

Tice, Terrence N., ed. *Faculty Bargaining in the Seventies.* Ann Arbor: Institute of Continuing Legal Education, 1973.

Tracz, George S. *Impact of Collective Bargaining on College and University Management Systems.* Toronto: Ontario Institute for Studies in Education, 1977.

Walker, Donald E., et al. "Collegiality and Collective Bargaining: An Alternative Perspective." *Educational Record* 57 (Spring 1976): 119-24

Weatherford, John W. *Collective Bargaining and the Academic Librarian.* Metuchen, N.J.: Scarecrow Press, 1976.

Weisberger, June. *Faculty Grievance Arbitration in Higher Education: Living with Collective Bargaining.* Ithaca, N.Y.: Institute of Public Employment, Cornell University, 1976.

INDEX

78; on medical insurance, 73; on medical leave, 82; on merit pay, 58; on office hours, 107; on other faculty responsibilities, 110-11; on outside employment, 114; on probationary period, 37; on promotion, 40; on re-appointment, 34; on retirement contributions by employer, 84; on re-trenchment, 45, 57; on sabbatical leaves, 79, 80; on salary increments, 55; on tuition waivers, 87

Professional duties of faculty: advising students, 108; assisting with registration, 110-11; attendance at faculty meetings, 110-11; committee work, 105, 107-8; course scheduling, 112; general, 103-5, 170; grading, 108-9; independent study supervision, 110, 112; office hours, 106-7; participation in commencement, 105, 109-10, 111; teaching, 105; thesis advising, 110-11

Professionalization: impact on collective bargaining of, 7-8

Professional schools and faculty, 139

Promotion in rank, 39-42, 167; awarded through the grievance process, 29; calendar of deadlines, 42; change of policies, 121; criteria, 40, 42; griev-ability of, 20, 41; initiation of recom-mendations, 40, 41; quotas, 41; salary increments, 60-61; stages in review and recommendation, 40; student recommendations on, 130

Public colleges and universities: iden-tified, 48n

Public colleges and universities com-pared with private institutions. *See* Private colleges and universities com-pared with public institutions

Purpose of collective-bargaining agree-ments, 134-36

Quinnipiac College, 30, 46, 61-62, 65, 73, 112, 143, 158

Ratios, student-to-faculty, 96

Reappointment, 34-36, 167; availability

of grievance process, 35-36; awarded through grievance process, 29; changes in policy, 121

Recognition clause, 134, 140

Regis College, 28, 29-30, 34, 56, 63, 65, 112, 142

Registration, faculty assistance with. *See* Professional duties of faculty

Rehabilitation, 47

Released-time: for union officers and representatives, 152-54, 174-75

Reopening. *See* Collective-bargaining agreements, reopening provisions

Reprisals: prohibited, 29

Retention of faculty: financial induce-ments for, 67

Retirement: financial contributions by the employer toward, 84-85, 90; financial contributions by the faculty member toward, 85; mandatory age at, 86; programs, 170; service award, 67

Retraining, 47

Retrenchment (faculty reduction), 167-68; determination of need, 45-47; linked to enrollment changes, 46-47; minimum notice, 46; procedures, 45-46; seniority factor, 46

Rhode Island College, 29, 65, 78, 82, 108, 111, 112, 124, 142-43

Rider College, 14, 26, 63, 153

Rights of faculty: exclusive, 118-19, 171-72; to a reasonable schedule, 112. *See also* Academic freedom; Affirmative action; Grievance system; Nondis-crimination; Personnel files, access to

Rights of management, 154-56

Rights of union. *See* Dues checkoff; Collective-bargaining agreements, dis-tribution of; Facilities for union; Information, access to; Released time, for union officers and represen-tatives

Robert Morris College, 26, 41, 46, 65, 80, 101, 108, 112, 135, 158

Roger Williams College, 24, 36, 137, 156

Roll-up costs, 53

Rutgers University, 14, 57, 103, 151

About the Author

RONALD L. JOHNSTONE is Professor of Sociology and Associate Dean of the School of Arts and Sciences at Central Michigan University in Mount Pleasant. He is the author of *Religion and Society in Interaction*, among other publications.